WARMED AND BOUND

VELVET
PRESS

WARMED AND BOUND
A VELVET ANTHOLOGY

Edited by Pela Via
With a Foreword by Steve Erickson

WARMED AND BOUND

© 2011 The Velvet Press
11120 Hartsook St.
North Hollywood, CA 91601
ISBN 978-1-61364-162-0

Edited by Pela Via
Printed and bound by Lightning Source
Typeset and designed by Pela Via

Cover photo by Chelsea Kyle
www.chelseakphotography.com

PUBLISHER'S NOTE
The writers of these stories are of a different breed. Their voices are inventive and their discipline unstoppable. They all have roots, in one way or another, buried within the community listed below. Please support their fantastic styles of literature, and help us support those writers yet to come.

The Velvet
www.welcometothevelvet.com
www.warmedandbound.com

What began as a love letter . . .

CONTENTS

FOREWORD

I've known about The Velvet for a few years now but I still don't actually know what The Velvet is. I suppose it could be called a collective but that sounds too benign; the implicit anarchy of the thing preempts anything so organized as a movement; and if you called it a school, for God's sake, its members would reach for their revolvers. They're an open conspiracy, is how I think these writers must be regarded, laying depth charges beneath a mainstream publishing business (which includes the likes of me more than I care for) that everyone knows is dead except the business itself. The writers of The Velvet are contemporary fiction's most effective and least self-conscious aesthetic guerrillas and obliterators of "literature," vaporizing arbitrary distinctions intended to tame a spirit that needs neither distinctions nor quotation marks. The result is fiction at once conceived from high artistic intent and executed with depraved populist energy. At some point in Craig Clevenger's story the narrator—for whom a series of ever stranger women serve as the odometer of his mortality, assuming the narrator isn't himself the stranger—utters this anthology's most dangerous sentence: "I've been good my whole life," and the moment you read this sentence you know there's a fuse attached to it, you can see in the distance its glint and hear in the background its hiss, this fuse that was lit before you ever picked up the book and which burns closer and brighter with every page turned. In the fiction of The Velvet, fixation and fetish swap meanings and moments, Brian Evenson's killer reaching out to the reader from the novel within a story, a mouth so mesmerizing to Matt Bell's voyeur that it swallows up his life, a glimpse of breasts that's won and lost in a card game dealt by Stephen Graham Jones, the touch of a breast that triggers a defiant meditation on God by this anthology's editor, a child's kiss by which Chris Deal bids goodbye to innocence and hello to an uneasy grace. I read *Warmed and Bound* over a number of one-in-the-morning nights with the Jesus and Mary Chain on my headphones and, if I were younger, a shot of tequila, until I knew nothing was left of any sleep pattern that I could dream to. For you, the Hour of The Velvet may be high noon and the Soundtrack may be Astrud Gilberto or Scandinavian death-metal. I'm proud to be in this book even in the form of a testament so inadequate as this; accept it as my humble application for co-conspirator, which asks not my height or weight or credit score or for evidence of my good character but rather the mug shot of my psyche, the rorschach of my shadow the last time I glimpsed it, and whether I swear with my signature that every single word I've ever uttered is a lie, except for these that you've just read.

Steve Erickson

INTRODUCTION
by Logan Rapp

You don't know what you're doing

It's the Year of Our Lord 2004 and I'm shouldering loneliness like a stick and bindle. I've been angry for three years now, with a weekly ritual of viewing videos on the Internet of smoke clouds and falling towers. I hadn't put pen to paper in that time, not for anything I'd deem worthwhile.

I would close the blinds at noon and sit in the darkness of my self-constructed cave. I memorized the CIA Factbook on Terrorism as though a test were coming tomorrow. Al Jazeera's English edition was top in my browser bookmarks. I kept my friends close, but my research closer. I feel bad now, because someone else must have taken on my freshman fifteen. I lost that much in the first six months of college.

It's what they want you to do

I listened to the cacophony of voices, all wanting to imprint their designs upon my clean slate. I fed off their anger and regrets and took a major that would get me to the front lines. I had hatred in my heart and an itchy trigger finger. I wanted to kill a motherfucker, and I wanted the

13

right ones dead. But I had to fire the shot. A girl in my philosophy class gave me every hint in the world, but I was ignorant, socially inept. Mechanical in my direction, I had thrown myself onto the Pyre of the Greater Good, built with the values of God, Family, Country and a Life for a Life. Then I picked up a book.

Dear Johnny

The dam I had built cracked, imperceptible at first, a cut from shaving where the skin fights to keep from bleeding. But bled it did. I remembered what it was like to create when for over thirty-six months I had wanted nothing more than to destroy. I wanted to know more. I looked up the author on the Internet, found some interviews, and his brother author.

Oh Lucy if you had only asked me for this

I wept. I hadn't let tears fall since I had acquired my target. I was alone, the beautiful yet foreign sounds of Sigur Ros filling my bedroom, and I was on the floor, shaking as if gripped by a seizure. I felt. I hurt. But damn, if it wasn't the most important moment in my life.

I read more books. I finished all of Baer and Clevenger. Read their short stories. Found Jones, devoured his work. I had the hunger and tasted the sweet ambrosia of creation.

Then I found they had an online community.

I dove for it, and I connected with people who had similar, but unique, revelations. No one was fighting. No one had an ax to grind. Solely from our connection to these books, we formed something larger than ourselves. It may have been longer, but I choose to believe The Velvet materialized overnight.

The Velvet warms and binds

It's a maxim no one officially claimed, but in the same unexpected way we came together, it came to be what defined us. I was no longer angry. I fed off of the encouragement of friends I hadn't yet met in person, scattered across the globe. People who defy exclusivity and clique mentality. People who duck away from conversations to write a thought in a Molesine.

I changed my major. I changed my direction. In 2008 I moved to Los Angeles. And my best friend, whom I met in this community, was there waiting for me. We proceeded to get wasted that very afternoon, but before the night was over, we were already editing each other's latest projects. And then one day, I opened my word processor and proceeded to write seventy thousand words within three weeks. They created, quite possibly, the worst thing I've ever made to completion. But when I came out of that fever dream, stumbling into the sunlight as though I'd never seen it before, I had resurrected myself.

I am Phineas Poe and this is how it begins

I cannot fully express what The Velvet has given me. I owe a part of myself to it, to the people who inspired it, and to the people who form its core.

As you read these stories, you'll find in them evidence of hearts that pump double-time.

Stay warm and bound.

—Logan Rapp

DEATH JUGGLER
by Axel Taiari

I'T's ALL LAUGHTER AND NERVOUS GIGGLES until the bombs explode for real. Then the audience's mood short-circuits fast as a brain stroke: a boom louder than staccato lightning strikes eardrums, a body skyrockets into the air, screams zigzag through the big top, people trample over each other for the swiftest way to the exit. The announcer begs into his microphone for everyone to calm down. A panicked clown runs around, hands flailing high above his head. A bloody stray limb lands into a crying kid's lap. Whatever's left of the blown-apart corpse splashes back to the blood-drenched sand. Dense black smoke chokes the air, saturating the massive tent in seconds. A few regulars stand up and applaud as the chaos flourishes around them. Floodlights die. Slaves carrying stretchers sneak through the bedlam. The death artist leaves the blacked-out stage as an unsolved puzzle of meat and guts.

Death as an art form took off when boredom set in. There are only so many tricks the audience can enjoy. Pull a rabbit out of an empty hat? Paint them fatigued. Disappear in a cloud of colored fog and reappear at the other end of the stage? Watch them yawn. Make an elephant dance, hacksaw a girl in half then piece her back together?

Snore. Card tricks, mind reading, hypnosis, straightjacket escapes, sword cabinets. They'd rather stare at a blank wall.

As the violence became a daily part of life in the city, Asher Marok realized magic was a professional job of upping the ante. On the way to work, humming citizens stroll past muggings in the streets. Zeppelins wandering between skyscrapers dump propaganda letters by the thousands, a paper rain of paranoid bulletins warning of more murders, more gang wars, let us pray the mayor shall forever keep us safe. Desperate basement-dwellers spike glasses of absinthe with tasteless date-rape juice. Door-to-door choirboys herald another apocalypse with seraphic voices. Conked-out link-heads fornicate with steamers in underground sex clubs. Junkies with jaundiced skins lick toads outside of schools and watch reality sunder beneath their skulls. The world is decaying at light-speed, and mouth-breathing wannabe tricksters expect the populace to care about a little sleight of hand? Please.

Asher understood it all, even before puberty sucker punched him with a fat boost of acne and strange stirrings. He watched his father step on stage night after night, doing your run-of-the-mill tricks. People came, sure. But they came once, never to show their faces again.

He managed to do what his father never could. He built a devoted fan base. Yellowed fliers on the crumbling walls in the ghetto advertised: Tonight in Sector 7, come see The Amazing Asher kill himself for your entertainment. Only tonight folks—we deal in death, not resurrection.

Asher wakes up to unblinking bug eyes staring at him over stiletto teeth.

The prodigal son returns, says Callahan, lighting up a cigarette fatter than a pinky finger.

Almost gave me a heart attack, you bastard, croaks Asher. He sits up, shuddering off the cobwebs of a coma.

Fucking welding goggles.

Callahan sucks on the cigarette, exhales a cloud of jet-black smoke. Heart attack. Funny, coming from a man hell-bent on killing himself. I'm here to patch you up, Ash, not turn you on.

Asher stumbles out of the dentist chair, nearly knocking over a tray full of tools in the process. Welder, screwdriver, bloody bucket, scissors, endless jars of multicolored liquids, oversized syringes, scalpel. An ugly process.

The artist cracks his fingers, neck, toes, pinches himself in various places, still not used to the patchwork of scars crisscrossing his ruined skin. He smiles and says, what's the damage, doc?

Callahan laughs, washing his hands under a rusted tap, drooling pale brown water. The damage, he repeats. Took the drones and me about eight hours to reattach all four of your limbs. Three hours more than usual. Your heart stopped beating for eight minutes. We made sure your brain still got oxygen, though.

Fuck, says Asher.

Callahan slides the goggles off, revealing eyes flooded with blood. Asher. You can't keep going. It's getting harder.

Asher nods and says, what else can I do?

The doctor sighs. Someone slid a present under your door, by the by. Catch.

Asher's nerves fail on him and the envelope slaps against his chest. It takes him a dozen seconds to pick it up and open it. He unfolds the letter.

FRIEND,
SEEMS YOU HAVE TROUBLE KILLING YOURSELF. WE CAN FIX THAT PROBLEM. PERMANENTLY. TODAY'S THE LAST DAY TO PAY BACK WHAT YOU OWE ME. COME THIS AFTERNOON WITH THE MONEY. OTHERWISE, WE SHALL SEE YOU TONIGHT.
DISRESPECTFULLY,
YOU KNOW WHO

Callahan studies Asher, then says, what's tonight's trick? Gotta get the instruments ready.

I think I have a rough idea, replies the magician.

It's not resurrection in the strictest sense, of course. That right there is a form of reality bending that's only been achieved in old tales and fables for kids—pure hogwash. Instead Asher settled for clever brutality, fixable injuries. The oversized pack of dynamite he unwrapped in front of the audience was a prop, mostly plastic, stuffed with heat-triggered smoke tablets. Before the show, he had strapped tiny blasting gelatin charges to his limbs, bombs no bigger than summer flies. Strong enough to shed various body parts, too weak to turn him into burnt stew. He wore thick metal plating under his loose sweatshirt. He coated his face with anti-burning ointments and a colorless protective residue he bought from a dubious shaman at the market, supposedly stolen from the city's firemen. He injected himself with morphine, swallowed enough pills to put a whale into a coma. When he pressed the trigger, his arms and legs were destroyed—good thing Callahan kept an army of cloned limbs at his workshop. After that, it was just a job of performing surgery and reality bending quick enough for him not to die.

The night before, an antidote already working its way through his bloodstream counteracted the poisonous gas he inhaled like a lung-scorching joint hit. He received the pain, the skin bubbling with tennis ball sized sores, teeth melting, hair falling out, all the usual radioactive horror, but no death.

Two nights ago, it was a self-inflicted shotgun shot right through the bare chest. He was on so much morphine he couldn't see straight, the trigger had to be remotely pulled by Callahan. Hurt like a bitch, took the doc four hours to remove the bullet fragments. Asher got a three minutes' standing ovation for that one.

The night before, a swarm of killer bees assaulted his face drenched with pheromones and anesthetics.

The night before that, he drowned in a giant aquarium.

Asher's cortex shifts gears as he walks over the bridge linking the rest of the city to Anachronos' Isle. The prison island now turned mutant ghetto always made him feel at home despite his skin color. The grey-skinned mutants with their deformities were seen as freaks, things innocent human children and pretty girls with rich dads should be kept away from. He focuses on tonight's act, reorganizing thoughts in the hopes of figuring it all out. He wanders the streets, passing shattered towers clawing for the sky, their sides lined with barred windows. Mutant kids run through the alleys—horns, wings, spikes and claws growing out of their flesh.

Another turn and he stops in front of the mansion. A mutant with a pair of hairy noses guards the door, cradling a riot shotgun.

Asher steps up to him and says, I'm here to see Carpat.

The guard shrugs, sniffs and spits. Don't know who you mean, partner.

Asher brings a hand to his forehead and rubs it, sighing. Look. I need to speak to him. Tell him it's extremely urgent. And he will be interested.

You look familiar, says the guard.

I just have one of those faces.

Hey, no, you're that freak from the circus, down in Sector 7. Saw your picture on the posters.

Freak, repeats Asher. He stares at the guard's noses and says, man, it must suck for you to get a cold. Snot city.

Get lost, human. Carpat won't see the likes of you.

Asher says, let me show you a magic trick.

The guard steps back and raises his shotgun, aiming for Asher's chest.

The trick, explains Asher, is you letting me in. Here's how it works: you step inside that mansion, you go get

Carpat, and you tell him I pissed off some squid bastards quite badly, and they want to do me in. The name is Count Voto. Funny part is, Carpat doesn't like him. Old grudges. And I have some information about him he could use. Valuable information.

What if I shoot you instead, circus boy?

Asher grins. Then Carpat receives a letter from one of my friends in a few days, informing him the pug-faced inbred lapdog guarding the door this afternoon shot someone who held precious facts your boss could have used to bring down one of his rivals. What happens next is between you and your easily angered employer. You know, the one renowned for violence and torture?

The guard frowns, and lowers the shotgun. Asher whistles.

Stay here. I'll be back.

Oh, I'll be waiting.

After a few minutes of shuffling cards and staring at the sky, the door opens. The guard steps out.

Well?

The guard nods, moves aside and mumbles, Carpat will see you now.

Why, thank you.

As Asher strolls past the brooding guard, he winks and whispers, abracadabra.

They struck a deal. Carpat listened. Asher shared his information. Carpat thanked him, and true to his reputation, offered his services. The young magician asked the gang lord only two things. First, a handful of armed henchmen. Second, the help of the most talented grave robber in the city.

Once all was said and done, Asher headed for the eastern market with enough coins in his pocket to buy himself a coffin he could rot in.

Showtime. Packed crowd, conversations stacking on top of each other in grumbling piles, the warm smell of sweat and unwashed bodies colliding, peanuts and sandwiches filled with questionable meat, spotlights making the temperature rise.

Peeking through the curtains, Asher spots them with no effort. Spread out and not even trying to blend in with the crowd, as discreet as dynamite. The squid-kin wear distinctive mafia clothing, summer blue military jackets with four sleeves, one for each arm. They wait, unblinking.

Asher backs away from the curtains and says, I left my will in the caravan. Make sure my mom gets her share. And there's enough money for you to open your own clinic. Or blow it all on shrooms, shrimps and sluts. Whatever floats your boat.

Callahan pats Asher on the back. Are you sure you can do this?

Asher turns around and smiles. Are you sure you can do this, doctor?

It takes Callahan a long time to hug his friend and whisper, I'll miss you.

Ladies, gentlemen, and inbetweeners. Welcome.

The crowd cheers and claps. Some devoted fans chant die, die, die, and stomp their feet in anticipation. Children chomp on popcorn while their fathers sip beer.

Asher stands in the very middle of the big top, multicolored lights blinding him. His lips almost touching the microphone, he says, tonight will be very special. More applause. He waits, then says, tonight, I will not kill myself. Silence. Confused faces study each others' for an explanation. Tonight, resumes Asher, I'll let someone else do the job for me. Why waste my own bullets when others are oh so eager to take care of it? He offers a devilish grin and the audience hoots and laughs, applauding louder than before. Everyone, it is my pleasure to introduce my assistants. Meet my murderers.

Asher steps away from the microphone and nods. The spotlights move, illuminating random audience members before finally settling down. Three different lights shine on three shub'nar, who hiss and look around, reeling from the sudden attention. The crowd eggs them on, cheering or booing them. Some hidden faces throw racial slurs at the shub'nar.

Asher says, our squid brothers are here to shoot me. Months ago, before this all started, I borrowed money from a less than honest character, you all know him by name. Count Voto. I needed money to pay for my mother's medication. I repaid him in full, but his bills keep coming to this day. When I stopped sending money, the threats began. And tonight, it ends.

One of the shub'nar shouts, we don't care about witnesses, trickster. This is your last chance to pay Voto.

Asher laughs into the microphone before backing away. He unbuttons his shirt and drops it to the floor. He spins around on himself, displaying a skinny sunken chest and an army of ribs lurking under a tapestry of tattoos, showing them all that there are no tricks tonight, no hidden armors, no misdirection, only a young man grabbing death by the jaw. Once everyone in the circus understands this will be Asher's final show, he grabs the microphone with one hand, raising up his middle finger with the other and says, everyone, I would like to thank you for appreciating my art and showing up night after night. Godspeed to you all. He pauses. As for you three bastards, you can tell Voto I'd happily rip his tentacles off with my bare teeth and shove them up his flabby ass. Blow me.

As soon as the last two words escape Asher's lips, the shub'nar whip out their respective weapons. Myriads of explosions bang through the tent. Sparks fly from the foaming mouths of shotguns. The audience screams and pushes for the exit. Bullets tear through the magician's flesh, lodging themselves deep within him. He feels it all, more pain than any of his previous deaths granted him but he forces himself to stand tall, blink through the red veil cloaking his vision. The shots keep coming, but too many for it to simply be the shub'nar and as he falls to his knees, blood pouring out of his mouth and filling his nostrils, he catches a chaotic glimpse of one of the squids' head blowing apart, Carpat's men landing a killing shot, an all out gang war blooming within the circus.

More shots echo but he can't see anymore and the sand is so warm, he may just rest there forever. Blackness shrouds his thoughts in tune with his crawling heartbeat and ragged breath. Flash visions of his father drinking and his mother trapped in bed, a young Callahan performing a back-alley abortion, the first girl he kissed, the last girl he kissed, the rainy day he spent performing coin tricks by the canal and his heartbeat is mute and the sand isn't warm anymore, turned to mushy ice against his skin. His brain offers him one last desperate grasp at beauty: a picture of the faraway city of Mallik, a place he only saw through a postcard pinned to the wall above his bed and at last, Asher Marok, the death juggler, gives up the ghost and understands what it feels like to truly die.

Callahan sits across from Carpat. The crime lord's scorpion tail dangles by his side, swinging back and forth like a poisonous pendulum.

My condolences about your friend, doctor. I wish his plan had worked.

Callahan nods, eyes glued to the carpet. Thank you.

I trust my men did their job?

Yes. Blew the squids to smithereens. Callahan locks eyes with Carpat. Seems this city will have to witness another gang war.

Carpat laughs. It will be a short one, I assure you. Your friend provided some very handy information. I expect Count Voto to be dead within two moons. Of course his numerous friends and family won't be pleased, but my people can handle them.

I'm glad to hear it, replies Callahan. The gods know this place has seen enough blood. Now, I believe this is for you.

The doctor removes a stuffed envelope from his jacket. He places it on the coffee table.

This is Asher's will and a good chunk of his money. I trust you will make sure his mother will be taken care of. There is more money than needed, feel free to keep the rest as a thank you.

Carpat shakes his head. No need. All the money will go to her. I will make certain she will never starve or have to worry about her living conditions.

Thank you.

As for you, doctor, if you are looking for a new home and a new job, my crew can always use a healing hand.

Thank you, Carpat, but I will have to decline. I am done with this city.

I understand. I'm sure you can show yourself out. I have a war to take care of. In the next few days, I will leave some flowers on your friend's grave.

Callahan offers a polite smile, then gets up and leaves.

Charcoal clouds leak dirty raindrops over the cemetery. Callahan kneels in front of Asher's resting place. He places a bouquet of black flowers on the marble. The tombstone reads:

HERE LIES ASHER MAROK
MAGICIAN, DEATH JUGGLER, ESCAPE ARTIST
DEAR FRIEND AND BELOVED SON

Twin blue pills down the throat chased by a splash of water and Callahan hopes the sickness won't get to him. He has no sea legs and the journey will be a painful one. The city of Nualla-Stem is long out of sight and there is nothing now but a flat stretch of grey, the ocean spreading as far as the eye can see. No collapsing buildings, no airships, no industrial chaos, no skyscrapers afire, no rot.

On deck, he passes by families enjoying the journey, fathers crouching next to daughters and pointing at the withering sun and packs of shrieking dolphins following the boat. The doctor smiles at the passengers and opens a door, plunges into the darkness. He makes his way down several flights of stairs bathing in red light. The ship's bowels growl through the walls. He reaches the lowest deck and walks down the hallway until he faces his room. He opens the door and closes it immediately behind him.

Thirsty, begs the bleeding man in bed.

The place reeks of maggots and damp earth and stale air. Callahan opens the window. He reaches for the water flask and brings it to his patient's cracked lips. Grey mutant skin lurks beneath the soaked bandages concealing his face.

There you go.

Thanks, the man croaks.

Callahan sits by his bed and lights up a cigarette. He exhales in the dark and lets the sea air steal the smoke away.

The patient coughs, a ragged thing. He mutters, what's . . . what's the damage, doc?

Callahan can't help but crack up. The damage, he repeats. The usual question. This body is rotting but I can slow it down until we reach shore. Then we'll need a reality bender or a shaman to cure it for good. Expect a lot of pain for the next thirty seven days. Longer if we get trapped in a storm.

Sounds peachy.

They don't trade words for several minutes, until the man coughs again then says, what did you do exactly?

The doctor scratches his beard, gathers his thoughts. Exchanged brains. Bent reality as best as I could. Rewired nerves. Replaced organs that were damaged. Ugly. Didn't think it'd work. Kept swearing the whole time. Wouldn't stop shaking. Blood everywhere. The grave robber recommended by Carpat was good, though. Got you a fresh corpse. Minimal stink. Rigor mortis had barely set in. Might feel some stiffness. So it worked, I suppose. I mean, gods, look at you.

I'm a mutant.

Yeah, says Callahan. Like you always dreamed. And Carpat thinks the procedure didn't work, and Voto will soon be dead. No one's the wiser.

Another successful death, whispers Asher. Greatest trick of my career.

What about your mother?

What about my mother? She won't starve. She'll get better. She'll heal. Maybe see the sunshine again, burn her wheelchair.

She believes you're dead, Ash.

I couldn't afford to let her in on it, and you know that. Think she can handle seeing me like that?

Doesn't matter what you are now. You're her only son.

It's begging for the word to get out, and for Voto's remaining family to hunt her down, eventually. Bastards wouldn't stop coming until I was dead. Squids are the best at holding grudges.

Sure, says Callahan, sure. He lights up another cigarette and invites the silence in. When he's done, he tosses the butt out the window and closes it. Funny thing, though.

What's that?

I placed your brain and a few organs in this new body, right. Some nerves and transferred some blood. Something's been bothering me, though.

Asher waits.

No soul, says the doctor. I didn't transfer no goddamn soul.

So what, replies Asher. You think we have no souls? Just walking bags of flesh with brains and nerve endings?

Callahan gets up and heads for the door. He opens it. The light from the hallway slithers into the room. I'm not too convinced about the rest of us, Ash. But I'm pretty sure about you.

CLICK-CLACK
by Caleb J Ross

SOME SAY THE TRAIN'S click-clack echoed his mother's escape, that the looming engine overtook and ultimately replaced the sound of her footsteps, leaving Ernie with only the train's passing heat for warmth and its lumbering weight to serve as the heartbeat he had nestled for the past nine months.

When Jack found the baby, newborn and discarded, webbed among the weeds and other failed carcasses lining the rails, birds pecked and sucked at remaining afterbirth. The infant's skin sparkled to the rising sun reflecting off bloated insects. Overnight rains had rinsed the mother's scent from the gravel and railroad ties, leaving the child without a single trail to follow, without a single strain of familiar air to feed its fading breath.

Jack scooped up the body with a shovel he reserved for roadkill. He named it Ernie and called his boss to request leave for the remaining day.

The surgeon met with Jack to discuss options, while Ernie lay in a room many floors away, kept alive by pumps and tubes and the hands of awestruck nurses. Both men folded and rested their hands atop the surgeon's oak desk, poised like opposite ends of a business negotiation. Ernie hadn't a hairline yet, so the surgeon agreed to cut and sew where he thought hair might grow. He sketched his plan with a green marker on a whiteboard propped beside the desk. The infant's head formed at strange angles, and the mother's apparently hasty drop-off only deepened the crevices, molded the already shifted bones to the difficult shape of rocks and metal tracks. Aesthetics meant little to Jack—his own grooming kit included one razor, a broken toothbrush, and a cracked mirror—so he told the surgeon, "I don't care how the hair grows. You're fine to just keep the brain in there however you can. Though honestly," and he leaned close, breaching the desk's perimeter with his large, hooked nose, "what are the chances it will ever work again anyway?"

The surgeon capped his marker. He shuffled through photographs taken upon Ernie's arrival. He rotated particularly strange images, searching to orientate himself to the correct angles among so much realigned skin. He let a long sigh ruffle stray hairs from his mustache. "I'll try to rebuild the brain back, but more importantly I'll try to just keep it in there." The doctor stayed with the photos. He stretched the sigh further. "I know you, Jack. You get paid by the carcass, and you're not the type to prioritize species. Why did you keep this one?"

"I think it's mine," Jack said. "Can't you see the resemblance?" He smiled for the doctor.

Hours later Jack occupied an emergency room waiting area with a family of three: one mother, two daughters. Between failed attempts to quiet the giggling girls, the mother dabbed her wet cheeks with a napkin. Jack met her glassy eyes twice, retreating quickly both times to his own projected pain. The girls played tag until one stubbed her toe. Only then did she join her mother's tears.

After the surgery, the doctor pulled Jack from the waiting room back to his office. "I've never seen anything like it," the doctor said. "My team swears it too, that he should have died. We laid him out, went through the motions, we basically prepared for a loss. But that sound, the heart monitor, each beep would fuel another, and so on . . ." Each beep-beep, the doctor said, encouraged the boy's heart to further share the rhythm.

Jack smiled past every superfluous word. "I have a son," he said.

Jack's home rests at the intersection of a strip of railroad he adopted fifteen years ago and a woody area known for spewing wildlife into the town's suburban sprawl. He enjoys watching from his window, the animals' adolescent pilgrimages from birthplace to a home of their own. But often the passages end interrupted. The years have trained Jack's ears to recognize the subtle thump of an animal cut short over the thundering locomotive beat. Utility bills and rent have their ways of changing the ear's physiology. The night Ernie dropped to the earth, that subtle thump against the ground woke Jack from a dream in which he cared for a child of his own. He cleared his head of the dream and stepped out into the dewy morning, still feeling the imagined child's hand in his. "His name was right there on my lips," he says to the empty field at his front door.

Anticipating no more than a single doe, perhaps a family of raccoons if he were lucky, Jack idled his rusty Ford the short distance to the tracks, letting the image of a son of his own stew in his head. He closed his eyes, let the muscle memory developed by years of traveling this same path steer his truck.

He saw first a foot, recognized from his dream. The leg cascaded down the gravel bank, ending at toes the size of infected mosquito bites. Jack accepted the child's limp body not as a professional token, but as a realization of the night's vision.

Home from the hospital, Jack lays Ernie upon the worn living room carpet. Twisted yarns cradle the tiny body, nesting the way weeds and rubbish did just weeks earlier. Unhappy to let the floor have his child, the new father builds comfort himself; he experiments with blankets of various textures and densities, settling on a half-complete afghan that a dead aunt willed to him during her final stages of dementia. The blanket dangles unraveled at one end, but otherwise suits the baby and his bandages. Ernie's chest pulses to the irregular soundscape of cricket songs and croaking frogs. Jack watches his son survive through the night.

The night's rhythm breaks with the day. As the sun quiets the crickets and frogs, Ernie quiets too, the faint rise and fall of his afghan slows to a scarcely perceptible blip. Jack, already attuned to the breath of this child, wakes by the silence, jumps from the floor beside the boy, and panics. The blanket soon stops beating. Ernie's lips blue. Forfeiting the moment, Jack considers the shovel in his truck. "At least you were real for a day," he says to the body.

A train whistles in the distance. Its wheels grind a familiar click-clack, click-clack, and with that click-clack little Ernie's lip gathers crimson back, click-clack, click-clack. His valve flaps, whip-whap, then Jack picks at the limp wrap, unrolls the child and holds him close, afraid for what the passing train will leave as the click-clack inevitably dies to silence. Jack wills his own heart to pulse with the rhythm of the train. "Stay with me," he tells the boy. The new father forces himself into a panic, imagining the worst for his boy, the worst for himself, a life as it was just weeks before, more pulling the dead from the ground without this chance to place the living upon it. He imagines the worst so to fool his body into anxiety, to keep his heart feeding the boy long after the passing train.

As the locomotive whistle grows and the click-clack rattles Jack's window glass and dusts the carpet with abandoned cobwebs and ancient flakes of ceiling paint, Jack pulls the boy tighter. The sound drowns even their shared beats. The whistle eventually fades, Jack can hear his own heartbeat still drumming from within. He envelopes the boy, coaxing him to transition to Jack's beat. Ernie opens his eyes for the first time. "Green," Jack says. "Just like me."

Ernie learns to walk. And soon after, takes to chasing trains. The engines' laborious and productive rumble mocks Ernie's own skewed gait. Jack anchors his boy with a shovel and brings him along to scrape fetid flesh from rocks and streets. Jack calls it the family business despite having no reason to fake pride in his work; Ernie's comprehension tops out at the awe of his own footsteps. Intangibles like pride and family loyalty offer no beat of their own, so are of no use to the boy.

Some say the boy chased his mother's heartbeat, that the trains' rumble pounded stronger than Jack's chest. These whispers, perhaps his own, never spoken outside his head, bring Jack nightly to tears, but still he stays close to the boy, charging the young heartbeat the way his mother never did.

Jack took to scattering his own collected dead animals along the track in hopes of keeping his boy occupied during passing trains. The boy's misaligned eyes would widen, his crooked smile would stretch, his distressed shirt—a gift from his father's closet—would throb at the chest as trains approached. "Mom," Ernie said, six years old, his first word. The following morning, Jack rose early and started planting these bodies of his own.

Ernie scooped. He dumped. Jack retrieved the carcass and returned it to the ground. Ernie scooped. This was the new rhythm, but could sate Ernie only temporarily. The routine weakened Jack's aging body, but strengthened his son's. An unfair but inevitable transition. Jack couldn't fight the train forever.

Ernie learns to wake to night trains. Jack builds alarm systems from rope and antique brass bells to intercept his son's escape attempts. Years pass. Ernie's awkward gait muscles to a skip, matures to a gallop, finally qualifies as a legitimate sprint. "Mom," he said at age six. "I'm coming," he learns at eight. One night, shaken awake by a railed monolith, larger than Jack had ever seen, he chases his boy, but cannot compete with the mother's heartbeat. Jack manages a final goodbye, but the deafening click-clack steals even that.

THE WORLD WAS CLOCKS

by Amanda Gowin

for Heather

DESCENDING THE STAIRCASE AS ONE, four legs in perfect time, the light was blue on four black braids.

Clasped hands parted with an electric pop as Tilly paused on a creaking stair. Her knuckles whitened on the rail. Rocking, she repeated the offending creak. Her eyes widened, cheeks reddened.

Tabitha, one stair lower and suddenly one plane removed, widened her eyes and laid a hand to her cheek.

Nothing.

Tilly said: "One day this place will fall in, and I will not be under it."

Symmetry disappeared.

Tabitha scratched the palm of her hand, scratched the itch of a phantom limb to see Tilly's half of the room stripped bare the following morning.

The oak tap-tapped at the window in sympathetic Morse code, but the sun and tree were too bright to be trusted. Finding Tilly's imprint on the bare mattress, she folded herself against the light and pressed the concavity of her sister. What tomb?

Sixteen years old, Tabitha was astounded at the world through one set of eyes. Pausing on the judge and jury stair, her parents' twinspeak crept up to her, peppered with words and phrases for the first time.

Tabitha stepped into their world.

A faded set? She stared. At five, the twins smiled from the sandbox and the mommy and daddy smiling down were vivid and flushed with youth.

Suddenly time was everything.

"I must acclimate myself into this world," she whispered into the mirror, into Tilly. Forehead to the cool glass she remembered their hatred for Alice—Alice didn't know. On the other side was another—where else would a twin come from? There had been much debate as to who belonged to this world, and who had daringly climbed in.

The tears her reflection gave back were a comfort until breath obscured the face in fog. Tabitha pressed, but the glass did not yield.

Ill-equipped, with naked eyes and thoughts, school whipped around her in a flurry of bodies, voices, and bells. Without Tilly the world was clocks. They hovered with round faces and she scurried away from their pointing hands.

"Their world."

Other girls began to fascinate Tabitha. Peering from around her melancholy, studying them, a picket fence of red lockers lit a vertical path to the circle they made. Deep breath and sense of falling, one big step. Surrounded. She searched the eyes of a redhead, murmured into the ear of a brunette, smiled at a dark girl so different and perfect as to almost be unreal—this girl flushed and broke her gaze.

"We are—no, I am beautiful," she told her conspirator in the long bedroom mirror.

Late nights in cars drinking gin from the bottle with a shy blonde who had never done this sort of thing, Tabitha kissed the girl's palm and placed it flush with hers, admiring the differences.

The ghost of Tilly itched and Tabitha cried, palms pressed to their cold reflections in the mirror, an aura of moisture welding them.

Tabitha blinked, the bell of her skirt had paced her. She opened her eyes and high school was over, the girls disappeared. Again, she was expected to recreate the whole world.

Tabitha studied her parents—aged turtle doves—and envied their stasis.

She discovered males.

Clumsy and oppressive, they lacked softness. But she rested in the crooks of their arms while they confessed the same fears as the delicate girls she had loved.

And what was love? Yellow urine on a stick turning pink, pails of blue paint obliterating the room she and Tilly had known. Her parents asked who it belonged to, their brows furrowed.

"Me," Tabitha answered, puzzled, hands on her warm belly.

She grew fat as the tree out her window unfolded tiny green hands. Love was color in the world. Her laughter drew laughter from the mouths and eyes of her parents—rusty notes that became well-oiled and silver, and came easily. Tabitha browned in the sun.

Her reflection no longer resembled Tilly's. The mounting wire snapped as she took the mirror from the wall, and mourning for her twin ceased.

Movement and rush, laughter and tears as they piled in the car. Headlights slicing through the sheets of rain, tiny green suitcase on her lap, Tabitha was too happy to scream. Palms flat on the suitcase of carefully folded nightgowns and handmade baby clothes, and two worn bears exactly the same.

Color grows slowly but disappears in an instant—in a click of teeth hard enough to make the tongue bleed. Alone in the hospital, the color and motion were sucked away into the fluorescent lights above, leaving only the drone of the doctors' voices.

Tabitha remembered nothing but the taste of pennies. She woke from the dream into this ugly grey world to hear about 'the accident' from a stranger. A story as preposterous as the TV ones her mother watched in the afternoons.

"So I dreamed it all?" She saw only her suitcase, tiny and insignificant in the corner.

The doctor didn't understand.

"Where's Tilly?"

All efforts to reach her sister had been unsuccessful . . .

Rolling to the wall, the better to forget the little suitcase, she cried without the comfort even of a mirror.

The clocks stopped, or spun backwards and forwards in apathetic bursts. The lights marked a forgotten pattern, off and on. Beeping machines, murmurs from the hallway. Scratchy, drab sheets around her and under her hands. Interrogations were called 'evaluations.' Armed with clipboards and scowls, white coats floated in like vultures, made their faces into question marks and scratched at their boards before leaving.

Finally, the word she longed to hear: Release.

The sad box of a room ejected her. A woman with careful hands tucked her into a car and followed familiar roads. 'Social worker' the woman was called.

Tabitha rubbed her eyes, waking, planted in the living room with the suitcase at her feet.

Not one clock dared tick. The house was a tomb.

No pain in the crescents her nails made in her palms, but the rage was consuming. She dragged all the mirrors into the painted room. Her father's hammer was found on the porch rail, laid to rest after hanging a wind chime from the rafter. She gripped the handle tightly as dragonflies spun and tinkled, leaving spots in her eyes.

Her heart swelled. Running up the stairs, the fateful step creaked and she released a howl that scratched her throat in its escape, blurred her vision, but did not slow her ascent. She raised the hammer, watched by a thousand overlapping Tillys and Tabithas, and did not put it down until the pieces were too small to reflect.

Yawning, she dismantled things little by little to know she was awake. Time was marked by Social Worker's visits—the woman arrived periodically to wear a face both worried and confused.

Mainly it was the dolls that worried Social Worker.

The project had been time-consuming—taking them apart and hanging the pieces by bright skeins in the branches of the big tree.

Social Worker warned about the group home.

The dolls belonged to the twins, their mother had dragged them from the attic back in the time of Tabitha's swollen belly. Discovering them in a sad pile on her parents' bed, she remembered the chaplain at the hospital saying her baby had gone into the sky. It was comforting. She mimicked it the only way she knew.

Sometimes when the wind blew, the plastic arms knocked together and she thought of babies clapping, and the dragonfly wind chime gave up a few rusty notes. For a moment her heart was light and so was the world, for a moment there was color, faint hues of blue and gold in the sky, blue in the dolls' eyes.

What could it matter to the warm body whose job was only to see that she was eating and keeping herself clean? Turning her head, Social Worker eventually went away again. Falling, change, upside down, all these words were forgotten.

One day a taxicab appeared, an improbability so far from town, and crunched to a stop in a cloud of gravel dust. She rose—the porch swing gave a perfect view, but she did not believe. From the cloud emerged Tilly, suitcase in hand. On her hip balanced a birdlike child of perhaps two, black hair and round eyes.

Tilly shuffled down the walk, head down, steps deliberate. The child's eyes flickered back and forth between the twins and her mouth made a perfect O, asking, "Who?"

"Tabitha," Tilly said in both answer and greeting, dropping the suitcase. Her eyes flitted over the tree.

"What's her name?" Tabitha's voice was a croak.

"Don't know. Won't tell me, won't answer to anything." A single braid snaked over Tilly's shoulder, scars zigzagged the arm enfolding the child. "Where are the others?"

"Dead."

Tilly nodded. "I'll come in and never leave again."

"No."

"I'll come in anyway." With sad eyes she plodded up the porch steps.

The little girl put out both arms and Tabitha wrapped her up, the weight comfortable against her, warmth unfamiliar. Tiny fingers linked behind her neck. The screen door slammed behind all of them and Tabitha's limbs tingled. The nameless child dropped to her bare feet and scrambled under the kitchen table.

"Can I stay in our room?" Tilly asked.

"It's not ours."

Tabitha watched her sister—Tilly's eyes swallowed every change, her hand fluttered over the stair rail.

The rattle of pans, crack of eggs, sizzle of bacon failed to draw the girl out. Tabitha fought the feeling of waking up, stirred and turned and blinked. She felt the child watching.

"What's your name?" Tabitha asked.

"Tabitha." A heart-shaped face appeared between the chair legs. Blue eyes. Voice like a bell, a wind chime.

"Yes. What's your name?"

"Tabitha."

Tilly reappeared at the foot of the stairs, pale.

Bending, Tabitha asked, "Will you be Tabby? We can't both be Tabitha."

"I Tabitha." Unblinking. She looked at the twins.

"Will you be Tabby?" Tilly asked.

Tabitha shrugged.

The afternoon passed untying the pieces from the tree. The yard became a giant chessboard of slowly reassembling dolls.

Tabitha looked up, her twin was gone.

The little girl wandered the rows of fragments, a plastic arm in hand.

Searching room to room, Tabitha finally stopped at the doorway she had not crossed in years.

The broken glass had disappeared, the wood floor glowed bright honey. The cradle in the corner was empty, and the curtains reached inwards, offering their wispy shadows.

Shaking, she climbed through the open window onto the roof.

Tilly stood near the chimney, hair loose and blown into the exact shape of a gingko leaf. Urn in one hand, lid in the other.

Approaching carefully, quietly, Tabitha extended a spidery arm to meet her sister's.

The metal container was the size and heft of a baby bottle when she wrapped her clammy fingers around it. Before thinking twice, Tabitha flipped her wrist and swung her arm in a wide arc, tearing a gash in time and space.

A rainbow of ashes caught in the wind, tossed into the branches of the tree. Rustling leaves spread them further. Some drifted into the old sandbox, but that was okay.

Below, the child Tabitha saw the twins on the roof, jumped up and down, and clapped her hands.

MANTODEA
by Matt Bell

FROM ACROSS THE BAR, I couldn't stop staring at her, at that breathtaking mouth of hers. Obviously as orally obsessed as I was, she filled that laughing cavity with whatever was close at hand: lime wedges, olives, tiny black straws she chewed between cigarettes. Gallons of vodka or gin, I couldn't see which. She cracked ice cubes between strong white teeth, the sound audible even above the jukebox and the clatter and clack of pool balls coming together, spiraling apart. I wanted to stick my fist in there, to get her bright red lipstick all over my watchband.

Getting up from my table in the corner, I steadied myself on chair backs and unoffered shoulders. The floor was the sticky history of a thousand spilled nights, and other couples danced between the pool tables and the bathrooms, their shoes making flypaper two-steps to the country-western songs spilling from the jukebox. I weaved between them until I reached the bar, where I took the stool beside the woman.

I lit a cigarette, signaled the bartender for another whiskey with a raised pair of fingers. From up close, the woman was all mouth, the rest of her thin, too thin, hungry and lean like cancer. I wondered about the nutritional value of her life, of everything that passed through the furious red smear of her lips. I imagined both our mouths working

45

furiously on each other, kissing with jaws unhinged as snakes.

I turned toward her, lifted my glass. Tried to remember how to smile without opening my mouth. Felt I probably wasn't doing it exactly right.

Her own mouth said, Whatever it is you're thinking of saying, it's probably the wrong thing.

I waited before I responded. Waited until the urge passed to tell her about my old life, about all that I swallowed in the months before the hospital. I wanted to tell her though. Wanted to tell her about the coins and thumbtacks and staples. The handfuls of dirt and crushed light bulbs.

I wanted to tell her that like a lot of poisons you might eat, you have to swallow a lot more drain cleaner than you'd expect, if you're trying to kill yourself. At least, the stuff hadn't worked on me, not as I'd once hoped it would.

What it had done was clear me out, get rid of all kinds of things that had once been stuck inside of me. That had backed me up.

What it had done was take away my lower intestine, give me a short throw of a colon that couldn't handle spicy food or even most solids. No citrus or tomatoes. No milk or milk products.

This new body, it wasn't supposed to be exposed to alcohol, but giving up the booze was never really an option.

What I said to her instead was, I like watching you eat, drink.

I want to buy you a meal.

A meal with courses. Appetizer. Soup. Salad. Fish. Meat. Miniature loaves of bread with mounded pats of butter.

I said, I want to watch you eat desserts that you have to chew and chew. Taffy. Caramels. I want to give you hard candies to suck thin and crush between your molars.

I said, I'd lick all the sticky sugar off your teeth for hours, if you wanted me to.

Her mouth laughed, said, The only meals I eat I find at the bottom of cocktail glasses.

She fished her olive from under her ice cubes and popped it into her mouth, then licked clear liquor off her dripping fingers. I watched a single drop spill down the back of her hand, trace the blue ridge of a vein from knuckle to wrist. I laughed too, but with a hand over my mouth, hiding the teeth destroyed by chewing steel, the gums peeled black by the Drano. She reached over and pulled my hand down, saying, When I was a little girl, I thought mastication and masturbation were exactly the same word.

She had a disorienting smile, and for a moment I didn't know who was aggressing who. She laughed again, slipped off the barstool with a swish of skirt. Drained her glass.

Her mouth said, It's not love at first sight, but it is something, isn't it?

She walked away, past the pool tables and the dancing couples, their temporary lusts. I watched as she pushed through the swing of the bathroom door. I stubbed out my cigarette, finished my drink, then walked toward the bathroom myself, my guts burning and my throat scratched with smoke, my brain brave and dumb as a lizard's. I put my hand on the cool metal panel of the bathroom door. I pushed.

The bathroom was two stalls and a single sink beneath an empty frame that once held a mirror presumably busted by some drunken stumble. She was inside the near stall, the smaller one. There was less room to move than there would have been in the handicapped stall, but there was enough.

The door wouldn't lock, but I didn't care. Her back was to me, that glorious mouth seen only briefly when she looked over her shoulder, the wet slash of her lips framed by the toss of her chopped blond hair. I wanted her to turn around, but I thought she was teasing me, even though she wanted what I wanted or something close enough to count.

She didn't look back again, just put her hands against the slick tile wall, planted her feet on each side of the toilet. Waited for me. When I got close, the nape of her neck smelled like bad habits, tasted worse. I didn't care. I wasn't there to feel nice. Neither of us were. She flinched slightly at the sound of my belt buckle striking the porcelain toilet seat, then asked me my name. I whispered a fake one, then told her the truth when she asked me to repeat myself, knowing she'd assume it was a lie.

Right before I finished, I felt her back arch toward me, felt her hands reaching for my face, pulling it close to hers. Her mouth opened, taking in my cheeks then my nose then my right eye, the whole side of my mouth. I felt her teeth tugging at the scratchy pouch between my ear and my jaw line, wanted her to keep going, to keep devouring me until I was gone.

I'd once thought I wanted to eat something that could end me, but now I knew I really wanted something else, something approximately the opposite. Something this woman could give me.

Later, after it was over, I realized she'd wanted the same thing, that I'd failed her by not tearing her to pieces, by not taking her inside me one bite at a time.

Too focused on myself, what I thought instead—right before I pulled out of her, before she pushed me against the stall divider with her tiny wrists full of their fragile bird bones, and definitely before she slipped past me without giving me the last kiss I so desperately wanted—what I thought then was, This one time will never be enough.

Still misunderstanding everything, what I said was, I'm going to need to see you again.

Her mouth laughed as she exited the bathroom, the sound so loud my ears were already ringing by the time I got my pants up. I raced after her, out of the bar and into the cold parking lot, where I lost her to the night's thick blanket of confusion, its sharp starlight and fuzzed out streetlamps.

I waited for the sound to stop, and eventually it did. Nothing she'd done would turn out to be permanent. Her smell would be gone by morning, and the teeth marks on my face would take less than a week to scab over and then, to my terror, heal completely.

For the first time in months, I went home to my apartment and emptied the kitchen junk drawer onto the dining table. I picked up the tiny nails and paper clips and stubs of pencils and erasers and whatever else I could find and then I jammed them into my system. I considered pouring myself a drink, then stopped and took a long hot swallow from the bottle. I smashed the unnecessary tumbler on the corner of the counter, watched as the cheap glass shattered everywhere. Stepping carefully so as not to cut my bare feet, I picked up the most wicked shard I could find. I held it in my hand, then set it in my mouth, rested it on my tongue. I swallowed hard, and when I didn't die I went back for more.

ALL THE ACID IN THE WORLD
by Gavin Pate

SUNSHINE

At thirteen they made the pact, swore they'd reign forever. The Acid King and Queen. He told her you have to do it this way, taking off his clothes in the middle of the woods and folding them on a patch of pine, because it's ritual, it shows a way to God. She nodded and peeled herself naked. He tried not to look at those freckled breasts, knowing she knew he was looking just the same. They couldn't hide anything.

This is ceremony.

She said she knew that too.

They scored the yellow blotter from her cousin's friend, the one who said it would burn right through their brains. No matter. They already couldn't concentrate in class, couldn't stop drinking their parents' liquor, couldn't wait the three months before they'd be policed at 4:00 a.m. in the orange chairs of the elementary school, Wizard of Oz singing Dark Side of the Moon off some teacher's VCR.

In the woods they held each other's hands and the trees bent into a portal blowing a voice through their flesh. She came down talking of a tunnel in her grandmother's basement, that behind a bookshelf burrowed not into the middle of the earth, but a secret passageway to the second floor restroom of JC Penneys. He said God lived in the dirt, and she agreed, said Hippo Penis, and they found laughter everlasting under the cap of a small red tree.

Mostly he rode his bike past her house morning and night tasting the air that watched her window and not feeling the crucible already hanging from his neck.

ESCHER

Fifteen.

The stairways went up and down and came around to beetles and fish, open panes of window glass dripping soaked and drowned.

She hung posters in her room, he drew imitations on the desks.

The hits were big—MC Eschers under their eyelids—and they went to class, laughed off lessons, learned walls can cry and breathe.

They ran away from home and stole her grandmother's Maxima with the factory equalizer and Guns N' Roses all the way to the beach, a mix tape with nothing but Sweet Child o' Mine and November Rain over and over again.

But later he'd remember not the strips of Eschers they ate like Twizzlers, but the way she willed their car into space and took him in a Motel 6, her hands showing him there were still some beautiful things.

He could look right through her skull.

She could taste him in her throat.

The Eschers got bigger, stronger, and sometimes he worried the acid would be too much.

Next thing they're at the 7-Eleven and she's just gotten her license and leaves the car idling outside. Somehow she's arguing with the clerk, her purple batik skirt washing away the white light, saying the rotisserie dogs are cold, the nacho cheese is runny, and by the way, where's the secret passage to the world under the sea? And there he is, his pupils wide as quarters, saying he's found it, right here beneath the Pennzoil display. Somewhere in the distance a clerk is saying Hey now, Hey now, and the words slip away even as they're said. Backing up, spreading his arms like Jesus Christ. At a full sprint he dives into the portal. Wow, she says. Wow, Wow, Wow. The bottom of the ocean shoots out of the hole, drips from the ceiling, spills from his scraggly blond hair. The clerk with a mop like a baseball bat, trying not to slip, pursuing and tumbling through the aisles. And because no one ever noticed, she rolls up the celebrity magazines and sidles out the door.

It was easy to blame the Eschers.

They found a way to hold hands at psychic distances and push their fingers safely through one another's skin. And he'd only just started to say there had to be another way, as something made her smile, laugh, even as he knew it wasn't funny anymore.

We're made of plastic, she said, her face in her hands.

To prove it: a shard of glass he'd found the universe in, an anatomy lesson of flesh and blood.

Later during the three-day hold, the ER wouldn't believe he'd done it for all the right reasons: not because he loathed himself or wanted to die, but because he loved.

There's a way to lose yourself completely.

Which got his hold bumped to a week.

MICRODOTS

This is when senior year never happened, when the holds and evals are steady and predictable, when she's in his room, showing him the acceptance to a college he swears does not exist.

From the Carmex container he dumps the purple microdots like caviar between.

To celebrate.

To push them all the way.

But she had given it up, too much unhinging the final door, coming too close to the God they'd been looking for all along. And she wasn't ready.

But there she is, eating acid all the same.

They stare at the acceptance letter written in a language he lost in a swirl of mental pixels by November of eleventh grade.

She tells him not to apologize or abdicate the throne.

He doesn't say it was always more than a pact, and she doesn't say he never has to.

Jesus Christ on a motorcycle: these hits are really strong.

The thing with acid is this. It's you in there, always has been, and just now, for this time, while your hand does cartwheels and your mind can't hold the seconds together tight enough, even then it's you.

Their clothes folded on floor instead of pine, their legs crabbed together, her hand in his stringy yellow hair.

They want me on medication.

Medication

Not like this.

The place where his laugh once was is disappearing.

Heavy.

She can see the word fall right through the floor.

Heavy.

Her neck elastic now, his hands working. She slips him inside and feels him crying Houses of the Holy and Wish You Were Here.

This is when you remember it's dangerous to feel too much.

He snakes through and she lolls her head back and forth. It rushes between: what her mom's boyfriend said he didn't do when she was twelve, what his dad had said so often in whispers and in rage.

So many ways to use a voice.

It wasn't about God, either. All the acid in the world. Because she saw through it that time they ran away, Guns N' Roses for 200 miles, his hand on her neck like maybe, just maybe, her head would dislodge and fly out the sunroof, and there he'd be, trying to explain to cops, parents, everyone, why she's lost her mind.

In the truck stop with the rigs lined like caskets, the smell of gas and yellow light, their seats reclined, the sunroof open, the night wide and forever above: they were too far already to double back. Dawn would beat them home and their parents would know the kids were not all right.

Sunshine, Escher, Microdots.

It gets into the hair, seeps into the spine.

He plucks one deep, the grey matter clinging to the follicle. She pushes her fingers through his neck, dips the hair into the spinal fluid, and they suck both ends like nectar from honeysuckle on a hot August day.

But that's not what's he's saying with the acceptance letter still unread.

It's about a squirrel.

Somewhere he remembers to roll down a window, clear his throat and spit.

She moves their hands, finds what might be a constellation and follows it to design. Gods and humans, November Rain again and again. A truck shifts into gear and a sun, their sun, blinks on the horizon.

Squirrels, microdots, medication.

Somewhere there are parents in an argument about who their children are.

It's really about how he and his brother trapped the squirrel at the bottom of the outside stairs, the ones with the three stone walls that led to the basement, and how the brother, older, already gone, didn't have to say anything to start the exercise, didn't have to explain why to the twelve year-old at his side.

There's a tunnel, don't you understand? And when we find it we can get away.

Their hands on the emergency break together, he tells her this is my family.

His brother who chased the squirrel into the pit, and how all he had to do was nod at their father's unused pitchfork beside the never-yet-strewn pine straw, the one his dad brought home, drunk, loud, standing in the front door with the porch light's silhouette casting him across the room.

Only a perfect throw would do, gravity and patience, aim and will.

Afterwards they didn't even bury it, just his brother slapping his shoulder, reciting lines from movies that never got made.

Already he knew God would stop listening and it didn't matter from here on out—what he did, how hard he looked—the world would hide its beauty.

They leave the truck stop, hole up in the Motel 6, and she tries everything she can to show him how to find it, swearing up and down that they will be enough.

But this is when she's not in the basement and losing her mind and crying on microdots, but when she's alone and crying at the face he couldn't shake, the one candle lit in the mirror, him picking at the corner of his pupils that refused to ever shrink, and she, rushing at him with the cup of water, trying to extinguish the candle and the mirror and everyway his face suggests all that has gone wrong.

LIQUID

But it was too late to wash it all away.

Sixteen years later, when the child they would never have is sucking down liquid, tripping her way into bliss, she awoke at a reunion with her husband and the story everyone was dying to tell.

How he had lived through a kid, a divorce, an institution with white walls and locked doors that called him its own. A deluge had come from God and he never found that olive branch or the return of his sweet white dove.

She could never be a sweet white dove.

How he swerved into the ER lane, ran to the waiting room and tried to untangle the wire and ball sculptures that kept the kids distracted while the hospital sterilized everything left unsaid. There would be no note except the article in the morning paper and the remaining silence was a hammer that began to smash her life away.

How he held the security guards with the .45 he stole long ago from his dad, backed his way into the small chapel, a few pews and a giant cross and a little piano in the corner. He sat, smiled, cracked his knuckles and soothed the opening chords of the next nine minutes of her November Rain.

And how he doesn't have to sing because by the time he reaches the second verse there are people at the doors singing for him, nurses and patients and a janitor tilting his life on a broom, knowing it's his wedding and funeral wrapped into one. He shakes more sound out of the piano than the chapel can hold, his color coming back, his arms tightening up, pounding away at the silence with his own little hammers to show her what beauty might mean and how to get there.

And then we're at the 7-Eleven, and the cops are at the door, pushing the rest of us aside, working their way into the pews and up the aisle. It's too late. He's started his crescendo. And we all begin to sing. You're not the only one, you're not the only one. And he raises his hands like Christ on the cross, sprints up the aisle and into the hall with the .45 in hand, tossing the unsuspecting deputy through the gift shop's still glass door.

And I know my part because no one ever notices. I reach into the toppled gift shop rack and grab the magazines, rolling them under my shirt, already outside before someone doesn't see he never stole the bullets.

I take the crucible and begin to run, leaving our kingdom behind, take it the rest of the way to the tunnel beneath the road, the one that digs down deep where God can never find us. I hurry inside, descending, descending, and knowing right or wrong this is the only way I can hear it if I ever tell it all myself.

CRAZY LOVE
by Cameron Pierce

SO YOU MEET A STRANGER ON THE BUS. The two of you speed headfirst into small talk about diminishing salmon populations, and that settles it. You will have a casual fuck. Two hours later, you float on the pillows that appear when the storms of good sex have ceased thundering. You're both vigorous cuddlers, so it's hard to tell in the half-light where your flesh ends and the stranger's flesh begins. You fall asleep, very much in love.

The stranger shakes you into wakefulness around seven in the morning and says, "You knocked me up." You insist upon the eternal virtues of prophylactics and tell the stranger to go back to sleep. The stranger gets out of bed and paces from one end of your room to the other. This irritates you. You have always hated pacers and morning people. It seems you have fucked the wrong kind of stranger again.

Five minutes later, the stranger yelps and gives birth to a child. Faithful to its strange origins, the child is a weird-looking thing. It could pass for one of those plush, cutesy-eyed hearts that pop up in grocery stores and boutique shops when February rolls around. You find it hard to imagine that your genes played any role in its creation.

"It sure is a weird-looking thing," you say.

"I think it is beautiful," the stranger says, and that settles it. You make coffee and eggs and the three of you take the bus down to the courthouse. You get married. With a child thrown into the equation, you see no option but marriage. Still, you're uncertain whether you really love this spouse-stranger. After all, the spouse-stranger is a pacer and a morning person. You return home from a honeymoon of takeout Chinese and an Italian horror film that the spouse-stranger claims to have seen precisely thirty-six times. "Once for every child born," the spouse-stranger says.

You think this is a lot of children for one person to have, but decide it is better to leave your separate pasts unspoken. You find yourself warming up to the fuzzy infant dozing between the two of you on the sofa. Family life might be okay after all.

A month of swell fucking and many diaper changes goes by. Then one morning at the crack of dawn, the spouse-stranger asks for a divorce. You pull the covers to your chin and say, "I thought we were happy."

"I am happy," the spouse-stranger says, "and I feel like I'm in Hell."

"How can you feel both things at once? What makes you think that?" you ask.

"Oh, a lot of things," says the spouse-stranger, packing a suitcase that belongs to you full of clothes that are yours. The spouse-stranger slams the front door three times on the way out.

You prepare to face the trials of single parenting, but first you sleep until noon. With the spouse-stranger gone, you can finally return to your normal habits. When you wake up, the empty bed saddens you. Prickles of loneliness scratch at your insides and turn your thoughts into some kind of lousy meat. Everything you think seems out of place in your head, dragging you to a new all-time low every minute.

You walk into the kitchen and spot a note on the counter. Your heart beats with the gusto of a Bach symphony. You clear your throat and restrain the great hopes the sight of this ketchup-stained note has bestowed upon you. You hold it between your fingers like a scroll from the heavens and read:

The baby died. I put it in the trash. Remember to pull the can to the curb tomorrow. I'm sorry I don't love you anymore. Don't feel bad about it. This is just what I do.

You pace from one end of the kitchen to the other. You hate yourself during every minute of it, but you're compelled to pace. You're a mad pacer. You were born to pace. The sun shines and you pace. The sun hangs itself on the blue horizon and you pace. The blue horizon fizzles into black emptiness and you pace. Black emptiness and you pace. Black emptiness. Pace.

Morning comes and you pass out on the floor. You dream that you die and meet the spouse-stranger on a bus taking you to Hell. The spouse-stranger shows you a ticket stamped PURGATORY in gold embossment. The bus drives off a cliff and you wake up. You realize what you must do.

You leave your house and stand at the bus stop. The bus pulls up five minutes later. Strangers occupy half the seats. The other seats remain unfilled. You sit beside a stranger near the back of the bus. The two of you speed headfirst into small talk about the poisoned cat food epidemic in China, and that settles it.

You go to the stranger's house because your own house is behind you now. You feel the stranger's stop approach like a historical compendium of all the strangers who have ever slept together.

But when you get to the stranger's house, you find that it is haunted. You stand outside and squint your eyes at the house's twisting spires, as if to gauge its spook count and decide whether the risk is worth the fuck. "I grew up in a few haunted houses," you say.

"It isn't that haunted," the stranger says.

Puffy white ghosts peer out from all the windows. The house is definitely *that* haunted. "Maybe it isn't," you say, and walk inside.

The stranger guides you upstairs to a room where a stained mattress lies in a corner. "I can't have sheets in the house because the ghosts poop on them," the stranger says.

"That would be a lot of dirty laundry," you say.

You and the stranger undress and lie on your backs. Then you turn and kiss the stranger and you fold over each other. The sex isn't that great because ghosts howl and fly through the walls. Lovemaking strikes you as a funny thing to do in a haunted house and you laugh. The stranger takes sex very seriously and does not laugh. This also makes it less great. The stranger sighs a ghostly wail and orgasms. You haven't come yet, but the stranger says, "I guess that's the end of our sleeping together."

"I guess that's it," you say. You dress in silence, recalling all the reasons you vowed never to live in a haunted house again. A ghost follows you down the stairs on your way out. You wonder if the stranger ever gets lonely and tries to sleep with the ghosts.

You stand at the bus stop and figure you'll have to try again some other day. The bus arrives a few minutes later and you step on. You spot the spouse-stranger you're still legally married to. The spouse-stranger sits beside another stranger who once meant something to you. You can think of nothing that made this stranger different from all the other strangers you have slept with. That stranger was not special, you think. Anyway, it took place in some half-remembered time.

It no longer matters that you engaged in brief encounters with either of these strangers. You still love them, but in the way people love the memory of a carnival funhouse. A gust of longing rises up in you because to hell with it. These encounters do matter. They must add up to something more meaningful than any of the strangers who make them happen. To think otherwise would be sticking a foot in the mouth of your own aimlessness.

Your stop is coming up and you want a stranger to talk with, but all of them converse with other strangers. Your thoughts no longer slosh around like bad meat, but you are hungry and a hamburger sounds delightful. Half a mile from your stop, you stand and tiptoe to the front of the bus. You tap the driver on the shoulder. You think that even if she's a pterodactyl and missing a front tooth, her blue uniform compliments her yellow eyes. You can tell this dinosaur has style and taste.

You ask if she's heard of an all-night diner that recently opened.

"No," she says, bubblegum smacking between her elongated jaws.

Before you can tell her about the diner and ask her on a date, the pterodactyl misses a turnoff because you're distracting her. The bus zooms straight ahead, right off a cliff. As the bus plummets into a canyon, everybody screams, including your ex-lovers.

The bus driver climbs out of her seat and takes you in her arms. She opens the door and leaps out of the bus. Her wings unfold like a lovely umbrella and you sail toward the sun. Deep down in the canyon, the bus explodes. Those strangers are dead now. It's just you and the pterodactyl. Maybe, if she doesn't have a nest full of babies somewhere, and she doesn't feed you to them, the two of you will hit it off.

CHANCE THE DICK
by Paul G Tremblay

now: the client

I say, "My fingers were stolen and replaced with someone else's fingers." I hold my left hand out to him as if he could take it, twist it, flip it all around up and down, inspect it like it was a jewel or a fossil or a photo of a crime scene.

I tell him that I woke up leaning against a toilet and my left arm in a bathtub full of ice. It wasn't my bathtub or my apartment. Only one light bulb in the vanity worked. There was blood on the aqua-green tile and all over my white blouse. I didn't remember anything.

He says, "Are you married?" He's wearing a pinstriped suit, like everybody else. His face is hard and rough and back lit in the neon spilling through his office window. I'm supposed to think about having sex with him, but he makes me feel tired instead.

I was woozy when I left the bathroom. Everything had a haze, a fuzz, the edges not sharp, not defined. My hand throbbed and burned, but I could move it and kept it huddled against my chest. I bumped into things in the apartment, overturned and broken furniture biting my ankles and knees. No one was there. I left and couldn't find a number on the front door. There should've been a number there, like 213, or maybe something with a 7.

I say, "I'm not married. See, no ring."

He says, "May I?" He lifts up the bandage on my index finger and does find a ring of angry red stitches. His touch is smoother than I imagined. He says, "Sloppy job." He's not surprised. He's seen it all.

then: the writer

It can't be **now: the writer** because I'll have written this before you read it. A minor detail.

I worry about the woman with the stolen fingers. Unless I go back into her past, I worry she'll always be stuck in the present tense, almost like she has no future.

I'll give the private dick a snappy last name. Something with two syllables. Or Frisk or Frist, or Chance. Chance's first name doesn't matter, no one uses it. His office is dark, like his city. I think all cities are dark places.

All the characters will say cool things and be smart and sexy and weird. I will like all the characters, and I will hate them. How else will they be real to me? I think Chandler hated Marlowe.

then: the client

I ran out of the numberless apartment building and into a laundromat. I had someone else's fingers, a blood-soaked blouse, and no quarters. The fingers worked, at least, but the hair on the knuckles was black and wiry. The place was empty and the lights had a green tint, like the bulbs were covered in pool table felt. Wait, the place wasn't empty. There was a slim man in a pinstriped suit and wearing sunglasses filling one of the machines. I watched him throw in mini-skirts, a curly blond wig, and three brown fedoras.

I wanted to do something sexy or deviant. I said, "Do you mind if I throw in my blouse?" and unbuttoned my shirt. My bra wasn't very sexy or deviant, but it was supportive and would have to do.

Sometimes you had to improvise.

The man threw his sunglasses in the washing machine. His eyes were green, like pool table felt again. He was young and he had a scared look about him that I find most intelligent young people have. He said, "Go ahead."

He had quarters and bleach. I leaned against the washing machine and let myself shake for a bit. He watched but it didn't make me feel sexy. Then we sat across from empty driers that he turned on, and he'd somehow rigged the machines to work with the doors open. The fried air poured over my skin. He sat on his hands even though I know he wanted to put them on me. My hand felt big and dumb. I tried telling him about my hand and how I didn't remember anything. I don't think he heard me because he didn't speak. When the washing machine was done, my once-white blouse came out the same color as pool table felt, and it came out dry and without the bloodstains.

The man didn't take anything else out of the washing machine. He lifted my hand, was real gentle with it as if people had always been gentle with me and said, "Find Chance," and left.

then: the writer

Near where I live there's a busy intersection that has a name. It has a laundromat, too, but with white lights. This past spring there was a man in a pinstriped suit, but this man was older, close-to-retirement age, and he stood on one corner, on the mini-manicured lawn that was owned by Mobil. Behind the man was mulch and shrubbery trimmed into letters that spelled 'Mobil.' I only knew that advertising shrub was behind him because it was always there. The man blocked the shrub from doing its duty with his very own advertisement. He leaned on a large piece of plywood with thick, desperate black letters that read: *"40 years of insurance/mgmt experience looking for a job. Hard working. Call 781-_ _ _-_ _ _ _ ."* He was grey and bald at the same time. He wore big glasses that were not in style and were never in style. He was there every morning for two weeks, then he was gone.

now: Chance the dick

She smells like a dryer. She has black hair but wears it like it's blond. Her green blouse stops a few buttons shy of being shy. I can't see her legs over my desktop but I hear them cross and uncross. A cricket chirping. Knives sharpening. I'm a dead man, aren't I?

She says, "I'm not married. See, no ring."

That's funny. Almost as funny the throbbing pain in my left hand. Wait, that's really not funny at all. It's the opposite of funny, though I get the subtle-as-a-sledge-hammer feeling that someone is still laughing.

I say, "May I?" I lift the bandage of her index finger and find a ring of angry red stitches. The skin is raw and swollen and the finger is bloated, throwing an antibody tantrum. The finger doesn't want to be there. It's a shame really. Those fingers of mine never hurt anybody that didn't deserve it.

I say, "Sloppy job."

She says, "You know who did this?"

"Maybe. But I know whose fingers you have."

"Who?"

"Mine."

I put my feet on my desk and feel sad. The world is running out of mysteries.

then: the writer

I was mad at the pinstriped-suit-guy. He shouldn't be there. Why didn't he just have a resume made and posted on-line? Why didn't he hire a headhunter or employment counselor or something? He had to know standing on the corner with a sign was fruitless. Was he taunting me/us with his management-level unemployment, trying to spoil the ritualized commute and coffee? I don't drink coffee. After anger, came superiority. I would never be like him. So passive. So not-in-control. After superiority came pity and a panoply of demise scenarios. Divorced, kicked out of the house, really was a swell guy just a relic of business-days long past, let go by a mega-corporation after a lifetime of service, just like my dad. Maybe I'd help him, make a resume for him, set up practice interviews, introduce him to people, maybe I'd save him, but then I'd convince myself that it wouldn't work that he'd be needy and clingy and that he wouldn't get a job that way and that he'd have to save himself, it was the only way. After pity, came . . . I don't what. I just wanted to forget. Forget that I was like him, only I might know the current rules better than he does. Or maybe I didn't. Maybe he knew more. Maybe he knew that none of us were in control and that things happen to us and we can't stop it. We didn't live, we reacted. And that's why I've inserted myself into this story because I want some control and that's why I love and hate my characters and that's why Chandler hated Marlowe because Marlowe was always in control even when he wasn't, because Marlowe was action and not reaction, because Marlowe wasn't real like Chandler.

now: Chance the dick

She says, "Should I believe you, Chance?"

That's a damned good question. One I don't have a good answer for, so I try the glib, "Why would I lie?"

"Can I see your hand?"

I give her my left. She smiles, like it's a present with a pretty red bow. I watch her teeth peek out from between those red lips. They're too neat and orderly. That can't be trusted. I say, "You like my manicure? Only the best for Chance."

She takes the index finger, her finger, into her mouth, and holds it there like a thought. I feel the tip of her tongue.

She slides it out and says, "Those are my fingers."

I take my hand back. With the shock of losing my fingers and the swelling of the replacements, I hadn't realized I had woman's fingers. Jesus, I'm getting old. I'm slipping. Maybe I need to wear those giant, never-in-style glasses my doc kept pestering me about.

I say, "What are the odds?"

She laughs and says, "Arm wrestle maybe?" She laughs harder. My office gets darker, if that's possible. She adds, "So what do we do now, Chance?"

Hell if I know. There is still so much I don't know about this dame. Who did this to us? How did we get here? How did we get to here? Maybe I could drop a fin on Mickey down at the boardwalk. He's a standup stoolie with good dirt. Then, I'll . . .

"Yo, Chance? Why don't we just swap digits and call it a night?" she says.

"What? I'm gonna get to the bottom of this. I'm thinking it's Coolie and his Alley Boys, as they're just sick enough to do this, and they hang out at the laundromat. Or maybe it's that new Asian gang. I've heard they've been doing black market organ stuff, and . . ."

She stands up and puts her hand with my fingers over my mouth, and then one into my mouth. It tastes like me. She's sexy and deviant. I can't help but stare at her blouse. She steps back and takes off my fedora. I will not tell you what's under there. She lays it bucket-side up on my desk. She plucks my fingers off her hand. The red stitches snap and fall away. There's no stopping this. It doesn't seem to hurt her as she's smiling, but it's a sad kind of smile, one that says I know what's really happening. That kind of smile is always sad. She puts my fingers inside my hat, though she saves one finger and has it trace the curves inside her blouse, tucks it under her skirt quickly, then back inside the hat. She's breathing hard and I feel nothing. She snaps at me with her good hand and nods. I know to give her my left hand. She grabs the hand and takes back her fingers. I don't feel pain, but there is an overwhelming sense of loss; it's huge, sitting in the room with us, making everything heavy. She twists her fingers back on her hand, flexes, and waves at me.

She says, "Which one will you put on first, Chance?" She lifts the hat, shakes it all around like the queen of some church bakesale raffle, then holds the hat above my head. "Come on, now, Chance. Take your pick."

And I don't know what to do. I just don't know what to do anymore. Maybe I won't do anything. I'll just sit in my corner office, underneath my neon sign that no one will bother to read, a sign as useless as an unanswered phone call.

SOCCER MOMS AND PRO WRESTLER DADS
by Bradley Sands

ANARCHY FUCKING RULES. My leather jacket fucking rules. The anarchy symbol on the back of my leather jacket fucking rules. The red paint that I used to paint the anarchy symbol on the back of my jacket fucking rules. Saying that things "fucking rule" fucking rules. Riots in the streets fucking rule. Pee wee soccer games fucking rule.

I sit in a folding beach chair on the sidelines, watching my little sister play out on the field. The chair is uncomfortable. A strip of polyester fabric is poking me in the ass. I do not like to be poked in the ass. But it is worth being poked in the ass. It is a really great pee wee soccer game. It is total anarchy, super-retardo anarchy awesomeness. It is the most anarchist thing on Earth, I think.

Oh wait, I forgot about riots in the streets.

But riots in the streets don't have little girls picking clumps of grass out of the ground instead of defending their goal, little girls chasing butterflies instead of the ball, little girls tripping over the ball, little girls kicking the ball into the wrong goal, little girls calling their opponents cuntbags, little girls screaming as they run away from the ball.

Riots in the streets don't have soccer moms. Riots in the streets don't have soccer dads. Riots in the streets don't have riots between soccer moms and soccer dads over pee wee soccer games. Riots in the streets are over real world

73

issues. Real world issues are fucking lame.

I say it out loud, "Real world issues are fucking lame."

Sometimes when I think strongly about things I blurt my opinions out. I can not help it.

My mom says, "Watch your language, Artie."

I sneer at her.

She removes a jar of extra hot mustard from her fanny pack.

Extra spicy hot mustard is not very anarchist. Extra hot mustard is the tool the overlords use to keep down the proletarians. It is what they threaten us with whenever we speak our mind. It is what my mom forces down my throat whenever I tell her to go fuck herself. Whenever I tell her that she is a filthy cuntbag. This is unfortunate because I really like the word cuntbag. It is very cute. It rolls off my tongue. The world would be a better place if I could use cuntbag as a term of endearment without feeling like a volcano has erupted in my mouth.

I hate my mom. I will kill her. I will kill her after everybody goes anarchy. I will declare war on her face. I will do this when it is legal to declare war on her face. I do not want to blow up her face before it is legal. I can barely handle a strip of polyester fabric poking me in the ass. I do not think I could handle prison.

I compliment my mom on her T-shirt. Compliments are the best way to prevent mustard volcanoes from erupting in my mouth. "Nice shirt, Mom. I like the soccer-playing bears. They are very cute. I also like that the shirt is ten sizes too small for you. I like how it accentuates your fatty-fattiness. I like how it shows off the blubber of your huge tits. I like how I can see every jiggle of your ginormous stomach. I like how it makes you look like you're having quadruplets."

"Aww, thanks, honey," she says, putting the jar of extra hot mustard back into her fanny pack.

She stands up to give my uncle a lap dance. I am

horrified. My uncle is sexually excited. My uncle is a chubby chaser.

My uncle is my new dad.

I will launch a Scud missile at my uncle's head after everybody goes anarchy. I plan to aim my Scud missile at his forehead. I will do this because he has a Fu Manchu mustache and Fu Manchu mustaches fucking rule. I am hoping his mustache will be able to survive the attack.

My little sister scores a goal. Mom and New Dad cheer.

Mom and New Dad realize their daughter had scored in her own team's goal. They stop cheering. My uncle starts laughing. His laughter sounds fake and melodramatic like he's a bad guy in a pro wrestling league. This does not surprise me. He is a bad guy in a pro wrestling league. His stage name is Kin Corn Karn. He stole the name from an old Nintendo wrestling game because he couldn't think of anything good. Kin Corn Karn is an awesome name, but my uncle sucks.

My uncle stops laughing. He and Mom call my little sister a loser. They tell her they still love her. They say she will do better next time. They blow her kisses.

I yell, "Anarchy rules!" I feel a little sad about not yelling "fucking rules."

The goalie for my little sister's team is very mad. She pulls my little sister's shorts down.

My little sister is not pleasant to look at. She resembles a muppet/tank hybrid. She is even more unpleasant to look at when her shorts are wrapped around her ankles.

My little sister shoves the bottom of her soccer cleats up the goalie's anus.

The goalie cries. She does not like to have the bottom of my little sister's soccer cleats up her anus.

My little sister is the epitome of evil.

But I still love her. I have a genetic disposition toward loving my little sister even though she is the epitome of evil. I also have a genetic disposition toward obesity. My genetic disposition toward obesity is responsible for my daily beatings at school. My genetic disposition toward obesity is responsible for my nickname, Chubby-Chub-Chub-Chub. If it were not for my genetic disposition toward obesity, I would not have to blow up my high school.

The goalie's father glares at my little sister. He says, "You are a terrible human being."

My uncle says, "Listen, brother. Don't call my daughter a terrible human being!"

My uncle calls everyone "brother." I think he stole it from Hulk Hogan. Maybe he likes to confuse people? People are very confused whenever he calls me "brother" in public. They probably think, I am very confused. I did not know he was Artie's brother. I thought he was Artie's new stepfather. Is he Artie's new stepfather AND his brother? Is that even possible? Something seems morally unsound about it. Doesn't anarchy fucking rule?

The goalie's mother calls my uncle a shitty father.

My mom takes the bottle of extra hot mustard out of her fanny pack, goes over to the goalie's mother, and squirts two servings down her throat.

The goalie's mother screams.

Her husband pulls down my mom's pants.

My uncle goes over and gives him a piledriver.

The goalie's father is now unconscious.

The goalie's mother is very angry. She pulls on my uncle's Fu Manchu mustache.

My uncle's fatal flaw in the wrestling ring causes him to howl.

The parents of the competing soccer team watch the confrontation. They look confused. They look left out. They pump their fists in the air and run across the field. They crush a few of their children. Either they do not notice or do not care.

My little sister's team's parents look a little scared. They pick up their folding beach chairs and attack.

The pee wee soccer girls pick clumps of grass out of the ground, chase butterflies, trip over the ball, call their opponents cuntbags, scream as they run away from the ball, and kick it in the wrong goal.

I march through the chaos. I smile. I take pictures. I stomp on the ground. I hoot. I duck to avoid flying beach chairs.

I feel a tear splatter down my cheek.

The glorious anarchy has made me think of my real dad. He died last year.

My real dad died during a riot at a pee wee soccer game. It was one just like this, except the opposing team's parents were wielding broken beer bottles. The mother of a girl who my little sister anally penetrated was one of those parents.

The mother of a girl who my little sister anally penetrated put a broken beer bottle through my real dad's brain.

I feel bad about saying that pee wee soccer games fucking rule. Pee wee soccer games do not fucking rule.

They fucking suck.

And crying is not very anarchist. I wish I could get myself to stop. I really miss my dad's ZZ Top beard.

TAKE ARMS AGAINST A SEA
by Mark Jaskowski

GETTING HIRED AT MOVIE LAND secured for me free movie rentals, what my college degree failed to deliver. The pay's atrocious but I think of the money I save on films as the check from a second job. I trot out of here every evening not much closer to making rent but with a B-grade horror flick or grainy forgotten detective story tucked under one arm, ready to pass the time with bourbon instead of popcorn until I fall asleep or Stephanie gets home. She thinks it's a sign that I should go back to grad school. She doesn't get that pulp enthusiasts are generally regarded as poor film theorists. I try to explain it to her but there's no talking to someone with convictions.

Andy got me the job when Stephanie called in one favor or other, which means I try to be civil and wait for him to tell me I owe him. He was vaguely apologetic about the piss test and rolled his eyes when I told him I didn't use anything. I'm trying hard not to count my blessings, stocking the romantic-comedy shelves much too far before noon.

Andy's house is ancient. He doesn't try to hide it. Powder-blue paint flakes off on my finger when I press the doorbell. He comes to the door, sleepy or stoned and wearing a bathrobe.

"Wow, Jim. It's late, man."

"We need to talk. About Stephanie."

He nods, yawning. "Sure, sure. Come in." He closes the door behind me. The place is about what I expected inside, with magazines and envelopes strewn around and a digital scale conspicuously alone on a coffee table. "How's she doing, Jim? Haven't seen her in a while. I was just going to call."

I nod, pacing around the room. "You haven't seen her?"

"No. Shit, what time is it?" I follow him into the kitchen. "You want a cup of coffee?"

He reaches for the pot and, following his movement, I see it. Set upright against the microwave. Stephanie's waitress pad. She had it yesterday.

"You haven't seen her."

He starts to shake his head, concentrating on pouring coffee. I swing, wildly and with all my weight behind it. A child could dodge the punch but Andy's not paying attention. The coffee pot shatters on the floor. Cold sloshing coffee under my feet. The mug rolls around on the countertop and I pick it up. It doesn't quite break against his jaw so I swing it again.

He crumples to the floor, fetal, and spits blood. He tries to form words but gets out nothing but bubbles. I lean down, forearm to his throat and staring him in the face.

"You haven't seen her. Fuck you."

I drag him across the kitchen, through a side door to the garage. He sputters and kicks but can't find his footing. I let him fall to the ground and shut the handcuffs tight around his wrists.

"What . . ."

"'Easier with the bitch gone,' right?"

Andy gives me a gurgling cough and spits. "What?"

I raise my eyebrows and let him work through it.

His face falls. "You dumb bastard—"

I bring my elbow across his cheek. Spatter against the walls, on his face. "Careful now."

"Jim, come on. It's not that. It's . . ."

He's scooting backward, away from me. I kick him in the ribs until he goes fetal again. "It's what?"

He whines. "It's just business, okay? A little scare. Hell, you think she's never threatened me?" He flinches back, waiting, but I don't hit him. "I just talked to her, okay. That's all I was going to do."

"Or else you break her nose."

His hands go up in defense. "No, man, it's not like that. I never, I'd never . . ."

My fist comes away from his nose dripping. He moans on the floor. I'm thinking scheduling and work and his cocky fucking smile and I grit my teeth with guilt and focus on Stephanie's bruised face instead. I rummage around and find a length of rubber hose and a power drill. I use the hose to lash the cuffs to the water heater. He's half-prone and struggling. I switch on the drill in front of his face. He bucks forward. He's writhing hard enough that the cuffs break skin. Trickle of blood. He lunges again and lets out a little moan and goes a little more still.

The power drill has a nice loud motor. The bit looks expensive, durable. I move the drill in circles in front of his face, letting him get the picture. His eyes go wide. He pushes himself back as far as he can.

I start with the feet.

Andy's stove is old and gas-powered. I turn everything on and toss my bloody clothes inside. There's an extra set in the trunk of the car. I leave his sink stained red from washing my hands, but if I understand pilot lights correctly, it shouldn't matter. I light a candle and nab three thousand dollars in crumpled bills from a drawer before walking out to the car nude but for my boots.

I roll the window down to the cool night. My clothes smell like dryer sheets. Stephanie's touch. She finds it funny, I suspect, to be all domestic sometimes. My heart tugs at my stomach and my head threatens to spin off and I tell myself to breathe, breathe. You did the right thing, Jim. I pull the threads all toward each other, piecing it together while trying to keep my eyes on the yellow line. It seems rather suspect. Overheard conversation, a good bit of assumption, the sneaking suspicion that I maybe flew off the handle a little bit there. Like maybe my head got muddied up. It does that sometimes.

But it didn't feel muddied when I left home. Two hours ago, the whole situation was all kinds of clear. Stephanie came home with a broken nose and a story, a story about the door to the kitchen at the diner where she works and how she'd been telling them to fix it for months, but I'd heard Andy talking to his druggie lackeys. I'd quoted it to his face back there and I saw the reaction all over him. And when your girlfriend has a dealer partner who's threatening things all over the place, so you can hear them, maybe there's only one thing to do if you want to keep looking in the mirror.

Running through it, it sounds pretty thin. I take a cigarette from Stephanie's pack in the cupholder. I quit years ago but it helps. I focus on the road, on the smell of my shirt, on the smoke. Have to get home. Need to get near Stephanie. She's calming. She's waiting for me, asleep, at the center of the world and all I have to do is drive.

I scrub the handcuffs clean with an old toothbrush. Pink foam collecting in the drain. I rinse them down and let the water take care of the sink before I tiptoe in the bedroom and clip the cuffs back to the headboard, slow and easy so the clicking doesn't wake her. She's wrapped herself in the entire blanket and spread out to take over the whole damn bed. She the-opposite-of-snores. Some nights I wake sweating and wonder if she's even breathing. She always is.

Her leg's sticking through the blanket, the only exposed skin on the bed. I can see the tattoo wrapping around her ankle, script doubling back on itself, but it's too dark to make out the "Don't mourn; Organize!" that she covers with her slacks or boots before going to work every day. She explained it to me once, but I don't quite remember what it means. Something about being the only communist around and without her organization when we moved to this town, she felt like she had to get it. She explained the dialectics of drug dealing to me, too, and though I'm a poor study at such things, I detected the sarcasm.

She's got the bed pretty well staked out, so I take the couch in the living room. I lie back and close my eyes but there's this restlessness I can't shake. My mind's clear now, empty, but there's this twitching feeling in my legs and I feel like I have to move. I feel alert, in control. Assertive. It'll fade tomorrow at work but for now I lie still and enjoy it.

The lack of sleep clings in a film to my eyes and I'm blinking too much. It's just the new guy and me this morning. When I told him to take the register, he didn't argue. It's a bit less work than stocking shelves if we're not too busy, which is always. He took a look at my face and decided not to ask questions.

I'm feeling good, all told, but I don't feel like dealing with customers, especially if one knows Andy, asks why he's not here. And it took me a bit to fall asleep last night, so I look worse than I am. The trick here is going to be to sink into stocking shelves, like I'm blocking out everything I'm thinking and just going through the motions. It shouldn't be too hard.

I get seven DVDs into the bin of new releases I'm working on, to which of course my free-movie perk doesn't apply, before a haggard, salt-and-pepper bastard hauls two young boys in and unleashes them on the children's section. I take one look over at the new guy at the counter and try not to grin to myself. The kids have voices like razor blades. The dad's face is resigned and tired and there's no damn way that he's getting the kids out of here in less than an hour. After a couple of seconds indulged watching the new guy sweat, I turn back to the bin of movies. Company protocol is to ask if you can help him every twelve minutes. I glance to the clock, not that I want to call the kid on it. I just want to see. He called old Andy "sir" when he first started a couple weeks ago, and though my stomach did a little tap dance, it set Andy anew on his rising-up-the-ranks, by-your-own-bootstraps kick, the fading of which I'd enjoyed. I try not to think about what happened next and focus on the shelves.

While the new guy handles the poor dad I slip a gory little slasher flick behind an animated children's film. I'm seeing a manicured mother storming in with fire and brimstone and offense taken at little Jimmy seeing such things, the new guy's flustered face as he calls the boss in to handle it, the other customers trying not to look like they're watching. It's beautiful and I'll be long gone by then. It's a pathetic form of rebellion, but here I am.

My last shift ends in twenty minutes.

I walk the thirteen blocks to Stephanie's diner after work and take a table in the far corner. It's like walking into a cloud of grease and disinfectant. Incandescent lights burn themselves low before anyone thinks of replacing them, so the place feels like a relic, a museum representation of a long-dead breed of greasy spoon. It's a charming little hole, run by an old married couple who probably remember sharecropping and treat their employees accordingly.

I don't recognize Stephanie at first, as usual. Her hair

is tied in a loose, functional ponytail and she plays up the Southern-waitress charm angle, calling everyone at the table next to me "hun" or "sweetie" as she gives them their receipts. I watch the transaction as discreetly as I can, by the reflection of the participants in the dirty window, and I still almost miss it. The leather booklet she hands them, filled as it is with four people's separate checks and credit cards, barely shows the extra bulge of a carefully-placed baggie. I smile to myself, masking it as best I can with the menu. She's at least better than Andy.

Andy's code was never particularly subtle. The customer came in, picked out a movie, and brought it to the register, making the joke about how his girlfriend or wife or buddy told him that, out of five stars, they'd give it ten, or twenty, or, on a lucrative day, fifty. I kept waiting for one of them to slip up and say "grams" instead of "stars," but Andy catered to a young, hip clientele, and they seemed to get off on the spy-film kitsch. He'd stuff a baggie, the large kind, so the shit was sufficiently spread out, into the movie case, under the counter where the well-accounted-for security cameras couldn't see it, and gave the customer far too little change before sliding the movie to them with a warning about the due date.

I catch her eye and she glides over. "How'r'ya doin' today, darlin'?"

"The accent is flawless."

"Why, thank you."

"Just brilliant caricature."

She pulls out a new waitress pad, without the worn edges or phone numbers in the back, borrowed, and flips to an empty page. "Getcha somethin'?"

"Coffee. How's business?"

She casts her eyes around. "Look at the place."

"Yeah. How's business?"

"Oh. It pays the bills." She nudges my leg with her foot. "It's a better system than Andy's got, anyway." I'm glad that the poor lighting has my face in shadows. I've decided I won't tell her. Just let it ride. She leans in a little, like she's asking me to repeat an order or explaining what's in a menu item in case anyone's watching, stalling for a little break.

The makeup she never wears anywhere but work is caked on a little more today so the bruises under her eyes just look like she's tired. I wonder how she manages the charm angle, sometimes, with how much she clearly hates doing this. The way I ride the movie rentals at work, though, she provides us with groceries lifted from the kitchen a few times a week. This is a bit more useful than my contribution, I suppose. I'm not saying that we wouldn't get by without petty theft, but it would be a damned sight harder.

She mock-scribbles in her pad. "You're heading home, yeah? Off work?"

I nod. "Slow day. I kinda like that job sometimes."

She snorts. "Yeah, I'm sure it's peaches." She's turning the Southern thing back on. "Coffee'll be up in a sec, darlin'."

She closes her pad and heads for the kitchen. I fold the napkin into smaller and smaller squares on the table, watching her go. She leans in through the order window and shouts something. Someone yells back, because she has to turn around and repeat herself. She touches her fingers to her temple, briefly, and I can only imagine what goes on in her head all day. She used to talk to me all the time about her coworkers, like a grand army just waiting to be mobilized. Maybe she's right, but in this town, when you talk about a union you're talking about the Civil War, and she left her organization behind when we left the city. She hasn't really talked to me about it since, but it seems like she forces it down when she goes to work and plasters that smile on her face. I wonder if it's something like schizophrenia for her, working.

Waiting for Stephanie to get home, I realize that I didn't tell her at the diner that I'd quit my job. It takes me a minute to process. I don't have any plan, and I suppose it'll raise a couple eyebrows with the cops, if they bother to look, that I quit right after Andy died. This should trouble me, I know, but it just glides into the mess of the last few days, another point I can't quite make sense of, and I'm starting to get those too-late second thoughts, the feeling the suicide case gets the moment after his feet leave the bridge. My breathing picks up a little bit and I can feel the sweat beading on the back of my neck until I turn on the television and flip to a movie channel. A diversion. I'm already missing the free rentals, but it's a third-tier horror film. The channel's got my number.

The killer in his rubber mask has just hacked a cellar door to splinters when the front door's kicked open and I jump so hard I spill bourbon down my shirt. Stephanie stomps into the house dressed in the black smock and white apron from work. She sets her waitress pad in its place next to the oven and dumps her coat on the kitchen table. The door creaks to a stop, short of closing. She curses to herself and walks back to close it, pushing it slowly closed with one finger held forward like she's miming a gun. She comes back to the kitchen and looks over at the television, to me, and back at the television. She very nearly smiles and goes to the bedroom.

I wipe ineffectually at the bourbon on my shirt and succeed only in spreading it around. The woman onscreen comes to a bad-omen gas station with dark windows and Stephanie slinks back in. I almost don't hear her footsteps. Her skin's blue in the light from the screen. She's changed clothes, something black, now, and not much of it, which means she's probably ready to talk.

I run my thumb around the rim of my glass.

"Hey you."

She walks toward me, slow, one foot in front of the other so heel touches toe. It has a distracting effect on her hips.

"Hello."

We exchange pleasantries and I find myself somehow blindfolded with silk, being led to the bedroom with a demented fervor that's still charming. Hell, she looks like a teenage babysitter when she puts her hair up, but it doesn't do for a blindfolded man to get too lost in thought. I focus on not tripping. There are no stairs, thank heaven, and I manage my way to face-up on the bed without embarrassing myself.

I know before I hear the clink of metal that she's going for the handcuffs, because of course that's how it would happen. I think I'm about to have a problem with this but she fastens my wrists to the headboard and puts one hand flat against my chest and I forget to.

We're well underway and I'm still cuffed and blind-folded, which is unusual. Most times she wants my hands free. She's having fun, blowing off steam. My head is clear. I'm picturing her face, thinking that I can imagine her expression and not thinking much else. She's all fingernails and teeth for the moment.

She bites down hard on my collarbone and my whole body jerks. The cuffs dig into my wrists. My voice catches in my throat. The silk over my eyes smells suddenly of dust and spilled coffee and the blood in my head is the faint whine of a power drill and I'm slipping, slipping. Long, jagged breath. I'm writhing around, slippery with sweat. Stephanie gets the cuffs and blindfold off one-handed. My eyes are confused. The first thing I make out is her smile as she pulls me over on top of her. She thinks my ragged breathing is a good sign, and maybe it is, I can't tell any-more, but I would have no idea where to start to explain and so I go with it. My mouth has gone dry but we're not exactly kissing.

Some time later her face is lit by the end of her cigarette. She's got the smile on her face that means she knows she's doing the Hays Code pose for me, smoking so the audience gets it without the director actually showing sex. Her body goes gradually limper and I can feel her drifting to sleep.

The bedroom is a sauna but I can't stop shivering.

I nudge her with my foot. "Stephanie."

"Mmm."

Deep breath, Jim. "You remember saying we should move?"

We pull together what little money we have saved and pile boxes into Stephanie's Pontiac. The landlord grumbles a bit about the late notice but mostly doesn't care; we were usually late with the rent anyway. Stephanie points the car west and it seems as good an idea as any. I'm trying to be dramatic about it, looking for new-beginnings sunshine or a symbolic rainstorm, but it's a boringly pleasant day. Partly cloudy, a little breeze. It's an un-cinematic move but it's a move, and I can fairly feel Stephanie trembling and grinning as we blow past the city-limits sign. She flicks her cigarette out the window at it, hits it, too, but suddenly looks a bit bashful about wasting half a smoke. I reach under her arm and snake one out of the pack when she flips it open, like somehow she won't notice. Seems I've un-quit since my intimate evening with Andy. There's probably something to that, but I don't have to think about that anymore, try to make sense of it. I pop out the car's lighter and hold it to her cigarette, meeting her very curious look with a rough approximation of a charming smile.

We trade off driving until we hit the desert and check into a sexy little motel, all peeling paint and mysterious stains. Stephanie flips the comforter off the bed with a sneer and sniffs at the sheets. She raises her eyebrows and shrugs, which I gather means approval.

She pulls the handcuffs from her overnight bag and closes them around the top of the headboard. "There. Home away from."

I think she's embracing kicking her uniform for the moment, in a too-big rag of a flannel shirt and incongruous combat boots. She turns the thermostat all the way down and flops in the chair and shakes her hair so it falls in front of her face. The hair is defiantly without ponytail and I start to relax for the first time in days.

We lounge about to network television a while until Stephanie sits up straighter and gets a serious look on her face. "Hey, Jim. I want to tell you something." She brushes the hair out of her face.

I shrug.

She looks down. It gets my attention. "You remember the other night, yeah? When . . ." She motions to the fading bruises under her eyes.

My stomach turns to ice and I focus on keeping my face still. I thought we'd agreed on this. I thought we'd agreed without speaking that we weren't going to go back there. No, Jim, no, that was just you.

I nod. "Yeah. Not real easy to forget."

She maybe blushes. I can't tell in the television light. "Yeah, well. It wasn't the door at work. Though they never did fix it."

I nod.

She hesitates a bit. "I went by Andy's after work."

"Oh." I think she hears something in my voice because she looks over, but lets it go.

"Yeah. He was pissed about, well, doesn't really matter. He tried to . . ." She snorts, a smile threatening the corners of her mouth. "You know how he thinks he's a hardass." She looks up and the smile spreads. "Anyway, I figured I'd let him stew for a bit, cut off contact. I can just see how his face'll look when he hears we split."

No. No, she can't.

I just want to get this over with but don't want to push too hard. Speak slowly. "I'm not sure I—"

"No, no, not anything like that. It's just, I needed to vent a little, yeah?" She shakes her head. "Went by a bar after. Rock show, right? Dark inside." She pantomimes with her elbow. "Caught one in the eye."

My mind jerks forward in little starts. I look over to the wall, fighting down the muscles in my face and some truly stupid urges to run from the room, scream, something. I breathe deep as I can. Easy, Jim. Easy. I swallow hard and look back to her.

She shrugs. "I was embarrassed about it."

Standing still is too much. I feel like pacing, fast, but lean against the headboard instead, slumping down until I'm lying on the bed. The floor has become unreliable.

THIS WILL ALL END WELL
by Nik Korpon

THE BUM WON'T TAKE NO FOR AN ANSWER, and when I finally push him aside, he stumbles on his blanket and a cabbie swerves around him, falling on the horn like it's his mattress after a twelve-hour shift. I pop the collar of my peacoat up over my neck as the wind shoves a stained diaper through the Dunkin' Donuts parking lot. Half the boards in the windows have been torn away, taken to fashion lean-tos, reinforce squatters' doors. Broken glass glitters under the streetlamp, a thousand green eyes tracking me, hiding between the spikes of grass spearing through concrete. Behind me on Boston Street, an ambulance screams past, tossing red and blue all over the place. Maybe the cabbie wasn't as quick as I'd thought. Maybe the bum should've found a job instead of relying on charity. There's a limited amount to go round these days, and I don't fancy wasting it on him.

Adele made Thai last night, but I could really go for it again. Something that makes me sweat when I eat it. If not Thai, at least talk her into throwing together some curry, coconut naan or something. Mom would've taken to her nicely, Adele being a kitchen alchemist and all. Mom never was one for culinary experimentation but if anyone could've done it, Adele'd be the lady.

She's a good one. By no means perfect—and with a penchant for creating situations I have to remedy—but she's a real good one. I should make her honest, one day.

The empty street slumbers. Sneakers pendulum on the phone lines. The chain fence slinking around our building is curled at the corners. Adele said it reminded her of flapper hair, probably trying to turn the place into something classy. Feigned elegance. I told her it was the humidity that did it, but that was just because my skull had been blanched after our window unit gave up the ghost. Can't blame her for ignoring me. With my knife, I cut two flowers from the vines clinging to the brick, twist the stems together.

Inside the hallway, sound is nothing but a memory. They marketed the building as a new artists' haven, but there's a high price tag on culture in this neighborhood, and WIC doesn't cover the esoteric. A few months after we moved in, there were still only a handful of tenants in four stories of studios and the landlord had become a ghost. The privacy is nice, but I figure it won't be too much longer till BGE turns the place dark.

A hint of Tom Waits slithers under the crack of the door. I imagine pale moonlight, a velvet rug and skin of sateen. Silk restraints and a leather flog hanging from the wrought-iron bed frame. I cinch my knife inside my pocket, drop a few dead petals to the floor and open the door.

Adele lies naked on the bed, bound by the wrists, with a silk kerchief over her eyes. Two dozen candles rimming the studio throw jagged shadows, make the slight line of pubic hair dance like a flame. She's biting her bottom lip, writhing against the restraints. Her ribs press against her flesh like a fish waiting to be gutted.

The light in the bathroom turns off.

A man enters the room. He unbuttons his sleeves and wears no pants. Black socks. Garters. He's laughing to himself, doesn't realize I'm standing here.

'What the fuck?'

He drops a cufflink. It skitters across the hardwood floor, under the bed.

Adele stops moving.

'Who the fuck are you?'

His shoulders pitch back. Chest out. Trying to stand tall. 'Now wait a minute. This isn't what it looks like.'

I peel off my jacket, drop it at the door. 'It's not.'

'This is just a big misunderstanding. Sherry, tell him.'

'So I'm not walking in on you fucking my wife, then?'

He looks genuinely confused. A bit horrified, too. 'Your wife?'

I smack my hand against the wall. 'You can't see the fucking ring?' I glance over at Adele, at her hands on the bed frame. 'Oh, Jesus, babe. Where the hell is your goddamn ring?'

The man backs up as I step towards him. 'We can deal with this like men. There's no need to get violent.'

'Motherfucker, you haven't seen violent.' The click of my knife makes him shudder. A smile creeps over my face, though I'm not sure whether it tastes blood or finds his southern-plantation accent amusing.

His wallet's out, bills falling like dead leaves in a storm. Adele's tiny hands ball into fists, stretch out. Working blood back to her fingertips.

'Let's be civil about this.' His voice is loyal, barely trembling or betraying himself. 'I didn't know she—I had no idea she was married. Sherry, you didn't tell me.' The candlelight glances off my blade, catching his eye and for a man who was just caught with a married woman—and an underage one at that—he is surprisingly composed. I suppose you need composure like that to make a living in politics.

He corrals the money with his socked feet, tries to shove it towards me.

'Now she's a whore? You can just buy me? We're just

trash and you can do whatever the fuck you want and let your wallet take care of it? I'd cram that money up your dick hole before letting you pay us off.'

'You're misunderstanding me. This was just—'

'And now I'm a retard? A whore-fucking retard? You need to draw pictures so I can understand?' To my surprise, it's my voice that shakes first. The throbbing in my temple makes the room shiver. Stay focused, man. Focus.

'No, come on now. Don't be—'

His hands barely reach shoulder-height before I'm on him, smashing the butt of my knife into his temple. He collapses, a foot snaring the lamp cord and yanking it to the ground beside him. The bulb shatters with a dull pop. His right foot, twitching slightly. No urine in his pants.

I turn to my right, kneel on the mattress. Cool sheets beneath my sweating palms, fingers cradling my knife. Adele's breath falls heavy, ribs breaching, nostrils flaring when she exhales. A few beads of sweat along the ridge of her brow. Climbing across the bed to her, she might be carved in marble for how little she moves.

Lips to her ear, I trace her lobe with my tongue, whisper, 'You should've listened to me.'

Between quick breaths, she asks what I mean.

'Because I was right.'

'How?'

Hands behind her head, I untie the knotted kerchief. 'I told you it would work.'

She blinks away the darkness. 'You did.'

'The little girl thing?' I gesture with my hands like a French chef. 'You were perfect.'

'I look sixteen, fifteen tops. Nowhere near thirteen and I told you this was a bad idea.'

'Tell it to me in Miami or Memphis or wherever you wanted to go, belle. We're but two days from there. Two days and you're far away from this. Besides, I wish you could've seen his face when I said we were married.'

She crinkles her fingers, hands tinted purple. 'I asked you not to use that anymore.'

'I was in the moment, I forgot.' I lean down, run my tongue along the side of her ribs, over the scythe of her hip. She presses her skin against my face.

'And I don't like you saying retard, either.'

I flip my hand, slide my lips and breathe across the apex of her legs. 'My apologies.'

Her chest rises hard, hesitant. A flash of stars when her pubic bone cracks against my nose. 'How much was in his wallet?'

Saying 'a thousand or so' makes her gasp, so I count up by fifties, telling her that with the pliers, lye and the videotape, he'll be more than willing to negotiate our relocation costs. An underage girl will precipitate the end of a politician, the beginning of a TV talk show host. I slide the blade of my knife along the inside of her thigh, create a tableau of lechery in thin dripping lines of red. She comes three times, and for a moment I almost stop, afraid I'll pierce the femoral artery.

When my face is damp and fingers stick to my cheeks, I inch away from her legs, letting the knife amble over the crest of her stomach, through the valley of her breasts. A thin red line and I'll know how to find my way home. She looks like she's been drinking wine, lips a deep shade. I straddle her settling chest, her skin radiating heat I can feel through my jeans, and set my face beside hers. A fleck of saliva lands in the corner of my eye.

'You did good, belle. You did real good.'

The bump in her throat falls, rises. I slice through the restraint around her right wrist, hand falling to the bed like a shooting star. Blush red pours into it, the circulation coming back. Free her left, then set the knife on the wooden apple carton beside the bed, sit up and stretch out my arms.

'Tell me again,' she says. Her voice is fragile enough to break with a harsh look.

'I love you, Adele. Vous, je aime te.' My pronunciation is awful. I need to practice more often, for her.

'Not that.'

I lean down again, press my forehead against hers, as if proximity had some direct relationship with certainty.

'We'll find a town that's made of circles, belle, one that's light all the time. No shadows, no black eyes. You're not going back. You can't and won't.' Her eyelids flutter beneath my lips. 'I won't let you.'

'Please, just—'

'This will all end well.'

She closes her eyes like fists, inhales hard to dry the tears. Nods a few times and inhales again.

'Now you say it.'

'This will all end well.'

'Again.'

'This will all end well.'

'Do you believe it?' I smooth her hair back against her head.

'I believe you.'

I can't help but smile and I unfold myself, dismount her chest. A pair of candles in the kitchenette burns out, first one then the other a few seconds later. The light on the coffee pot glows like a distant red planet. Three frying pans stacked on the two-burner stove, the sides turned black with scorched coconut milk and chili. I get a glass of water from the tap, watch the sediment swirl while Adele lies in bed, staring at the light show on the water-stained ceiling.

'Can you bring me some?'

'We'll get cleaned up first.' I cross the studio with her water, stand next to the bed while she drinks. 'Get ourselves together before we wake him.'

Her eyes open wide, lips contorted, water spilling over her bare chest.

I open my mouth to speak and all I see is static, swirling

snow outside a frozen window. The sound of Adele's scream trickles through the haze, filling my skull. My hands land on something soft and cool—I can only assume the bed—and find a cold cylinder. Like it's a developing picture, I see the lamp that sat next to our bed, now jagged at the top and rimmed with blood. Furious breathing behind me. I slide my hand over, ready to grab the base of the lamp and impale the fucker, and when I spin I taste metal in my mouth, hot copper and bile. Once, twice.

The fucker's face is flushed with murder, his arm extended towards me. He's shaking hands, he's pushing me away. Gnashing bugs swarm through my stomach. I look down at the knife bobbing in my gut, look up at the floor hurtling towards me.

Adele screams and then there's a wet thump. She holds her mouth, blood streaming through her fingers. The room turns strobe, slivers reassembling in random order. He looms above me, foot raised and ready to stomp, then he's barking into the phone. His arm is cocked back to hit her again, then he's dragging me towards the door. My head hits the hardwood floor, sends shockwaves through my vision. His silhouette in the doorway, saying he'll be back in ten minutes with his people.

Warmth spreads through my cheek. Adele, her breath enveloping me. But when I open my eyes I see the dozen candles he swept from the counter lying sideways on the ground, spilling fire across the floor.

She yanks on a pair of velour pants, a hooded sweatshirt with a streak of wine down the center. I reach out to her, feel the cold handle of the knife kiss the back of my hand. Rustling around my head. Her hands wedged in my armpits, shattered French whispers, heels dragging along the carpet. Acrid smoke, her whole box of incense, cheap perfume, burning at once. I look up and she's crying, lips moving but I hear no words.

'This will all end well.'

She doesn't respond to me, just cries harder. Every step shimmies the knife in my gut, opens the hole wider and wider. Sends bright blue shocks across the hallway, but that may just be blood-loss. My legs have disappeared.

I can see my breath. The light hasn't changed but we're outside. The wind burns uncovered skin. Heels smack against the concrete steps, her cries accentuating the thuds. I tell her that it's okay, that she doesn't need to apologize, that I shouldn't have turned my back on him, that we'll be in Memphis or Miami soon, but watch my words drift away in the wind. My knee brushes against the cold steel of the fence when she lays me down. She crouches, presses her face to mine and whispers something I can't understand.

Her lips on my eyelids. We'll be okay, belle. This will all end well. Icy puckered depressions over my eyes. 'I'm so sorry.'

I have no body, no arms. I am a head resting on the sidewalk, the bottom of my neck sticking to the cold concrete. I can feel my lips move but can't fashion words.

'I'll pray that someone finds you.' She kisses me again and hurries away, out of my sight. I close my eyes, try to absorb the echoes of her heels, try to pull myself along the whipping current and follow her.

Something touches my face. She's come back, caressing me. Her hand is made of paper. I open my eyes. A crumpled bill. Brown fingerprints. A small pebble in my back. The memory of her breath. A chill down my side. The squeal of brakes, thick southern shouting. The black sky.

This will all end—

MIDNIGHT SOULS
by Christopher J Dwyer

SHE MOVES LIKE A CRIMSON GHOST. Every motion flutters with the glittery viscera of a million shimmering butterflies. Hair as black as ash swims in a sea of endless auburn and for the fifteen seconds it takes her to saw through the nameless man's arm I'm sure I've never loved anyone as much as her. A crimson geyser sprays plasma the color of broken rubies and a single miscible scream penetrates the layers of the dank hotel room, lost somewhere between the moon and the stars.

Penny takes a breath and sits at the edge of the bed, the weight of our world pressing into her shoulders like an angel's fists. The man falls forward, clasps the fresh stump with white-knuckled fingers, and softly moans until a thin layer of saliva escapes his lips and collects into a mirrored pool on the carpet.

I stand up, dig my soul out of my chest and kiss Penny's forehead. A trail of comet dust spins between our bodies when she looks down at the unconscious man. I collect the thirteen-inch blade from the center of the bed and wipe it clean with a beige handtowel. Penny crosses her legs and removes the small makeup container from her purse on the side of the bed. She checks her eyeshadow, blinks three times, and smiles with cheeks the color of Christmas morning.

The man squirms beneath me and when I place a pillow under his head, he looks at me with eyes of desperate abandon. Neither of us knew his real name and he paid the full three thousand in crisp, unmarked cash that was housed in a briefcase that smelled of whiskey and regret. Penny reaches over for the phone on the mahogany nightstand and hits the button to reach the front desk.

"There's been an accident in room 217," she says, and leaves the receiver disconnected to hang from the side of the nightstand. She takes my hand, immediate warmth and comfort spinning in my veins like fiery heroin, brings her lips to mine.

I grip the small of her back and bring her body closer to mine, dewy lavender scent of her tingling the edge of my nose. "Let's get out of here," I say.

She smiles and nods, blush of her dimples radiating the dark light streaming from the silent black-and-white television in the corner of the room. We walk past the dead limb separated from its host and as I flip the duffel bag over my shoulder, I silently hope that I forget the momentary look on our client's sodden face as he awakes from the foggy nightmare of a dry October evening.

Penny sips her wine as if she's never had a glass before this evening. She licks her lips every few seconds as if to savor the years the liquid lived in the opaque green bottle. "You've never wondered what it feels like? What it means to experience it?"

I shake my head, down another gulp of Guinness. "Not for a second."

It's when she smiles that I picture the first time we met. The balsam forest green of her eyes twinkles with stray moonlight and for a moment I'm a child again.

"I can't believe that for a second," she says. "After all

we've done together, you must want to know what lies on that other side, you know, the words and thoughts and visions they all claim to have after we're done."

Another long sip of beer, another cool burst of autumn wind from the open window in the corner of our kitchen. "No. I can't. I never have, Penny, and I never will."

She sighs and finishes the glass of wine, downing the swirling purple remnants with a final swish of her tongue. She stares out into the midnight sky. "That man tonight, when he had called, it was almost as if he believed everything he heard. How he could one day see them, the ones all around us."

It's right here that I stop drinking, grit my teeth together with the force of a thousand wild boars. I've heard it all before, the talk of their shadows, the way they dance in the empty matter floating above and below us within every step we take. The truth is that I don't want to know what's living next to me. The truth is that the amount of pain experienced in one of our sessions isn't enough for me to believe that there's more to this existence than the physical world around us.

Penny's cell phone rings and the warmth inside my chest dissipates into a broken silhouette against the celluloid behind my eyes.

His name, he says, is Kleyton Parker. Red leather cowboy boots, black jeans and an arrogant smile. His eyes slink back-and-forth as if they're baby black garden snakes. He sits in the hotel bar and sips on a clear martini. Every few seconds he checks out Penny's cleavage and makes it hard for me to forget that he handed us just over five grand in cash just ten minutes ago.

"You're a lucky guy, muchacho." A wink and another gulp of his drink.

I nod politely. "Yeah."

I can tell Penny's getting anxious because she slides a black-painted fingernail against the edge of her glass, the other hand reflecting through the liquid like a patch of baby black widows. She looks at the neon orange clock above the bar and nods at me. "Let's get this started," she says, and picks up her purse.

"You guys don't want another drink? It's on me."

Kleyton stands up from the bar and raises his glass to the air.

"No thanks. What room number are you in?"

He downs the last of his drink. "Two seventeen."

Penny leads the way and Kleyton and I follow her directly into hell.

The radiance of a dozen shattered rays of moonlight pierces the open hotel room air like a rainstorm of silver knives. Penny drops her oversized purse on the edge of the pine desk and fishes out a syringe and two small bottles. I pour myself a scotch from the bar in the corner of the room. Kleyton smiles as I drop an ice cube into my glass.

"I see it's your lady that does all of the heavy lifting." A sharp chuckle and he leans against the window, facing my wife. "It's okay, though. I like me a lady that's a hard worker."

Penny draws a few milliliters of morphine from the first bottle and sprays the tip of the needle into the air. "I need you to sit down over there and be quiet."

Kleyton raises his arms up and scoots over to the other side of the room. He sits in the armchair next to the bar. "Don't worry, little lady. I promise not to squirm."

"Good, because that's a fantastic way of making this a lot worse than it could be."

I finish my scotch in two large gulps and place the

glass at the edge of the bar, halfway on the edge of the pine and halfway into the rest of the room. I've done it enough times to know that if the glass falls, the evening won't go as quickly as I'd like it to. Kleyton fidgets his fingers on the arms of his chair as Penny pulls up the sleeve of his designer flannel shirt. A crow on the edge of the windowsill catches my attention and in the ten seconds that its eyes dance with mine a sharp shriek pricks the calm, dewy air.

The next black shape I see is a gun. Kleyton jams the weapon in my face and in a quick swirl swipes it across my cheek. The pain is nothing compared to seeing a near-stranger with his arm around my wife's neck.

"Don't fucking move," he says, pulls Penny to the other side of the room.

I wipe the blood from my face and taste the rust of rage against the tip of my mouth. "Let her go."

Kleyton laughs, pulls the side of Penny's hair so hard that I can see the hurt in her rosy cheeks. "I don't know how many of these the two of you have done, but along the way, something like this was bound to happen."

"We'll give you our money, Kleyton. Just, please, let her go."

He shakes his head, holds my wife tighter against him. "It's not about the money, cowboy. Believe me, if I was short on cash, I would have never been able to pay that god-awful deposit the two of you required for this here visit. What I'm here for isn't something you can give." He pauses for a second and I swear his shadow dances in the moonlight. "I promise this will be quick."

What happens next occurs in blocky, blurry shapes that radiate with a prismatic glow. A jumbling arrangement of sharp noises and metallic whirls spin in my head like a broken symphony. I ignore the tinges of pain beneath my skull and lunge at Kleyton but I'm greeted with a jagged whip of the pistol butt. Blood spills out of my mouth like a spider web and when the first of Penny's screams pierces the air, I can't tell if I'm alive or dead.

Fade into white and back to grey. Ten seconds or ten days pass and she's lying next to me, her right hand on my chest and clenching my shirt with cherry-stained fingers. The other hand sits ten feet from her body. Kleyton backs away from the scene until his boots scrape across the floor and hit the edge of the opposite wall.

Penny's fingers release the fabric of my T-shirt and she lies motionless and pale. She rolls over to her backside and pushes her body away from me and into the corner between the bar and the window. Her eyes are as black and dead as a newborn demon's and a comet streak of albino white dresses her once auburn locks. She pays no attention to the blood escaping from her new wound.

"Look at her hair . . ." Kleyton's lips nearly swallow his entire face. "Jesus."

Kleyton grabs the doorknob and struggles to swing it open. My last sight of him is the serene wrinkle in his forehead, the two morose eyes locked onto my wife as if his actions changed all of our lives.

I stare at the various stains on the hotel room ceiling and within seconds our shadows have collected our consciousness and dropped us into a frozen slumber.

You were barely seventeen and perfect. Lips of an angel, dimples that could hold a man's soul. You held my hand during the rainstorm and pointed at every shooting star, leaning in for kisses whenever there was a gap in time and space. You smelled of lavender and an autumn afternoon, skeletons of leaves as brown as dead pumpkins.

"Look," you said, and pointed to a fiery trail in the October night sky.

I gazed above and when my eyes were ablaze with the reflections of glitter and hail you pressed your mouth against mine and sucked the memories from the back of my throat and swallowed them. Your eyes shifted from blue to grey and back again.

Our fingers entwined, alpine purple nails trailing the edges of my palms, we let the rain beat down upon our hearts as if nothing could ever stop us.

Penny's eyes draft from side-to-side as if she's following a tennis match. I hold her hand in mine but it's been at least a week since she last squeezed back. Her breaths are consistent and slow. The white streak in her hair remains cold, a reminder of the events before us. Every few hours she smiles and points behind me.

"They're right behind you," she says. "Red eyes like fire. They're all around us, baby. I don't think you should be scared."

I can't turn around, can't bear to think of her this way anymore. I kiss the back of her hand, remember the days when we'd watch the geese in the Charles River and drink coffee and follow the moon back home.

Another kiss on her forehead but she doesn't look directly at me. She keeps pointing to the empty hospital sky. I leave her behind me when the night beckons and I walk to the only place in Boston where the one person I need to see could possibly be.

I spot him walking in through the front lobby. Eleven hotels on this strip of downtown and I was bound to be lucky. I keep a distance from his back, careful not to let my reflection catch the rugged look he still wears on his face. He sips a beer at the bar across from the lobby and it's only a few minutes into his first drink that his client walks over and sits across from him. I study the client's mannerisms, the nervous twitch at the tips of his sneakers, the wavy cowlick that shoots into the sky with an awkward sway. I wait another ten minutes for them to get the small talk out of the way before I move from the velvet couch in the lobby.

Kleyton walks away first and the man follows suit within the next eighty seconds. I walk quickly until I reach the set of elevators near the bar. Kleyton is smart and gets on the first elevator but lets the man catch the next one. We're the only two in the next ride and when he pushes the 'four' button a bright hurried pinch of light escapes from the metal panel.

We reach the fourth floor and he exits first. A quick scan of the hallway shows there's no one else breathing here except for us. It happens almost too quickly and when his windpipe slams against my knuckles it sounds like a popping soda can. I toss aside his cash and license and credit cards but instead grab the key ring from his inside jacket pocket and catch the momentary trance of golden light from the '423' on the ring.

The room's only a minute walk away from the elevator. I knock once for each time my heart beats through my ribcage.

"Thanks for waiting a few minutes to—"

Kleyton can barely finish his sentence before I shove my weight through the door and onto his chest. For a man that's only a decade or so older than me he's not nearly as strong as I'd imagined. He gasps for air between my fist cracking the side of his head. When he stops moving I slam the door shut behind me and smile.

Kleyton's eyelids swing open. The fear in his pupils dances behind the sweat and blood that have caked into his sockets.

"What . . . the fuck." Only three words from a man who, with our situations reversed, wouldn't be able to shut up.

"The quieter you are, the less this will hurt." I only had to fish through his duffel bag for a few seconds before finding the polished cleaver.

Kleyton's eyes follow the moonlight's reflection off the knife and a single swift blow to his jaw is enough to rattle him one last time. He stops squirming when the cleaver hits the open air and slams into the flesh. It takes three swipes to cut through completely and Kleyton is silent as soon as the forearm is split from the wrist and hand on his right side. Lips part open so wide that they could swallow himself and the chair he's sitting in.

"So . . . beautiful . . ." Tiny strands of fresh saliva fall from his mouth and onto his lap. "In the air, behind the bed, all around us . . ."

I launch the cleaver against the side of the desk on the opposite side of the room. Telephone off the hook and Kleyton bleeding out, I nod at the scene and leave the room and the hotel as fast as a ghost falling from the heavens.

Another shot of tequila with no chaser. I stare at the butcher knife Penny used to use on our clients. The wooden handle is beaten and raw. I'm surprised the splinters never found their way into her palm. I finish the rest of the tequila and move onto the half-empty bottle of whiskey across the table in our kitchen. Penny's asleep in the bedroom but nowadays slumber to her isn't really rest at all. She says they talk to her when her eyes are closed. They tell her about what's beyond the arc of this world and the next.

I toss my black T-shirt onto the kitchen floor, feel the cool breeze of an October evening across my bare chest. I stretch my fingers, crack the knuckles with a deep breath.

Eyes closed, I grip the knife, let it sway over my wrist before swallowing the last mouthful of whiskey. I let it fall with a resounding screech and picture Penny's face in the moonlight, her smile as soft as a seraph's voice.

The first one skitters from the corner of the kitchen and over my head. The next one sniffs the new wound, its horns and oval head shifting from side-to-side with a magnetic swing. One of them walks into the kitchen, a pure obsidian form nearly blanketed by dark light. Its eyes glisten with a scarlet glow.

THE TREE OF LIFE

by Edward J Rathke

'YOUR EYES ARE LIKE FIRE.'

'Sounds like bad poetry.'

He gives her his back. 'Never mind.'

'Aw,' she wraps round him, 'don't be such a baby.'

'Sometimes it feels like you don't want me around.'

She sighs and lets go, falling to her back and blowing black hair out of her silver eyes. 'I'm going for a walk.' She gets out of bed and dresses.

'It's the middle of the night.'

She pulls up her pants and throws on a coat. 'It always is.'

'You can't go for a walk.' He rests on his elbow. 'It's not safe.'

The streets glisten and a veil hangs over the sky, blotting the moon, the sun, and stars. She pulls her hood up and pushes her collar high and lights a cigarette. Smoke blooms from her mouth into the thick air where it fingers apart, snakes winding through a desert. She hurries with no direction, each step carrying her further from him and his heavy blue eyes, curly hair, and thin lips. Duned and waved, long cracks and deep chasms fill the roads.

Drifting through the streets like a fog, she loses herself outside looming cemetery gates. She wanders past, her shadow clinging to the high fence, cast by the streetlights.

She stumbles, a tug at her feet like hands wrapped round her ankles.

Behind her, her shadow climbs the cemetery wall and hops over. The cigarette drops from her mouth. She inspects her feet, lifting one boot at a time and seeing no shadow left beneath. Her hood falls, hair dancing in the wind, she turns back and forth, but the streets are wide and empty and silent. Another cigarette in her mouth, a cough pushes from the back of her throat, long strides bring her over the pavement, away from rogue shades.

Her phone vibrates.

'Hello?'

'Where are you?'

'Walking.'

'Where?'

'Around.'

'Are you smoking?'

She exhales loud for him to hear.

'It's not safe out there. Please, Jenny, come back. I can't do this without you.'

'I'll be back soon.'

She thumbs it closed and turns off her phone. The new sodium light pours onto her and she watches the smoke linger and surround, like fairies in flight. Spotlighted there, her thoughts reach after the phantoms, and she turns in all directions looking for her shadow. Closing her eyes, she gives her face to the overhanging light. The hum catches her ears, the sound of fireflies in heat. The roar of fire returns and the warmth is real.

She finds herself an hour later sitting on the stoop of his apartment building chaining cigarettes.

'We can't do this.'

'We don't have to.' He kissed her, long, and she wanted to swallow him.

'I have a boyfriend.'

'I don't care.' He kissed her again and tugged down her pants, tasting her skin. She writhed in his hands and bit her lip.

'Should I tell my boyfriend?'

'If you want.'

'I feel like shit.'

'Do you love him?'

'I don't think so. But, still.'

He kissed her again. 'You should tell him.'

She buried her head in his chest, tasting sweat.

'This is the last time.'

'It doesn't have to be.'

'I can't keep doing this to him.'

'Then tell him.'

She curled away, but he pulled her waist to his.

She put her palm to his beard and kissed his cheek, the hair tickling her nose. 'I don't want to hurt him.'

'Then stop.'

'I don't want it to stop.'

'Stay with me.' He brushed the hair from her face, his fingers glancing against her skin, and kissed her. 'I want you.'

She rolled, face to face, and bit his lip and pressed their foreheads together. Smiling, she pulled his ashen hair, and whispered into his mouth.

He inhaled her words and slipped inside.

'The sky looks weird.'

Butterfly kisses on the back of her ear, his beard grazing her neck, he propped on an elbow and looked to the sky out his window. Far away, past the skyscrapers and highways, at the edge of the horizon, a bloodred line erupted, biting into the sky. It flashed in furious shades, filling the air like an accidental dawn. Buildings toppled near the edge and the street waved, displacing concrete and homes and businesses. She screamed and he covered her when the apartment vibrated, shaking loose the pictures and shattering the windows.

Their ears rang and there was nothing but.

'The fuck was that,' his words gasped, quiet and unheard.

He knew she screamed from the vibrating of her throat and the pounding of her heart. Out the window, carlights flashed, streets glittered with broken glass, water fountained from broken pipes, and blood spotted the sidewalks beside broken bodies.

The ringing dissipated, but the world remained muffled, a cacophony of sirens and car alarms and screams. The night glowed in orange shades.

'Jack.'

'Hm.'

'Is it over?' She whispered to his chest.

'I don't know.'

She raised her head and followed his eyes. 'What time is it?'

The clock was empty. 'Power went out.'

Her phone rang. 'It's Ricky.'

'He survived.'

'Should I answer it?'

Jack got out of the bed and put on his pants.

'Hello.'

'Baby, you okay?'

'Yeah, I'm fine. What was that?'

'I'm on my way over right now.'

'No, don't. It might be dangerous.' Her heart increased its pace and she felt it would rip through her chest.

His breath was heavy like he was running. 'I need to know you're okay.'

'Ricky, don't. It might happen again.'

'If I die, at least I'll be with you.'

'Jesus, stop. Stay home and be safe.' Her hand clutched her phone.

'I'm going crazy thinking about what might happen.'

'We're fine, but one of us won't be if he keeps running here like a madman.'

'Are you sure you're okay?' Ricky's gasped breath.

'Knowing my white knight is safe would help.'

His breath slowed, heavy. 'Okay, call me when you're ready. I need to see you.'

'Okay.'

'I love you.'

She hung up. Her eyes welled and she cried.

He put his hand on her shoulder and ashed into the carpet.

She flung her arms around him, tears streaking down his chest.

'Think it'll always be like that?'

'It's beautiful.'

'Ricky writes me poetry sometimes.'

'He would.'

'He talks about sunsets and sunrises and the horizon after a storm. About me and my eyes.'

'There're no words for something like this.' He grazed her arm with fingertips, up and down, his feet resting on the windowsill.

She nestled her head into the crook of his shoulder. 'That's why I like you.'

Out the window, the sky was on fire and had been since it erupted days before and sent the world into chaos. A lake of fire hung above the earth casting life in permanent daylight. It lapped down towards the earth, like staring inside a volcano, flamed demons reaching from hell with long claws and sharp fangs and curved horns. It made the air sticky, thin, and hot.

'If you look at it long enough, it feels like you're falling in there, like it's gonna suck you right up, you know?' He blew smoke out his nose and tossed the cigarette outside.

'Icarus.' Breathless and whispered.

'It might burn till we're out of oxygen.'

She rubbed a finger through his beard. 'Suffocate.'

He kissed her forehead. 'Someone'll figure something out.'

'What would you do?' Her eyebrows curved in and up, but her pupils were discs, shining with the fire's reflection.

'Your eyes're like fire.'

She smiled and pushed him to the floor, straddling him.

'I love you.'

She removed her shirt.

'What is this?' She traced a finger over his back along branches painted in his skin.

'Hm.'

'On your back.'

'Yggdrasil.' His mouth muffled by the pillow.

'What?'

He turned his head, dark eyes drooping. 'The Tree of Life. The Norse believed that every plane of existence,' he yawned, 'was a part of it.'

'But why do you have it?'

'Hm?'

'Are you asleep?'

'Hm.'

She nudged him.

'As long as that tree lives, the world will too.'

'I like that.'

'Hm.'

'Jack.'

'Hm.'

She sang his name softly into his ear and touched her fingers to the wrinkles beside his eyes.

'You get one wrinkle for every crow that you outlive.' His voice was soft, dripping from his dreams.

'You've outlived a lot of crows.'

He smiled.

'Sleepyhead.'

He opened his eye. 'Hi.'

'Hi.'

He closed it, smiling.

She watched him sleep and caressed his back, running her fingernails lightly over the branches and roots.

'I don't get why you won't stay here.' His blue eyes dimmed by the constant burning sky.

'I like my place.'

'But it's dangerous. Those men out there could get you and I'd hate to think about it.' Ricky pulled her close to him, laying her head on his chest.

'It's too much to handle right now. I can't just move.'

'I could move in with you.'

She stared into the lake of fire and felt the pull, the flames cycling towards her, calling her deeper and higher. 'I don't know.' His dark eyes were out there, deep and muddy, calling her name and tugging at her chest.

'Why? It doesn't make sense to be apart anymore. The streets are wild and it's not safe for anyone to leave. The looters and gangs are everywhere and no one cares to stop them. More and more people join every day. It's madness. Every time I think of you being so far away when I hear those screams and see all those stacked bodies, I feel my chest collapse. What if one of those bodies was yours or what if one was mine?'

'Don't think like that.' Her voice was thick and her mind flew out the window to him so far away, each thought an outstretched hand reaching, if only to touch fingertips. 'They'll burn out.'

'Like the sky?'

'Like a sunset.'

He kissed her head, taking in the scent of stale sweat. 'I'm just scared. For you.'

'Don't be.' She shifted so they were face to face. 'I'm a big girl.'

'Why won't you stay with me?'

She touched his bare chin and rolled to the window and waved a hand where the glass once was. 'Do you ever wonder if there's someone else out there for you?' She stared into the street where five teenagers beat a bald man in a suit and stripped him of his clothes. His screams echoed against the fire. She brought her eyes to Ricky.

He kissed her hand. 'No. There's no one else for me.'

'What if there is and you just haven't met her?'

'You're perfect for me.'

'How do you know?'

'Where is this coming from? I love you. Believe me.'

'No, I do. I know you do.'

'Then what? Do you think there's someone else?'

She blew hair out of her eyes. 'Of course not.' Heat ran up her back and touched her face.

'Then stop. I love you.' He tried to kiss her, but she leaned away.

'But you've loved other girls.'

'Not like this.'

She pulled his face close and kissed him. 'You know how to make a girl smile.'

'You're not smiling.'

'I will be.' She kissed him again, hard, and pulled him on top of her.

'What?'

'I'm sorry, Ricky, I just can't.'

He sighed and bowed his head, the blond hair tickling her chest.

'It's just there's so much death outside. I can't think of anything else.' She pulled his chin up so he could see her.

He studied her face seeing his own reflection in her wide pupils. 'You get me all worked up like this, though.'

She frowned. 'I know. I'm sorry, but I just can't. Not right now.'

'It's been weeks.' He rolled off, crossing his arms behind his head, staring at the ceiling.

'I'm sorry.'

'Will you stay here tonight?' His eyelids weighed down his wilted eyes.

'It's never night.'

'You know what I mean.'

She rolled over and watched the fire rage.

'We're almost out of food.'

'Don't go out there.'

Jack pulled on boots. 'We need something to eat.'

'You said almost.'

'I meant, All gone.'

She stood and grabbed his hand. 'Please, Jack, don't. It's scary out. It's not like before.'

He kissed her fingers. 'They won't bother me. I've nothing they want.'

'It's not the same out there. They're desperate and getting crazier. I saw them cut a guy apart. The screams were terrible and they lasted all night because they just left him

EDWARD J RATHKE

to bleed to death out in the middle of the street. No one tried to help him.'

'I'll manage.'

'But the radio's out now, too, and, I don't know, you can't. If you die.'

His lips were on hers and the words were lost, never spoken, but carried between them. With tears, she wrapped her arms round him and kissed him longer. They separated, slow, their lips touching like fluttered butterfly wings. She whispered into his parted lips and he took it inside, deep, where he could taste it, live on it.

Her phone rang.

'You still have Ricky.'

'Not anymore. I live here, with you. I need you.' She kissed him, ignoring the phone.

'I know. I know.'

Her lip shipwrecked and her eyes drowned.

'I'll be right back. Trust me.' He kissed her through her sobs and was out the door.

She collapsed.

She leaves the stoop and tosses the last cigarette into a puddle. Skeletal trees line the road back, replacing the streetlamps, most of which no longer work. The wind blows cold and she looks to the infinite cloud above. It hangs low, suffocating the earth with grey. The colors rot off the world and she is left only ashen shades.

The sound of her footsteps echoes off the tilted buildings that bow in mourning for the world. The streets stretch forever before her and the lamps return, droning beneath the clicks of her aimless feet. The wind whispers in her hood, his voice soft against her ear, the caress of his beard on her neck. She turns and sees her shadow across the street, waving.

She waves with fingertips, not sure if a shadow can see. She almost speaks, but knows not if shadows hear. It jumps down the street and she follows. Through puddles and over breaks and beams and collapsed buildings and monuments, she chases, running till her lungs fill with glass. It stops outside Gate Park and she falls to her knees and weeps.

He did not return nor did her tears stop. Her phone rang incessantly, but she could not move to answer or smash it. She was curled in his bed, afraid to look out the window or see the sky burning. The scent of him, his sweat, was all she wanted and she bathed in it. Screams ripped through the air, but they stopped meaning anything weeks before, so much a part of the airwaves that she forgot how the world sounded without them.

Her fears played inside her eyelids. Blood pouring down the street, his body in pieces, his head staked by ruthless Kurtzes, vagabond savages. The streets— more temperamental than the sky and infinitely more frightening—were full of them and he, Jack—her Jack— was out there amongst them, him, all of her love into his mouth, so that he could walk through hell and pull her from the flames.

The neverending day confused time and place. He had been gone for a week or only an hour, but she knew he was gone. Dead.

All sensation slipped away, her body hollowed out. His black eyes and smokey hair carved into her mind, there was naught else to see.

The phone rang and it was in her hand.

'Ricky,' the sobs choked all words he or she had.

She crept through the city back to Ricky's apartment. Her heart plummeted with every trickling sound, the blood rising in her chest till she wanted to vomit, but forced herself to keep pace, almost running.

She avoided blood stains and forgotten bodies. The city stunk of decay, fire, and blood. Broken glass and burning cars and headless bodies plastered to buildings. Gate Park had a head mounted on each post of the fence. She turned her eyes and carried on, sure she would never go outside again. Every face, contorted in agony, screaming their dying wish or curse, blaming god or devil or man. Bodies forged together, cut up and sewn in monstrous contortions, grotesque sculptures of pain.

Jumping over a pit full of blood, her eye caught the tattoo of a great ash tree and muddy eyes. She could not look away, the world muted and the light blew out. Her eyes clouded, her mind a fog, she staggered to the body. Black ink in the skin, the branches flowing to his shoulders, full leaves, the roots reaching down to his legs, and all the world stemmed from it. His face staring at her, looking always behind. She wretched, emptying all of her into the street, and put her hands to his back, tears filling the cracks in the pavement, her sobs breaking through the sky. She unstrapped him from the fence and his head fell from the shoulders, rolling on the ground. She kissed his rotting bloodless lips and vomited again. His arms were skinless, his scalp gone. Eviscerated, his body was an ocean of maggots. Closing his hollow eyes, she fell apart and could walk no more, could breathe no more, could see nothing else, could live no more.

'Jesus. I've been terrified. Where have you been?'

The tears still streamed down her face and words could not form, her lips trembling.

'Come here.' He wrapped his arms round her, kissed her head, and closed the door. 'Want some coffee?'

She shook her head and collapsed onto a chair.

'I've been so worried. Where have you been these last couple days?'

Chest heaving, her head in her hands, she wept.

'Shh.' He put his arms around her. 'It'll be okay. You're here now.'

She coughed and pushed him away, spittle falling from her mouth, snot running from her nose, her eyes, red and inconsolable. The silver worn away, blotted out by the blood of his mutilation.

'What's wrong?' His voice was soft, trying to weave through her, bring comfort.

'It's over. Everything.' She shook and wretched, but there was nothing left inside.

He brought a blanket and wrapped it over her shoulders. 'It's going to be okay.'

'No, it's fucking not. Everyone's dead and I wish they'd take me.'

'You don't mean that.'

'I do. I fucking do.'

'Without you, I'd die.'

'Then go fucking die.' She threw the blanket at him, grabbed her knees and put her forehead to them, her body quaking.

He watched her and did not speak. He let her be, but stayed close, waiting for the casket to unlock so he could rock her back to life.

'Jenny, look.' He pointed out the window, his eyes cobalt and wide.

She followed his finger to where the sun shown. A moment unregistered, the image struck her breathless and her knees buckled. Her lips opened, tried to speak, but only ate sunlight.

He kissed her cheek. 'Can you believe it?'

'No.' She whispered and she felt the warmth fill her.

The sun risen, the fire gone, she touched him to make it real, his face bathed in sunlight, in real daylight, his curled blond hair haloed from the dawning sky. She turned to their apartment and it was lit, not by a permanent fire, but by the sun, like angels dove in and touched every corner, every particle of dust floating in the air. Back to the sun, she could not look away and tears filled her eyes. 'He would've loved this.'

'Who?' His eyebrows arched.

The world returned, lungs refilled, and legs straightened. 'What do you think it means?'

'It means things are going to be okay.'

She smiled.

'This is good news. People will feel less hopeless and someone will stop the gangs.'

'But who's left?'

'I don't know.' He watched her stare out the window, catching every movement of her lips, memorizing them, how the light made her eyes glow, and how it touched her porcelain face.

'What if it happens again?'

'I'm so glad you're here.'

She smiled and lowered her head.

'I love you so much.' He ran his hand through her black hair, holding the back of her head. 'I can't imagine seeing this without you. A brand new sun, a day we never thought we'd see again. It's the sun, Jenny. The world's going to be okay.'

'I hope so.'

He kissed her hair and took it in, the sun, her scent, the cadence of their hearts, and each new breath.

She hears footsteps and runs, the tears still stinging her eyes. Shouts and howls stab through the air, and she ducks into a crumbling building and hides. Her heart pounds, weakening and stinging her chest, pins sticking into every inch of her, climbing up her back, down her legs. Reality snaps back, and death reaches its talons into her heart.

The howls grow louder, accompanied by percussion of metal on metal and wood on concrete and two sounds she cannot distinguish, but their timbre is softer and higher in pitch. Afraid to look or breathe, she cowers behind a wall and closes her eyes, like a child becoming invisible.

Footsteps come close. 'It might've been nothing.' The voice, soft, a boy's.

'Nah, I heard some bitch cryin.' Like sandpaper, his voice scrapes the inside of her skull.

'Yo, what you guys waiting for?' A third voice, boyish as the first, but rasped, as if the second tore off the youth of the third.

'It couldn'ta got far. No more footsteps to hear.'

'Could have been a dog or something.'

'Nah, it was a bitch. I know a bitch when I hear it.' A tapping of the unfamiliar noises trickles into the night.

She opens her eyes and peeks round the corner. They are fifteen feet away, circled in the middle of the street. Two look between fourteen and twenty, and the third is a heavyset man. Warpaint or blood or both cover their faces and the big man has a necklace of bones with a small skull, like the skull of a child, centered on his chest. She puts her back to the wall, her hands clutching her mouth, stifling screams and swallowing vomit.

'Everyone else is going up Fifth or down Third. I'ma meet up with them. See ya'll later.'

'Later, Finger.'

'What you wanna do?'

A snort and a cough. 'Les stay on Main. Bitch is dumb enough to come to Gate, it's dumb enough to stay on Main.'

'Yeah.'

She waits till the beats and howls are faint and far away. She creeps down to 2nd Street and follows Fitzimmons to Ricky's apartment. Barely able to breathe or cry or walk, she prays, muttering syllables.

Opening the door, she finds Ricky with his phone in hand. 'Where have you been?'

She runs to his arms. 'Just hold me, please.'

And he does.

They lie awake in each other's arms, her eyelids never touching. The clouds wander like the waves of an ocean, but there is no reprieve. 'It's different than it used to be.'

'What?' His voice drifts through dreams.

'The sky doesn't change, but it's worse than before.'

'How do you mean?'

'It was always terrifying, but now that it's always dark, I don't know.'

He spoons her and kisses the back of her head. 'The sun will come back again. Remember how beautiful that was?'

'Yeah, but it was only a day. A single day and instead of constant daylight, we're drowning in darkness. My shadow ran away tonight.'

'What?'

'I think I'm going crazy.'

He pulls the hair away from her face.

'Things are much worse now. The people out there, they're completely out of control. I saw them tonight.'

'Jesus, are you okay?'

'Yeah, but I wasn't. I thought I was going to die, thought they were going to get me. They wear the bones of the dead. This one guy, he had an infant's head hung around his neck on a string of bones, like it was his prize. I think they're eating people now, and I could smell it, their jaws on me, their hands grimed over me. And I really thought I was going to die, and I was terrified, but I wanted them to. A part of me really wanted them to take me and kill me.'

'I'd die without you.'

'This isn't about you. It's not about me.' She turns to him. 'I'm ready, Ricky. Really ready.'

'Don't say that.'

'I mean it.' Her eyes are deep pools and he sees her drowning in them. The silver tarnishes, black tar spreading over her irises.

'Things will get better.'

'What if they don't?'

'They have to.'

'Why?'

'If they don't, then this is it. And I can't believe there'll be nothing after us.'

'There's already nothing. Those people are all that's left. What if they start raiding buildings? We won't be able to stop them. They'll come in here and kill us, maybe eat us. What if they're the future?'

'Think we should leave?'

'I don't know.' She kisses him, lightly, feathers on lips. 'I wish the sky would catch fire again. I can't take this, this endless night. Everything's dying. Everyone.' She cries, wetting the pillow.

'I promise things will be okay, as long as I'm with you. You're all I need. And if we die, we'll die together.'

Her sobs increase and he kisses her forehead, her cheeks, and her nose. He takes her hands in his and kisses each finger. 'I promise you, even if it kills me, we'll make it through.'

The sobs strengthen and her voice cracks, torn apart. 'You just don't get it.'

'What's wrong?'

'I don't want to just survive. I want to live.'

'We are living.'

'We spend all day in this fucking room in the dark. There's no electricity, no water, no food. There's nothing and there's never going to be anything again.'

Her voice was rasped and sobs cut through her words. 'Is that why you left tonight?'

She gives her back to him. 'I don't know.'

'When did you start smoking?'

'Jesus Christ.' She sits up, her face furrows. 'Does it fucking matter?' Her tears stop and her voice flattens.

'What do you want me to do?' His face is long, his eyes well, like a dog, loyal to the end, willing to give anything and everything to her.

'There's nothing to do.'

'Don't lose hope. It might not be much, but it's all we have anymore besides each other.'

'How do you do it?' Her voice relaxes, her face slackens.

'Do what?'

'How do you keep going? How do you smile when everything's just . . . just so fucked and, I don't know, fucked?'

He looks down and slowly moves his hand to cover hers. His fingers are light, the skin barely touching. His eyes return to hers, the fading light, the emerging blackness consumes them. 'You.'

She puts her hand to his face and pulls him to her. His pale face, his breath hot and sour, she kisses him on the lips like the first time, tentatively, like toes dipped in cold water.

'I love you, Jenny.'

The clamor of the city cuts through the air, howls and cheers and screams and the percussion of bones and metal and wood penetrate their room. They cling to one another, quaking, their hearts splintering, and the riot rages. They are close, right outside their building. The darkness crushes them in bed, stealing their breath, stabbing their every vein, and the tears spill from their eyes like open wounds. She prays, though she has not in years and can remember no words. She prays for it to be painless, for Ricky not to suffer, but mostly she prays for dark eyes and greying black hair, for the face that saturates her every waking moment and haunts her every fitful dream. The voice that whispered in her ear, the lips that kissed her neck, the hands that gave her hope, the man that is lost, but unforgettable. Her shadow appears on the windowsill and motions for her to follow. It jumps and soars into the eternal night.

The rabid revolutionaries storm the apartment building, but their tumult is far from her, held behind a curtain, for she drifts out the window on the wings of his memory, trailing her shadow. The man beside her clutches her, holds her tight, whispers hope and bravery into her ear, but it is nothing, only meat and bones in the bed with him. Doors collapse before the ravagers, one room at a time over each floor. Explosions of shattering wood, droning of drums, and shouts cut through the walls.

She follows her shadow across the sky where his voice comes clear. Surging through the unbreakable cloud, she feels sunshine once more, for the first time in weeks, and his hands are on her, pulling her through atmosphere and space and time to a great tree, miles high and piercing the endless cloud weighing down the earth. The branches stretch for miles and they stand in each other's arms bathed in sunlight watching the earth die.

THE KILLER
by Brian Evenson

With a razor, Santon reads, *the killer slit the intravenous sack. The fluid gushed out, spattering onto the
floor. Ruiz, drugged and immobilized in the hospital
bed, could do nothing to stop him, could do nothing but
wait for death.*

It is the end of the page. *What is the killer thinking?*
wonders Santon as he turns the page. *Who is the killer? Is
the killer a man or a woman? What has led the killer to com-
mit such an atrocious crime?*

On the subsequent page, Santon finds that the
unconscious Ruiz is not, after all, unconscious. He is
disturbed, barely coherent, but he is conscious. *Ruiz stared
at the figure above him, knowing the form to be familiar but
unable to grasp the name. What,* Ruiz wondered, *could the
killer be thinking?* With that, the plot flees to make way
for the slow death of Ruiz. His thoughts spin idly through
sunlit and sentimental years of childhood much to Santon's
annoyance, until the memories slowly darken, take a sharp
downward course into *systematized depravity* until page
420 when the memories collapse into a free association
chain which, by leaping from the word "genuflect" out into
empty space, leads to the novel's resolution and climax.
The killer is—, thinks Ruiz, and dies. Four pages later the

book concludes, with an imaginary newspaper headline— *Mysterious Killer Still at Large*—and a subtitle—*Promises to be heard from again.*

Santon puts the book down. He walks from the chair to the table, running his hand along the table's surface. The table is ordinary. It is dusty. There is nothing on it.

What does the word "genuflect" mean? he wonders. *Is there perhaps a meaning for it which cannot be seen with the untrained eye? For Ruiz, who is dead, there was. Why not for me?*

"Ruiz," Santon tells Alma, "dies."

The bar is dark and nearly empty. The table is lit by three paste-white candles as thick as Santon's forearm, none of which give off more than a tiny flame. Not quite paste-white, Santon thinks. They are the color of two fish that Santon found once in an underwater cave. The fish were nibbling at his legs, not hurting him, just nibbling. He could not see them. He caught them and killed them and then swam out of the cave to look at them. *Not quite pasty-white*, he thought, upon seeing them in the light.

The patrón, wiping off the bar, asks Santon and Alma to lift their cups.

"Genuflect?" asks Alma.

"Yes," says Santon. "Yes, for Ruiz that's the key."

"What does it mean?" she asks.

"I don't know," he says. "To squat?" he says.

Santon has some idea of what genuflect means but is certain that it meant something more to Ruiz. Words, when they brush up against people, swell and split and branch. They become unmanageable. He explains this to Alma, who listens politely, her index finger touching her chin. It is a gesture he has never seen her make before.

"Swell and spit and branch?"

He shrugs and buys another round of drinks. He drinks something clear. Her drink is opaque.

He explains to her how he wondered what the killer was thinking just an instant before Ruiz wondered the same thing!

"Is that a coincidence?" asks Santon. "I ask you."

Alma says nothing. Santon goes on to explain that he was curious about other things as well.

"Sex."

"Sex?" asks Alma, coloring.

"Sex," says Santon. "The killer: which sex?"

"Oh," she says. "I see."

They are outside now and walking. The area they walk through is a park of sorts, poorly lit. It is dark. There are trees. There are spots of grass that have been pressed down and, off the path, dark shapes.

Santon puts his arm around her as they walk. Alma does not try to move away.

"Who in the book do you think the killer really is?" she asks.

Santon stops. "I can't even make a guess."

"He could be anybody?" asks Alma.

"He could be anybody."

"You'd better be careful," says Alma.

"What?" asks Santon.

"Perhaps I am the killer," says Alma.

"Ruiz could tell me," says Santon. "But he's dead. Murdered."

He takes his arm off from around her shoulders.

"Genuflect," he says tentatively, watching her reaction from the edge of his eye.

She does not react. They walk next to each other in silence.

Reading another book, a "true crime" story, Santon remembers the novel's last words: the killer will be "heard from again."

He can't concentrate. He puts the book down, gets out the novel with the killer. He takes out his telephone guide, calls *Biblioteca Fidel*, asks if they have another book by the author of *The Killer*. There is only the one book, he is told.

"Isn't there a sequel planned?" he asks. "The killer promised to be heard from again," he says.

"I don't know anything about a sequel," says the bookseller.

He thanks her, hangs up the telephone. He sits down again, looks at the novel in his hands. On the cover it says "Based on a True Story." It doesn't mean anything. Most books, he thinks, claim this.

When he opens it, he discovers the final pages have been cut out with a razor, cleanly. Six pages gone.

Perhaps a joke of Alma's, he thinks. Nonetheless, he is deeply disturbed. If a joke, it is in poor taste. Is Alma capable of it? How could she get in? Practically speaking, she hardly knows him.

Perhaps it is not a joke. After all, anyone could be the killer.

For several weeks he avoids her, does not answer the telephone. The telephone keeps ringing. He encounters her accidentally on the bus. She is already sitting when he boards. She looks up and sees him and he has no choice, he feels, but to smile and join her.

One thing, another thing, and soon she and Santon sit in the dark on a wrought-iron bench. He has explained how when his grandparents came to the island their name was not Santon at all, but rather Sànton.

"Is that significant?" asks Alma.

Santon looks at her. Her body is cut in twain by darkness, her far side vague.

"Is it, Santon?"

"Is what?"

"The name."

"Rather significant."

They sit silent for some time. *Why significant?* Santon wonders. *What makes it significant? What if she asks why?*

"So, you're going to college," he says quickly.

"Yes," says Alma.

"Well, I'll be damned," says Santon.

Silence. Santon is thinking, *I'd give anything to know where the killer is right now.*

He wakes. He washes his face and puts on his robe. When he goes to have breakfast, he looks out the window.

There are people passing on the way to work. He watches them pass. So many faces, but none of which he recognizes. He wants to close the blinds but cannot. He stays watching, anxious, until it falls dark.

He wants to ask Alma if she removed the pages from the novel. *If she admits to it,* he thinks, *maybe we can have a good laugh about it and forget about the whole thing.*

But what if she will not admit to it? What if she did not do it? If it is not her, he can only conclude that it must be the killer. He would prefer the uncertainty over knowing that it is the killer.

Even if she does admit, it does not mean that she is not the killer. She may admit and laugh with him, to throw him off guard. And then kill him.

If she admits it, she might be the killer. If she does not admit it, she might be the killer.

He cannot bring himself to ask.

He is walking by a dilapidated theatre when he sees a poster. On the poster a hand slices an intravenous sack with a glinting razor:

THE KILLER!
A True Story!
Based on the Book!

The names of the actors are French, Spanish, Italian. None are names he recognizes. Beside the killer's name, there is no actor listed.

He wanders around the district until it is dark, returns to the theatre in time for the first showing. The theatre is mostly empty, a scattering of people through it. He sits in the back, near the door.

The film flickers onto the screen. Light plays oddly over the few faces near him. He smokes a cigarette to make his hands stop shaking.

The movie begins much as the book, with the philosophical conversation between the curate and the well-dressed gentleman and then the subsequent murder of both, shortly thereafter. Then the bodies begin to pile up, while Ruiz begins to gather evidence, goes undercover, is nearly killed, uncovers the child pornography ring, catches malaria, is run over by a car, is brought to the hospital.

It is in its ending that the heretofore faithful film changes, for there is no sign of consciousness on Ruiz's part, no flashbacks into childhood, no free association chain. Instead, there is a transition and the hands and torso of the killer are shown in an apartment. He walks about, straight razor in his hand, as if stalking someone. The scene fades, comes up again in a hospital. The killer slits the bag as Ruiz's breathing slows. The killer leaves, the breathing stops. There are no closing gestures or credits, the film simply spools out.

He stays for the second and third showing, falls asleep. When he wakes up, he seems to remember, while groggy and before falling asleep, catching a glimpse of the killer. The killer had walked past him and sat three rows before him. Santon had noticed it, but had not realized the person was wearing the same coat and gloves as the killer in the movie until now, waking up. Unless he imagined it. The seat is now empty.

After the second reel, the film stops. The light shines white on the screen. Santon sees he is the only person in the theatre.

He waits, but nothing happens. He goes out into the lobby but the lobby is empty. He opens the door to the projection booth and moves up the stairs. There is nobody in the room. The film reel, still spinning, clicks against the tail of the film.

He waits for a moment, then threads the third reel himself, returns to his seat. When the movie finishes, he makes his way out into the lobby. The theatre is still empty, the lights extinguished. He pushes quickly into the streets, is relieved when he finds people around him again.

He is nervous about returning to his apartment alone. He is as much afraid that nothing will happen as that something will. If nothing happens, there is something wrong with him inside. If something happens, there is something wrong with the world. It is easier simply to avoid returning home, at least for one night.

He finds a card house called "The Five Aces" with a bar, a few rooms with beds above it.

He arranges to take a room for the night. The room is squalid, the wallpaper puckered and yellowed. He can hear mice in the walls. The bed has a cheap metal frame, a mis-woven blanket atop the uneven mattress. On the wall beside the bed is a black house phone, an internal line, no dial.

In chipped enamel at the bottom of the mirror are four aces, spread, one from every suit. *Where is the fifth ace?* he wonders.

Santon picks up the receiver, waits. He hears it click at the other end. "¿Mande?" a voice says.

"Where's the fifth ace?" Santon asks.

"Pardon?"

"From here I can see only four aces. Where is the fifth ace?"

"The fifth ace?" says the voice. "Sir, you are the fifth ace."

"Where are you?" Santon yells. "What is your name? Where are you?" The line seems to have gone dead.

When he is sufficiently drunk, he pays the bartender to let him call Alma. He tells her to come meet him.

"You can be the sixth ace," he says, forcing a laugh.

She says she might come but she is not certain she can make it. She'd like to come, she says, then asks him if he's been drinking.

"I'll wait for you," he says. "I'll wait in the bar. We can go upstairs and talk. All we have to do is talk."

She gives some answer or other. He sits down to wait at a table that gives him a good view of the door, orders another beer.

He awakens to find the bartender jostling his shoulder, the rest of the bar empty. He lets himself be led upstairs to the bed, is quickly asleep again.

When he runs into Alma again, she asks if she can borrow the novel. She would like to read it, she says. She has seen the movie and liked it and wants to compare it to the book.

He shrugs. He invites her to his house that evening, says he will give it to her then. Smiling, she accepts.

Later, he will claim it did not turn out as he expected it to. His only intention is to give her the novel, which she herself had asked for, but when he has given it to her, she seems reluctant to leave.

Out of reflex, he asks her if she wants a drink. Then, through a series of events which Santon fails to understand, they are in the bedroom together, without clothing, on the bed. She has straddled him, her hands resting lightly on his bare chest.

"The book," he says. "The last pages have been razored out."

She hushes him, presses her finger to his lips.

"But—"

"What's the matter?" she asks. "Not afraid of me, are you?" He doesn't respond. "Relax," she says. "It's not going to kill you."

She covers his eyes with her hands, brings herself tight against him. He can hear her body move, as if at a distance. It terrifies him. "Don't open your eyes," she says. "Don't look now."

HEADSHOT
by Gordon Highland

INT. LIVING ROOM - NIGHT

STEADICAM through posh, modern furnishings
inhabiting a spacious 1970s floor plan. SOFT
JAZZ suffuses the room, its vinyl crackling
along with the fireplace casting amber hues
on the suede furniture, wildlife paintings,
and taxidermy. A GRAND PIANO with no sheet
music props up many FRAMED PHOTOS of celeb-
rities, each with their arm around the same
man (40s), always in gold aviator shades
and spiky salt-and-pepper hair. LAUGHTER
and VOICES slowly fade in O.S.

>   FEMALE VOICE
>   Besides, everybody does June.
>   Too hard to find a place.

>   MALE VOICE
>   How 'bout right here, then?
>   Set it up out back. Erect
>   that thingy, the hoopla,
>   whatever it's called.

>   FEMALE VOICE
>   (laughing)
>   Huppah!

INT. DINING ROOM - CONTINUOUS

The man of the voice and photos, SAM DAWES,
sporting a grey blazer over an emerald-
green shirt, charms his companion by sum-
moning phlegm to imitate her Hebrew.

                    SAMMY
         Hchchuppah.

The woman, CARI (30s), elegant and dressed
for her sexual prime in a burgundy cami-
sole, raises her wine glass in mock-toast
to his effort. They sit adjacent at the far
end of a long table, CANDLES burning and
spent linen topping their dinner plates. It
could be a jewelry commercial. Looks exchange, the arch of his brow and her bitten
lip suggesting the carnality to come.

EXT. HOUSE - THAT MOMENT

HANDHELD POV outside the window. Darkness
vignettes the warm, MUFFLED dining-room
scene as the couple converses whimsically.
Tree limbs rake the f.g., WIND rustling
through them. Sam puts one hand over Cari's, then pulls her close with his other
for a kiss. WHIP to CAR HEADLIGHTS piercing
the night and pulling into the driveway.
The gate is already open. The car stops,
then reverses back the way it came. WHIP to
the window again and the couple is gone.

INT. KITCHEN - MOMENTS LATER

Vised between the black stockings of Cari's
thighs, a high-tech CORKSCREW atop a wine
bottle resists her efforts. Sam scrolls
his CELL PHONE screen and swipes a finger
through the hummus dish on the counter,
licking it.

> CARI
> (re: corkscrew)
> I can't believe you -- er,
> we -- have one of these.

> SAM
> Careful. Eric Roberts gave
> me that.

He steps behind her and guides her hands.
She purrs and tosses her auburn hair to ex-
pose her neck, which he nuzzles.

> CARI
> You like screwing from be-
> hind, dontcha?

> SAM
> How many more glasses you
> think that would take?

INT. LIVING ROOM - THAT MOMENT

HANDHELD POV. A rougher, frenetic imitation of the opening shot. Piano. Artwork.
Fireplace now licking more fiercely as if
challenged by a gust of air. A cork POPS
O.S., with more tipsy LAUGHTER. WHIP to
the couple waddling into the room, joined
at the waist and balancing their replen-
ished glasses as they devour one another.
Cari breaks away, and her bedroom eyes
instantly sober as we SNAP ZOOM into her.
She shrieks.

Cabernet douses the white carpet, the
dropped glass rolling beside it.

> CARI
> Hello?
> (then)
> Sam, who's this?

GORDON HIGHLAND

Picking up Cari's glass, Sam turns and
sizes up an intruder. Cowgirl boots, black
cashmere sweater, purple ribbon choker--

                    GIRL'S VOICE (O.S.)
          Yeah, "Sam," who's this?

--and stringy blond hair framing a pale,
raccoon-eyed face (20s) with a diamond stud
in her nose. Five years ago she might've
been adorable or in rehab.
The color drains from Sam's own face.

                    GIRL (CONT'D)
          Expecting someone else, were
          you?

He glares at her the way one might at a
caged tiger before realizing the bars are
too far apart. He swallows.

                    GIRL (CONT'D)
               (to Cari)
          That's gonna stain if you
          don't treat it right away.

Cari nods absently and steps out of frame.
The girl approaches Sam, who backpedals
until falling into an oversized chair.

                    SAM
               (sotto)
          Are you serious? The fuck?

                    GIRL
          Oh, I think you know I am.
          You're the one who never
          was. So who's the flooz?

                    SAM
          Please. You can cut the act.
          Just... go home before this
          gets out of hand.

>   GIRL
>   Before I cause a scene, you
>   mean?

Sam digests the bitter medicine of her
words.

>   SAM
>   I'll call you tomorrow and
>   explain everything. Promise.

Cari reappears with a dishtowel, a dog
brush, and a shrug.

>   CARI
>   I didn't know where--

>   GIRL
>   (locked on Sam)
>   Utility closet. On the left
>   past the dead son's room
>   with the boy-band posters.
>   (to Sam)
>   Not exactly a domestic one,
>   is she?

Cari tosses the supplies at the Girl, who
just watches them fall to the floor.

>   CARI
>   You clean it. I'm not the
>   one breaking into people's
>   houses.

>   GIRL
>   Door was unlocked. I know
>   it's Encino and all, but
>   still. Sammy.

Cari also turns to Sam and crosses her
arms, speed-blinking for an explanation.

                         SAM
              What. I didn't...
                   (sighs)
              Cari, this is Joelle. Jo-
              elle, Cari.

JOELLE (formerly GIRL) sneers at Cari, then
drapes herself over Sam's lap. He struggles
to avoid her lips and she settles for his
cheek while eyeing Cari.

                         CARI
              I'm guessing she's not your
              niece.

                         JOELLE
              Bitch, I was you a year ago.
              But without the stretch
              marks. Or a Valtrex com-
              mercial on her reel. And a
              helluva lot more to live for.

                         CARI
                   (embarrassed, to Sam)
              I don't have herpes.

Sam closes his eyes and shakes his head,
imploring Cari not to provoke their intruder, who stands up and crosses to her.

                         JOELLE
              You. Sit here, right across
              from him. Sammy, stay where
              you are.

Joelle pushes Cari backwards into the
matching oversized chair and straddles her,
measuring her. She clasps both of Cari's
hands, fingers intertwined and cycling them
like an exercise machine, then leans close
as if to kiss her, and headbutts her at the
last second.

Cari's eyes flutter and water as she sucks
air between her teeth. Sam winces but remains silent.

Joelle holds up Cari's limp left hand,
examining the DIAMOND RING on her engaged
finger in the flickering light.

>   JOELLE (CONT'D)
>   (to Sam, disappointed)
>   Seriously?

Her mouth slowly engulfs Cari's digit from
nail to knuckle, and the ring is gone when
she resurfaces. She displays her tongue
for Sam, the gold band ringing the barbell
pierced through it like a carnival game.
She spits the ring back into the dazed Cari's face. It tumbles between her cleavage
and Joelle reaches up underneath her cami-
sole to retrieve it, throwing a seductive
grin back over her shoulder.

>   WHIP TO:

Sam, stoic. Blinks. A deep breath. As if
she'd vanish if he only stopped believing
in her.

Cari flexes her eye sockets wide and rubs
her head. Joelle climbs off and massages
the length of Cari's arm like a phleboto-
mist preparing to draw blood. Unable to
break the skin, she trails the ring with
her black fingernail, digging into the
flesh until Cari yelps and blood surfaces.
Joelle's eyes light up like Christmas
morning, teeth flashing.

>   SAM
>   Enough! What do you want?

                    JOELLE
          What's my motivation, you
          mean? Aren't I supposed to
          be asking you that?

                    CARI
               (groggy)
          I want a Band-Aid.
               (beat)
          And a big wedding.

                    JOELLE
          Aww, of course you do,
          sweetie.

                    CARI
          In a nice hotel. Bon Jovi
          tribute band...

                    SAM
          Let's just get this over
          with.

                    JOELLE
          Oh, no no no. Doesn't work
          like that, Sammy. There's no
          little magical transition to
          Happily Ever After on the
          Jersey shore.
               (then)
          Wait.
               (she freezes, whispers)
          You hear that?

                    SAM
          What?

                    JOELLE
          Is that a... SWAT team out-
          side?

Sam's eyes dart to the corners of the room
as he listens. Cari perks up her head.
Nothing but the TONE ARM COCKING as another
LP drops onto the turntable and MUTED TRUM-
PETS begin. Joelle laughs it all off.

                    JOELLE
          Course not, dumbass. But I
          do have an idea.

                              SMASH CUT TO:

Crime-scene slides project themselves onto the wall inside Sam's skull, dust motes suspended in the lamplight arcing through his grey matter. Each advance of the carousel one potential scenario, all flattened to two dimensions by blue-tinged, overexposed flash.

Ligature rings around a purple neck. Next.

River bloat. Next.

Bludgeoned face. Next.

Amateur vasectomy.

In his business they call this *pre-viz*: crude video storyboards created for approval before animators rend their artwork in full detail. But Sam's vision had been compromised from the beginning.

Joelle seemed such a sweet girl when they first met on *Transplanters*. It was only a few days. He'd hired the special effects company where she apprenticed, glueing on silicone prostheses, blending makeup, and mixing batches of gore. Despite being starstruck by the actresses whom she disfigured so intimately, her people skills outshined the mouth-breathers back at the shop. She fantasized about someday being the one in that makeup chair, though Sam encouraged her continued craft specialization. Later, Joelle would toe the waters of many trades, each but a stepping stone to the Walk of Fame.

For five months they both got what they wanted from each other. He charted the territories of her young skin, sowing seed, while her networking tree took root. She loved finishing his sentence whenever he told someone she'd stolen his heart . . . "but only to make a mold from it." And last Thanksgiving they shared his candlelit table much like tonight, when her pregnancy scare trumped his bent-knee proposal.

Her scare, not his.

Sam beamed at the news, pledging his eternal commitment while praying for a son to redeem the one he'd lost to depression and vomit inhalation two years prior. But Joelle only saw the career derailment that came with birthing a child at twenty-three. Their embryo was already spoken of in past tense before its father could object. She wouldn't say where or how, and flashbacks of the animatronic latex and red-dyed corn syrup in her old creature shop gave Sam nightmares for weeks.

Though she didn't want to marry, Joelle wasn't ready to abort their relationship. Sam cut the cord. His assistant delivered a carload of her belongings to the wardrobe department in Burbank where she'd most recently been working.

When Sam found gashes in all four sidewalls of his 7-Series parked outside the studio bungalow, he didn't file for an *ex parte*. He didn't employ an investigator, didn't even bring it up with his therapist. He did change his house alarm code, but never saw Joelle again until tonight.

"How about," Joelle says, "we play a little game. Like a twenty questions type thing." Crouched next to Cari's chair, she remains fixated on the woman's fingers, once again holding a handful up for inspection. "Actually, ten makes more sense. Ten questions. Yeah?"

Sweat trickles down Sam's nose, clinging under the

tip until accumulating enough mass to drop and stain his trousers. "Something you wanna know, Joelle, just ask it." He wriggles out of his blazer and tosses it onto the couch.

Joelle clocks his every motion, coiled, irises dilated like anime. "Oh I will. But we need to establish the stakes. I mean, what happens when someone gets one wrong? Or lies?" She draws the word out like an accusation.

He takes off his cufflinks and tables them. "When have I ever lied to you?"

"Not to me. To her." She rubs Cari's shoulders from behind. "Though, by extension, to me, yes."

Cari remains silent, not wanting to stoke any pre-existing drama. None of this is her doing, yet she can't say she didn't sign up for it. Producers make enemies, and she's known her complicit role from the start, fiancée or otherwise.

Sam rolls up his sleeves.

"One finger per question," Joelle suggests with all the levity of a roulette dealer. "Sounds fair, right?"

This gets Cari's attention. "Wait, one *what*, now?"

"No," Sam grumbles, "it doesn't."

With a rattle of her arm, a roll of black gaffer tape shimmies down from Joelle's elbow into her hand. The tape screeches like a wounded alien as she whips it around Cari's torso from above while holding her in a headlock. Cari squeals.

Sam sees his chance and lunges for them, but in the ten feet and one second between chairs he takes a boot heel across his chin.

"I told you to stay there!"

His fluttering eyes distorted through Cari's spilled wine goblet, Sam picks himself up off the carpet and follows Joelle's pointing finger back to his chair. He rubs his jaw and numbed lips, and spits a mouthful of blood tasting nothing like corn syrup into his palm. Nowhere to wipe it among the all-white décor. Resigned to sully his green shirt, he knows he'll forever associate this memory with Christmas. Another crimson stain begins to set next to the neglected cabernet.

After four tape passes, Cari can only flap her forearms like a T-rex. "Don't worry, this stuff is great. No residue," Joelle says. "Oughta be, for twenty bucks a roll. This part, though," she binds Cari's ankles, "is a community service."

"Fuck. You," Cari snarls. She wonders how much damage one of her own four-inch heels could do to an eye socket if given a chance and sobering reflexes.

"Allrighty. Let's do this." Joelle takes the woman's flailing hand and grips its pinkie like she would an ATV throttle, thumb against the side for leverage. "Samuel. First question: what's Cari's middle name?"

Sam's brows raise in anticipation, then twist, and Joelle sees Cari's pantomiming lips in her periphery, which she thwarts with an elbow to the temple.

"Ellen!" he blurts, impeded speech from his bitten tongue drawing looks from both women. "Jethuth, it'th Ellen, okay?"

Cari's head sinks. Joelle fishes a driver's license from the purse now on her lap and chuckles at Cari. "Says 'Cari H.' *Helen*, I'm betting, right?" She licks her lips as she applies pressure. "Okay, here we go—"

"Wait! Dubuh or nothing!" Sam pleads. "Dubuh or nothing. C'mon."

"Intriguing. Shoulda figured you might bargain." Joelle opens her grip, then grasps both Cari's pinkie and ring fingers. "Sure, why not. Because I know you don't know any of this shit. Okay—for *two* fingers—question number two: what's Cari's favorite movie?"

"Oh, thath eathy. *Jerry Maguire*. Ith thtill in the pwayer upthtairs." He's a better negotiator than liar, but they're complementary skills.

Joelle looks to Cari for confirmation, who feigns relief

and nods quickly. "Bullshit. It's gotta be *Pretty Woman*," Joelle says, and Cari's torrid howl wrenches Sam's heart as her tendons snap.

From her pants pocket, Joelle slips what Sam figures to be his engagement ring back over Cari's gnarled finger. Despite being oversized, there's no way it will fit around the swollen flesh now, and her trembling makes it all the more futile, but Joelle persists.

"Oh God, no!" Cari thrashes in the chair like a shark, bound feet flailing. "No! Why are you—" She screams and throws her head back as the veins in Joelle's neck tense repeatedly.

Her tormentor's hands come up bloody and accomplished, palms on display. One holds two severed fingers, the other a chrome guillotine cigar cutter identical to Sam's.

Sam gags, coughing and sputtering some combination of fluids between his fingers and down the front of his Christmas shirt.

Cari's mutilated hand lies limp, blood flow pulsing in rhythm with each heartbeat. Her skirt is already spotted red, and the dripping armrest begins to flood the floor. Tears cascading, her head lolls side to side in shock on the edge of consciousness. Panicked breaths seething through her nose and grinding teeth. She thinks only of Gabrielle, light of her life, who's probably asking the babysitter right about now if she can make popcorn, negotiating bedtime and their movie library.

Four bars of Miles Davis swing through the silence as Joelle stands dazed before her work. Then, "Damn. That was . . . way easier than I figured."

Sam vaults from his chair and breaks for the kitchen. "I'm cawing an ambulanth." Joelle jumps onto his back and stamps her foot behind his knee. They tumble to the floor, rolling until her knees pin his arms down, face to face.

"And dialing with what?" She air-snips the cutter, its

blades already sticky with platelets. "Also, you sound like Down's Syndrome."

"She'th gonna fucking bweed to death!"

"Got a couple hours. I looked it up," Joelle says, catching her breath. "Though that was probably for just one finger. And with help."

"Then hold it up, at leatht, for god'th thake. Elevate it."

"You hear that, *Carrie*," Joelle joins in and climbs off of Sam. "Plug it up. Plug. It. Up!" she chants, invoking one of her favorite films

Cari's forearm raises and shudders as if trying to curl a weight, rivulets of blood streaming, before falling limp again. She draws a jagged breath between sobs, and a long note resembling *whyyyyy* bleats from her throat.

Joelle turns back to Sam as the base of an Emmy award fills her vision and shatters her nose. *Outstanding Made-for-Television Movie.* She stumbles into the piano with a cluster of discord. Shoulders heaving, Sam drops the statue and opens the display cabinet next to the fireplace. A stuffed Alaskan red fox proudly watches.

Blood mushrooming from her exposed nasal cavity, eyes running black like a fourth-quarter linebacker, Joelle comes at him with a congested battle cry. He selects the Mossberg 12-gauge from the arsenal and pumps the action. *Welcome to the cutting-room floor, bitch* flashes in 12-point Courier on a page in his mind, too late to deliver it aloud. No time to shoulder the gun, he pops the safety and squeezes the trigger at waist level. Double-aught buckshot shreds Joelle's mandible and ear, as bloodied feathers scatter from a wall-mounted pheasant. The girl glances off a bookshelf, misting the spines of dozens of screenplays arterial red, and slumps to the floor.

Gurgling and immobile in her waning moments, only her eyes follow him as he stands over her. Each judging the other.

Sam digs Cari's phone out of her purse. Thumbs 9-1-1,

then hesitates over the Send button. The screen times out.

His so-called fiancée hasn't blinked in ten minutes. Still bound to the chair, her flesh lifeless as those in his imaginary slideshow. Drained like a box of cabernet into a patch of carpet . . . smaller than his bearskin rug. . . .

This could all go away, he thinks. *Actresses disappear all the time. Like hookers.*

He ponders the difference, wondering how Cari could have agreed to play fiancée for an evening without feeling exploited. Despite Sam's nonsexual reassurances, twelve hundred bucks opens a lot of doors, and all day he'd questioned how far she might take the role. Everyone knew she slept with one of the writers on that day-spa pilot.

Who else knows she's here tonight?

Sam had contacted her directly, so no official trail exists. But for the first time he finds himself considering whether she had family. Kids. Or god forbid, a vengeful and resourceful man.

The ex-girlfriend on his floor missing a third of her face was going to be the bigger problem. Sam plucks a Cohiba Cuban from the box on the shelf and settles wearily onto the corner of the piano bench, elbows on his knees. He noses the cigar on instinct, rolling it around and around with his thoughts.

The fuck just happened? And Joelle? How'd she ever break in?

He slams his eyes shut, tries to rub the night's images out of them and some sense into them. Doesn't even notice Coltrane has been blowing the same scratchy lick for who knows how long.

Sam shakes his head, bites off the cigar cap, and pats his shirt pocket for a lighter, when the unmistakable action of the Mossburg ratchets in his ears. A spent shell hits the soiled carpet in front of him where Joelle is no longer. Raising his gaze to meet hers, he finds only a blurry mass of red and black and blond, the barrel at his nose

GORDON HIGHLAND

commanding cross-eyed focus. Burnt gunpowder and cleaning oil.

Feral, vindictive syllables erupt from what remains of Joelle's mouth.

"I'm thorry," Sam says, hands up and spitting out the cigar as his slideshow accelerates. Exit wounds. Skull fragments. Dental x-rays. "I— I thoud've been more thupportive. But how could I've known? I mean, the cointhidenth. . . ."

One eye rolls, the other blown-out red. Her moan produces a bubbling froth. She firms her grip on the shotgun.

"Okay! Anything you want. We could write and thoot your very own—"

The blast yanks the plug on his projector as his literal memories splatter and crack those captured in the framed photos behind him.

"Deb-bie," he chanted into the phone as if rewarding an obedient puppy. "Debra. Debs."

"Mister . . . Dawes?"

"C'mon, now, it's Sammy. You know that."

"Of course, darling. Just didn't recognize the number."

"Yeah, we moved offices again." Sam propped his feet up on the slab of mahogany that so often barricaded him from those pitching awful story ideas. "Look, hey, need a favor."

Her computer keys clacked as she input this new contact data. "So how'd Fernando work out on that commercial a couple weeks ago? Was I right, or what?"

"He lathered up nicely, yes."

"You know I'd be lying, Sammy, if I didn't admit hoping you're getting back down to making features soon. Don't get me wrong, a day's work's a day's work—and my folks do appreciate it—but most of them would prefer to get in a few weeks at a time, you know?"

"Not to mention your twenty percent off both ends."

"There's that, sure," Debra said, a grinning confession. "Hey, speaking of eighty-proof . . . you're coming to our holiday shindig, right?"

"No way I'd miss a chance to drink back your billings in Red Label and Blue Ribbon. Count on it."

"Should I put you down for a plus-one?"

Shouldering the receiver, Sam spun his chair and rifled through a file folder. "Well, that's actually what I was calling about. . . ."

Debra removed her bifocals and rubbed the bridge of her nose. "Ah, let me guess, she's an actress."

"No no, nothing like that. Well yeah, my, um . . . my fiancée is, but this isn't about her so much. I'm needing someone for a thing Friday evening."

"A thing."

"A gig, yeah."

She uncapped her pen and tore off the densely-inked sheet that topped her note pad. "Is this AFTRA or SAG?"

"Strictly non-union. It's actually not going out anywhere, more of a performance piece. Just a couple-person audience for now."

Debra clicked her tongue. "What exactly are you producing, here?"

He paused. "We've known each other a long time, right? I remember the year your agency opened its doors, I cast that entire TV movie exclusively through you—"

"Sammy, I get it. I'm keeping a kidney warm for you, babe. But tell me what I can do in the meantime."

He takes a deep breath. *Here we go.* "Okay. This stalker chick, some old scorned flame, right? She shows up at my place one night—I'm talking off-her-meds batshit—while I'm wining and dining my lady by candlelight. . . ."

"My god, when did this happen?"

"Day after tomorrow, Deb. *She's* the stalker. The role."

"Now why in Jewish hell would anyone want—"

"Consider it a . . . I dunno, paid audition."

Debra shut her office door and cupped the microphone of her headset, whispering. "I love ya, Sam, you know you're my motherfucka, but that's not what we do here, that fantasy fulfillment shit." She paced in front of the window and its hazy view of Century City. "I think you'd better call a pro, if you know what I'm saying. I could . . . probably get you a number, if—"

"I need someone passionate, Debs. Fiery, frustrated— whatever. Someone eager to take that next dramatic leap into alternative theater."

"Oh is *that* what they're calling it over in Chatsworth now?"

"This isn't sexual. Don't even care what she looks like. Surprise me. Gotta be able to improv, though. That's key."

"Why don't you just call up a real-life ex? I've seen you with a starlet or two on your arm."

"Right. They're exes for a reason, Deb." He ran his tongue over his teeth, eyeing his gallery of track-lit film posters and all the regrets they held. "Now surely you've got little pet projects, certain actors you shepherd and try to break in, right?"

"You said *audition*. So what's the project?"

He cleared his throat. "We're developing a reality series with a bait-and-switch. Middle of the season we introduce this scripted dramatic element—with actors—that the cast is unaware of."

"I've seen this before."

"Big screen, maybe, but not network. You go into a theater expecting and wanting to be manipulated. But if, say, you flipped on the news and saw your favorite *anchors* being hijacked at gunpoint. . . ."

"You figure it's real."

"Bingo. Might even plant some cameras around the house Friday, just in case. Don't tell her that, though, I don't want her playing to them. I'll e-mail you what we've got by the end of the day."

"Ooh-kay, Sammy," she scoffed, shaking her head. "I'll make some calls. And by the way, *mazel tov* on the engagement."

INSIDE OUT

by Sean P Ferguson

Smoke 'em if you got 'em.

The words ring true, but there is no echo. State of the art sound-proofing makes sure of that, despite the studio's cavernous loneliness. Stage lights still burn and the beacon red light of the live camera feed tells me to focus on stage left, camera three. The electricity of a television show still courses through the building's veins, beaming my image out across America. Millions of viewers watch me light up at home, listening to the isolation of my insides sloshing to the floor. It alienates me. I feel hollow, if you'll excuse the poor timing of such a statement.

I'm not mad. This is my predicament, and if I happen to make it out of here, spectacular, even better if I'm alive while doing so. However, my internal hose reel shows no signs of stopping, and the effort to shove it all back in just seems like too much work.

I play introspective.

The fellow disguised as a member of the studio audience, the one that's cut me open, for all of you to witness, he's a childhood friend. We used to have sleepovers where we'd eat ice cream. We would watch scary movies on late night cable. He and I would sneak out and play tag with flashlights in the woods behind our houses.

SEAN P FERGUSON

I'm not assuming to know why my best pal from high school appeared like an arch nemesis to gut me. Doing so insults the heart and the drama of the story, removing all probabilities and leaves a big stinking gap for chance to slide right in and take over. If I were to assume the reasons behind my attack, I would lose what little control I have. It would mean that life simply happens and we're all floating in its ether. Buoys trapped in a raging demolition derby played by oil tankers with madmen at the helm.

This is why I was stabbed, this is why he slid the knife from hip to hip, opening me up so the entire world could see what I'm made of; it gives me control.

I pull hard on the cigarette and wonder if I'll see the smoke come out of my wound.

My comrade in adolescence had me over one night. We had pepperoni pizza until we were sick to our stomachs from the grease. Tommy took the pink circles of spiced meat and stuck them to his face. He pinched his voice and sucked in his cheeks, forming circles with his hands around his eyes. My friend's round face had transformed into a geek with soda bottle glasses and delicious acne.

"I'm Tiffany Hartman!" he said.

I picked a piece of the meat from his face and popped it in my mouth while he squealed, "You horrid boy! You ate my gross pimple! I cherish each and every one of them. I've named them all while studying to be Mister Mortimer's butt kisser."

We howled like this until Tommy went upstairs and passed out, ignoring the tape his mom had gotten us about the superhero turtles with camp catchphrases and a wild obsession for skateboards. I was terrible at falling asleep. The harder I tried, the longer I stayed awake. I found the channel with all of the naked people. Watching them writhe around and sweat on each other, making ugly faces and uglier noises, it did something to me. I wanted to change the channel out of sheer embarrassment.

The wood paneling spoke to me, though. It shook every time the plumber with shag carpet for hair and hideous teeth thrust his hips. The view of the camera would change positions with the couple, and each time something like an errant arm or a curious pile of linen would block my first image of a woman's nipple. It eventually got so bad I heard myself growl a little in my throat.

That's when Tommy's mom finally laughed.

I smashed buttons on the remote to change the channel and hoped she had only just walked in, maybe I could pretend like I had been surfing through, looking for cartoons. Something age appropriate. Clothed.

"Put that back, it's one of my favorites," she whispered.

She grabbed the remote and sat on the other end of the couch, pushing buttons until she found the sunbather doing things to her pool boy. The lady in the yellow bikini pushed and pulled at her employee's appendage with her mouth, reminding me of a magician with a long string of colored scarves. I could see the reflection of the movie in Tommy's mom's eyes. She started chewing on her lower lip and sliding her palms up and down her thighs with the grace of a dancer, the light airy touch of a secret.

"Can you change the channel, now?"

I didn't quite mean it, but watching this with a woman that knew my mother by her first name made me sick, the weight of guilt and fear pulling on the insides of my stomach the way a small car would inside of a balloon. She pushed the round red button and the television went black. My best friend's mother stood up, opened her robe and sat on my lap, facing me, reaching down and pulling away my sweatpants with one hand.

I was suddenly wet all over while she slowly did what the women in the movie did. She pulled me close, held me tight until I couldn't run, I couldn't move, I couldn't breathe. Until I felt free. Every move she made was slow and soft like the bubbles in a bath, loving like a mother. And in the dark reflection of the television, over her shoulder, I saw Tommy watching us from between the railings of the stairs.

Matt Styles' birthday was great, almost like a carnival. He had colored balloons, cotton candy, popcorn, pony rides, and a clown. The magician was the best part, though. I watched him do tricks and tell jokes while my fingers clung to the cement walkway that looped the pool. The big finale was incredible. Tommy's mom shuddered on top of me, and I thought she'd pulled an innocent white rabbit out from between my legs.

And then I slept.

I woke up to a police officer standing over me in Tommy's room. Without a word, he led me down the same stairs that Tommy watched me from earlier. I looked to see if I was still on the couch, if Tommy's mom's nipples were still in my mouth, but the officer ushered me outside. He wrapped me in a scratchy brown blanket and sat me on the curb. All kinds of people in suits and uniforms were on Tommy's front lawn, in and out of his house.

And later that morning, I watched my best friend in the whole world be driven away in the backseat of a police car for what seemed like eternity.

A woman that smelled of cats and old chewing gum came and put me in her car. She sat with me and my parents when the news cameras came. They used words like monster, rape, victim, and tragedy. Watching myself talk about my best friend on television was weird at first. I wished he was there with me. It eventually became a game, a script as the telling and retelling of the story became larger, more than it ever was. Old news.

And then, a couple days later a news crew from New York came and asked the same questions. The cat lady looked prettier then. She used words like litigation, said victim a lot louder than before. She was almost passionate. After the interview, she stood at the end of the driveway crying. I'd seen the bun of her hair bobbing up and down in the lap of the sound guy from the news crew in her car. The woman wanted to go back to New York with him as he disappeared in the shadows of the van. It was probably the cat smell.

I went back to school. All of the guys worshiped me, let me cut in the lunch line. They would pat me on the back and call me hero. When the girls were in groups, they treated me like I had a disease, but when they had me all to themselves, they wanted me like I had the cure. That's when cutting class started. That's when I'd started showing whichever girl I was with that day her own magic trick. I'd promise that it was special, that this was my body, broken for her, for the forgiveness of all her transgressions.

My parents spent the rest of their lives on the phone. When I wasn't in school or in the company of a girl, I was telling my story to someone who would later palm a wad of cash to my parents. I overheard my mother say that it would help pay for my therapy. After the reporter left my father asked when I'd started going to therapy.

"He isn't; get real." That's what my mother said.

I could feel my body root for my father. It started in my toenails and worked its way up the slender digits of my feet. The electricity was warm and binding, like velvet, like my best friend's mother. It was almost too much to bear without crying. My vindication would come when Dad found the error of his ways. It was one thing to bask in the love of camera lights, but to be making money off the destruction that I had caused would be too much.

And I really wasn't too far removed, either. No one at school was more popular. I had successfully made my way through all the girls at my school and even some of the staff. I'd moved into the pants of schoolgirls in neighboring towns as the nicknames started creating a wake of whispers behind me. Agents with ponytails called the house about movies of the week featuring my father's son and the woman who died because of him. At some point he would put a stop to all this. A chair would fly, he would scoop me up and kick out the front door screaming that enough was enough.

But instead he said, "Okay good, I really want that television we were talking about."

A few months later a movie premiering on the cable network for women by women was viewed on the television paid for by my sold rights. Mom seemed to enjoy it, but my dad had to reassure her that even though the movie said I conspired with Tommy, it wouldn't ruin the possibility of future projects.

"If anything, it sells the drama," he said.

In college, my girlfriend said she hadn't heard about me, and I instantly loved her. She made me feel safe and needed. Her hair was the color of dried wheat but smelled like pressed flowers scattered over clean sheets, beautiful and airy but not overly fruity, just simply perfect. She was perfect, and she laughed in song. And the sex video she sold to the internet porn company paid for both of our tuition, with my face in a nice night-vision-green on the cover.

At graduation a woman walked up to me wearing a pantsuit, greeting me with, "Mongrel."

She said that despite her better judgment, followed by her pleas of absolution, she had been sent by her employer to escort me to Hollywood. A reality show circuit had my name all over it, perhaps a Christmas album, and as I drifted off into obscurity, a satellite radio show. In the meantime I could work the talk shows, pepper in an autobiography and really finish off the life my parents had made for me.

Which brings me here, America. As you all know, the reality show had a successful run. My drug rehab farce carried it a year beyond its life expectancy, and then the celebrity reality shows, the dancing, the weight loss, the season when I was center square on a game show revamp. This interview here was to mark the twentieth anniversary of that night I watched television with my best friend's mother.

I wash my hands in the bile pumping out, the blood that's been spilled, my organs on display. My eyes find the stage lights while the strike team bursts into the studio looking for my killer, my reunited best friend. One of the officers throws up as another screams for a paramedic. I feel myself fall, wooden floorboards waking the numbness in my knees.

"Jesus Christ, where's that medic?" he yells. "Hold on, man."

This is the blood, shed for you.

I find his face through the tears welling up in my eyes.

Please, forgive my sins.

"It's all right, son," his hand says as it grips my shoulder.

And it all fades.

The clapping is what I hear next. The lights come back and an assistant comes and unhooks the props from my abdomen. The officer that was gripping my shoulder is wiping sweat from his eyebrow and asking an intern if he thought he should ask for another take. The director calls for the union-mandated lunch break and people pat me on the back for a job well done.

LAWS OF VIRULENCE

by Jeremy Robert Johnson

INTERNAL MEMO: 08/07/2010

CASE: F-DPD0758 (CDC NORS-Water Report ID VEC147, Received 08/03/2010 via State Report OMB No. 0920-0004, Submitted by: Dr. Lorena Santos of Pacific Grace Clinic)

ETIOLOGY: Unknown (comparative specimen analysis in progress, genus/species/serotype may require new designations)

CONTAMINATION FACTOR: C-N/A, Unknown

SURVIVAL FACTOR: S-N/A, Deaths can be attributed to case though comparable pathogens have displayed symbiotic behavior

DOCUMENT INSERT: Verbatim transcript of post-containment etiology determination interview with Subject 5 (Matthew Hall). Due to active vector status (transmission mode remains classified as Indeterminate/Other/Unknown although enteric Phase 1 possible) subject interviewed in iso via 2-way audio. Dpdx program active/engaged. Elimination & Control team at ready.

Recorded at Director's Request/Classified Confidential 1-A. Speaking: DPD Director Cliff Selzer, Matthew Hall

CS: Hello, Mr. Hall.

MH: [No response]

CS: I'm going to be frank with you, Mr. Hall . . . Can I call you Matthew?

MH: You can call me whatever you want.

CS: Very well, Matthew. I need you to understand the situation we're in right now. How important you are. How much you can help us.

MH: I'm not important. I'm the least important person you've ever met. And I don't give a shit about helping you. And if you don't get me something stiffer than this glass of fucking tap water then I'm not saying a word.

CS: Matthew, I'm afraid that water is all we can provide you right now. But if you cooperate there could be adjustments to your Stay Profile.

MH: You get me a bottle of Maker's and a shotgun. You promise that. Then I'll tell you everything.

CS: You know I can't do that.

MH: I don't know what you can or can't do. I don't even know who the hell you are. You strip me naked. You spray me down with some kind of goddamn fire extinguisher and make me sit in the dark in three smaller and smaller rooms. I thought you were cooking me alive in the last one.

CS: Matthew, that was all for standard decontamination protocol. We're trying to protect you and others.

MH: So am I safe now?

CS: "Safe?"

MH: Decontaminated?

CS: [Long pause] We're not sure, Matthew. That's why it's so important you tell us what you know.

MH: [Garbled] fucking shitbirds. Just let me die. Please.

CS: That's very selfish, Matthew. There are millions of people in this country who don't want to die, and you're putting them at risk. If you won't speak with me will you at least consider filling out the form we've placed in front of you?

MH: [Sound of pen being thrown across room, striking floor. Sound of Subject 5 expectorating on form CS115.]

BREAK IN RECORDING

MH: Now that's more like it, chief. Aaah, that's more like it.

CS: I suggest you slow down, Matthew. We don't know how alcohol will affect the specimen or its interaction with your body.

MH: [Sound of gulping.] Shit on your specimen, chief. [Sound of belch.] Oh, Jesus, that fucking burns.

CS: It's 100 proof, Matthew.

MH: No, not the booze. That stuff is silky. It's the fucking crawler. Sonofabitch never stops working on me. I knew it. Your precious little detox rooms were a waste. [Sound of fabric rubbing on skin.] See, my mouth is already bleeding. Then I'll get the fucking seaweed eyes. Then you guys will wish you already would've given me that shotgun.

CS: "Seaweed eyes?"

MH: Yeah. It's like lace under the eyes, or like . . . like they're bloodshot but the blood is dark green.

CS: And your wife displayed this condition?

MH: Claire had it first, and then . . .

CS: Then your daughter?

MH: [Long pause. Sound of gulping.] Yeah . . . Myra.

CS: We've performed a full sweep of your apartment, Matthew. We're aware of your loss and I promise you we understand how difficult this must be.

MH: Did you burn them?

CS: No. Our procedure dictates a course other than destruction . . .

MH: Quit fucking around and burn them. Please. Give them that. Claire always wanted to be cremated and . . . I was going to do it myself, before you guys booted in my goddamn door . . . please. It's the last good thing I can do for them.

CS: The sooner we know what you know, the sooner we can honor your request.

MH: Promise?

CS: We will do our best to keep funeral processing in motion.

MH: Well, cheers to that. [Sound of gulping.]

CS: So, at what point did you notice the discoloration in your wife's eyes? And were there any notable signs or symptoms prior to that? Vomiting? Fever? Abdominal cramps?

MH: There are probably some symptoms I didn't even notice. To be honest, we weren't talking that much. I mean, this all happened last week and it happened so fast. But she was always bitching and crunching on Tums and popping Tylenol, so . . . I mean, running a daycare center is hard work. She used to joke that children could only grow by stealing your energy and happiness. But she liked it, she really did. Hell, she was pretty much raising Myra without me.

CS: Our records indicate you lived together.

MH: [Brief laughter.] Depends on how you define living, chief. We split rent on an apartment and had the same last name, you know . . . Sometimes I'd take Myra to the park. She was too little to go on the swings or anything, but she liked to smell the flowers and watch the other kids play . . . But Claire would have been the second person, after me of course, to tell you that I'm a piece of shit. A real charity case. So the truth is that I didn't notice how wrong things were until they'd gone way past wrong.

CS: What did you observe first?

MH: Well, I woke up after Claire every day, and I'd make the bed to pretend I was useful in some way, and I noticed some little spots of blood on her pillow. Nothing too serious looking. But then she got home that night and had a hefty cough. Plus, her breath had become pretty toxic. She'd block it with her hand but the smell would float across the whole room. And this smell, chief, it was like a dead hooker's pussy stuffed with old shrimp. But worse. It crawled into your nose like it was living. She started burning nag champa incense, so she must have smelled it too.

CS: Is that when she decided to go to the hospital?

MH: No. Claire is . . . Claire was a tough one. I was starting to feel a little sick, too, and Claire figured we had some food poisoning. It was her birthday a few days before, and I'd been out "job hunting" at the Pussycat Palace. You know the place?

CS: I'm aware of it.

MH: So you've seen Cherry Headrush dance before?

CS: No, Matthew. But I'm aware of many venues and chains because of their prominence on our regional disease vector maps.

MH: Oh. Shit. [Sound of gulping.] Well, I'd flipped for this girl, Cherry. And they'd just extended my unemployment for another three months so I was feeling flush. Spent almost my whole check in one afternoon, hogging up the lap dances. Milking a cheap beer buzz for hours. And then my cell started vibrating and a Reminder message pops up: CLAIRE B-DAY DINNER TONIGHT. Only the "tonight" is spelled like 2-N-I-T-E which means Claire programmed this into my phone so I'd remember.

[Long pause.]

CS: Please continue. The food poisoning?

MH: So I'm running late, very buzzed and most of my cash is already in the Pussycat's sterilizer. But I have to try and pull myself out of this so I hit Chinatown and looked for something fancy to cook up. Chan's Market has a beautiful red snapper on discount, so I cop that, pick up some lemon and capers, and get two fancy chocolate Cupcakes at Dreampuff's.

SEE SEPARATE DOCUMENT INSERT FOR RELATED DIRECTOR ORDER: DPDx multi-venue deploy/search/ surveil. Full containment authorized. Andolini appointed Team Leader.

CS: Sorry about that break, Matthew. You've been very helpful.

MH: Do I have any choice? Really? I appreciate the second bottle, but you might want to give me a bucket if I'm going to keep going. Although I'd have no problem shellacking your little desk here.

CS: Consider us well advised. Please continue.

MH: Shit, man . . . it seems obvious, doesn't it? I barely had any time to bake the fish before Claire got home with Myra. I brushed up and changed my clothes and put on some Alicia Keys even though I can't stand that shit. Lit a couple of tea lights I found under the sink. But I still fucked it up. I still fucked it up. [Pause] The fish looked good by candle-light. Looked delicious.

CS: You think the red snapper was the original source of the sickness?

MH: Thing is, I was pulling off the sober act, but I had to burp. And that just ruined it. One hundred percent. Like a strip club came out of my mouth. Claire pegged it, and laid into me, even though Myra was sitting in the room in her little bouncy chair and we'd sworn not to fight in front of her. And I mentioned that and we tried to enjoy the dinner and pretend that something was okay and nice and we didn't even notice how raw the snapper was until we'd taken out half of the fish.

CS: So Claire was guessing that the raw fish had given each of you food poisoning?

MH: Yeah. She was toughing it out until Myra got sick, too. Because that didn't make any sense. Myra was still breastfeeding, so she never had any of that nasty snapper. But she was coughing and having the blood speckles just the same.

CS: That's when she visited Pacific Grace, toward the beginning of August?

MH: I think so. I was sort of on my own thing (delete) while this was happening. Sleeping on the couch at night. Hiding at Pussycat's during the day. I told myself I was in exile, giving Claire some space to forgive me. But I was really just doing the same old shit. Living in a worn down strip club booth, paying Cherry to hip-hump me. Hoping that Claire and Myra would start feeling better. That maybe Claire would start feeling so good she'd build up the mojo to finally drop me.

CS: When did you find out she wasn't feeling better?

MH: Well, Pussycat's kind of extradited me back to my family. I was already putting off that rotten jellyfish smell and . . . let's just say there aren't enough dollars to make a stripper let you cough blood in her face. I didn't even see it coming. Just sitting there half-chubbed and dead drunk and BOOM! No tickle in the throat. No warning.

CS: Do you happen to know Cherry Headrush's real name?

MH: You're kidding, right? [Sound of bottle opening/ sound of gulping.] All I know is that I was home and starting to feel pretty rotten myself, and I can't imagine how Claire was managing to run the daycare like that. All those little people screaming. "I want. I need. Watch me. Love me." Jesus.

CS: This was the Morning Sun Daycare on Stanton?

MH: Yup. So, Claire stumbles into the house and she and Myra are both coughing and they have those triple-dark circles under their eyes, and seeing them like that makes me feel like I managed to sneak into Hell without dying. Just worthless. No, worse than that—fucking evil. [Long pause] Claire said the lady at the hospital gave them both two I.V. bags to rehydrate them, and that they needed to go back tomorrow for more diagnostics. But she thought it might be a parasite, like one of those squiggly little gut worms you get from eating sushi in Ohio.

CS: Did she suggest you go with them?

MH: Of course. And I was thinking it was the right thing to do. I was starting to feel weak in my bones. But the next morning I wake up and they're already gone and there's a text on my phone saying that they're both "feeling much better." Which was weird, because they'd been coughing like crazy all night. Just brutal sounding. Wet. Like I'd guess TB used to sound.

CS: So . . . a productive cough followed by an apparent return to vigor?

MH: Sure, chief. However you want to call it. It spooked me because I was still under the weather. But I pegged that up in my mind as booze-related immune suppression. All those sauced little white blood cells getting bitch-slapped by the bugs in my system.

SEE SEPARATE DOCUMENT INSERT RE: Viability of ethanol [or variant] ingestion as chemical deterrent to life cycle of [un-named parasite/parasitoid CASE: F-DPD0758].

CS: So when did it become evident that Claire and Myra were still . . . unwell?

MH: [Prolonged sound of gulping.] You want to hear the rest, you get me a loaded shotgun. I promise I'll only fire it once.

CS: Not an option, Matthew.

MH: Okay. Fuck it. I better get the truth out before the goddamn crawler starts telling my story. [Pause/sound of shuddering exhalation.] I knew they were still unwell when I found their tongues. Claire's was in the bed, tucked under a pillow. Dried up already, like jerky. And Myra's . . .

CS: Please, Matthew.

MH: Myra's was in her crib, next to her favorite pacifier, the one with the orange dolphin on the back. And I've got to tell you, chief, between my half-sick, half-drunk stupor and lack of sleep, I felt like I was dreaming. So I did what seemed like the right thing. I threw the tongues in the garbage and kept on tidying the apartment. Like I could organize away what I was seeing. Like I could clean up reality.

SEE SEPARATE DOCUMENT INSERT FOR RELATED DIRECTOR ORDER: DPDx forensic detachment to attain SW Sanitation schedule/potential combing of landfill [use of trailing dogs authorized]. Retention of tissue from Subjects 3 and 4 Top Priority, presence/absence of eggs to be communicated ASAP.

MH (continued): So I had the place pretty spruced, and I was waiting for them to come home. Claire wasn't answering her phone. And my nerves were on four alarm blaze, so I had some bourbon close by, just to keep things mellow until I could figure out what was going on. I'd call her phone. Five rings. Voice mail. Nothing. Take a swig. Five rings. Voice mail. Nothing. And they still weren't home by 9:00 p.m.

CS: Records show you called Claire's mother.

MH: Three or four times. But she never picked up. And I thought about calling the cops, but I knew my speech was slurring by that point. What would I tell them? There was no crime, and they'd probably guess it was just another wife bailing with the kid, leaving the stew-bum behind.

CS: But their tongues? That must have . . .

MH: Can't see that impressing the cops either. Just a way to induce them to pack a straight jacket. Besides, if I mentioned finding their tongues . . . I'd been on a steady drunk trying to bury that detail, hoping I was just losing my shit.

CS: So when did you next see Claire and Myra?

MH: Never again. I think the night they came home from the doctor's was the last time I really saw them.

CS: Matthew, the chronology we've established shows the three of you were in that apartment for almost two days before we . . .

MH: Before you decided to bust into my place and stop me from finishing my work? Listen, chief, this is hard enough to talk about. So let me lay it out for you without all of your interjections and then we can clear up your questions later.

CS: [Long pause.]

MH: That's more like it. So what I'm saying is that I saw Claire and Myra again, but they sure as shit weren't my Claire and Myra. At some point that night I'd finished my bottle and given up on my phone crusade. I remember thinking, "She finally left me." And I remember feeling so relieved. No one would expect anything from me after that, you know? I'd cop some menial job, enough to service a studio apartment and child support. I'd push for a few weekends a month with Myra, just enough to not feel guilty when I show some stripper a picture of my kid. I think I'd been waiting for a long time for a chance to fall apart.

CS: Matthew, I need to know more about your wife and child, and time is a factor. We have a staff psychologist you can speak with later if you need to get more familial issues off of your chest.

MH: Courtesy is a short-lived thing around here, huh, chief? All right then, shitbird . . . So I passed out on the couch, if you can believe it. Noble. Noble guy. And when I woke up they were sitting at the foot of the couch, both of them, very quietly and . . . holy shit . . . and Claire was nursing Myra, and her head was tilted, and she was staring across the room at nothing, like she was back on Paxil, and they both had those goddamn seaweed eyes. And Claire had both of her breasts out and the one that wasn't in Myra's mouth was . . . it was kind of lumpy, like it had been stuffed with tapioca, and the nipple looked raw, just red meat raw, with these blisters around it, some popped, some filled up with the same dark green that was in her eyes, and . . .

CS: Hold on for a moment please, Matthew.

SEE SEPARATE DOCUMENT INSERT RE: Confirmation of multiple gender-specific intra-species transmission methods as seen in CASE: F-DPD0674. Student population under Sector 6 Quarantine should immediately be grouped same sex for confirmation/testing of all fluids for presence of concurrent microparasites.

CS: Okay, we're back, Matthew.

MH: [Garbled/indistinct vulgarity.] My tongue is starting to feel numb. [Sound of coughing/spitting]. Aw, Christ, chief.

CS: I'd suggest drinking some water. We need you to finish your account.

MH: Yeah, well . . . suggest in one hand and spit in the other and see which one fills up first. [Sound of laughter/sound of gulping/sound of empty bottle set down on table.] What you have to understand is that I thought I was dreaming, seeing Claire and Myra like that. Between the guilt and the hooch, that kind of nightmare fits right in. But then Claire put one of her bony bird hands on my ankle and she turned toward me and smiled. And I swear to God, these two wiry antennae uncurled from in between her teeth and started swaying in the air. So of course I lost my shit. I rolled onto my side and chucked out my guts on the shag carpet, and it's just bile and bourbon and I get that post-puke rush where things feel okay for a moment and I'm thinking I'm awake now and then I turn back towards Claire. [Long pause] She's still smiling at me and this voice comes out of her mouth and says, "Empty. Feed." And she's got her other breast cupped and I swear it's dribbling this shit like fucking wheat grass juice. [Pause] And Myra . . . Myra pulls off of the other breast, or at least her lips move away, but there's something else pushing out of her mouth, something with those same feelers wiggling, and it's latched on to Claire, right on her tit, and it's got these two tiny claws pinched on and its body is pulsing and hunching, and these plates on its back are clicking together and I can see through this thing's belly, where the skin is clear and its guts are filling up green. And Myra's eyes look almost black, but I can still tell they're rolling back in her head . . .

CS: Claire could speak?

MH: They both could. But Myra . . . she didn't have any words yet, so she would smile and her lips would pull back, but all that came out . . . Have you ever seen that footage of dolphins being massacred in Japan? And Claire's voice was different. There was a lisp, like her mouth was too full, and there was a sort of hissing to it, like cricket legs or . . . [Pause] And the smell that came from them filled up the room. It was like being stuck in the dumpster behind a seafood wholesaler on a hundred degree day. Made me throw up again.

CS: So why didn't you call 911?

MH: Are you listening to me, chief? This strikes you as a rational response fucking situation? I had no bearings. I asked Claire a question, thinking that this time she'd give me a normal answer in her old, sweet voice and I'd be all the way awake, but it came out with no authority and just made me feel smaller and detached and more alone. But I told her I was worried and that I wondered where she was yesterday and she smiled again . . . I'm thinking that's the only way the thing could move around in there . . . and all she says is, "Work. Feeding." And I say, "You were at the daycare?" She nods and says, "Feeding. Growing. Most will be born." Then she looks down at Myra, and her nose curls up like she's disgusted, and she says, "This one is dying. This one is too small." [Long pause/sound of soft crying.]

CS: Matthew, I'm sorry. I'm so sorry. But the more detail . . .

MH: Details, chief? Go fuck yourself. I did what I did. I tried to save them. I tried to fix it. To fix them before anybody would have to know . . . But it was too late. I could barely stand, but Claire was always pretty frail, and this fucking bug thing had wiped her out. So I tried to help her first and it wasn't too difficult to get her hands belted behind her, but that thing . . . that thing had teeth or mandibles or whatever and Claire started to shake and even with all the lamps in the room turned on my head kept making a shadow over her face and Myra was squealing and stomping her heels down where I left her on the carpet and I couldn't tell where the thing in Claire's mouth ended and the rest of her tongue began and when I cut in with the box knife it started bleeding so bad . . . But for just a moment Claire was looking straight at me, and even with the green lace it looked like her old eyes and then she spit right in my face. Right in my face, and she meant it. And her mouth was half-filled, and I noticed the blood from the thing and my wife wouldn't quite mix, so there's your details, chief. Then her lips pulled back and the eyes were still Claire's eyes and she said, "You did this to us."

CS: Matthew, she . . .

MH: She was right. She was right. Even after I managed to finish cutting through, and I'd pulled the goddamn thing out of her face and smashed it under my foot . . . You want more details? The shell of the thing started changing colors and it hissed and sprayed a yellow mist out of its mouth after I set it on the floor. What the fuck does that? Even after I got the thing out of Claire she still had her eyes trained on me, just bullet-eyes, and she couldn't have hated me any more. And I couldn't fix her, because she was already weak and I don't think she could stop from choking on all that blood. But I thought that Myra . . . [Long pause.]

CS: You didn't try to remove the "crawler?"

MH: I didn't want her to bleed like Claire. So I thought if I could just kill the bug that maybe it would just detach and . . . and I was thinking of how they cook lobsters, and I tried to keep the water in a tin can and hold her over it, but the steam was making everything slick and I couldn't get her mouth open at the same time and . . . so I thought that the burns would heal, you know how they say that the inside of your mouth can heal so fast, and then at least she'd live, and I didn't put the sponge in there for more than twenty seconds, but the thing was hissing and it tried to curl in on itself, and Myra started shaking and making fists and then her eyes were open and they were looking right at me, right into me, and . . .

CS: Matthew?

MH: They were right. There's nothing . . . [Sound of empty glass bottle being shattered.]

CS: Matthew, please. There's no need to . . .

MH: I did this. I did this. I . . . [Sound of Subject 5 collapsing on floor. Sound of wet coughs/exhalations. Faint sound of specimen clicking/squealing from interior of Subject 5. Sound of door opening/boots shuffling/Subject 5 moved to stretcher.]

CS: Goddamn it, [REDACTED]. I said plastic bottles only. Triage?

DPDx: Subject 5 at ISS 75. Both major sources of blood flow to brain severed, trachea punctured. He was committed to it.

CS: The specimen?

DPDx: Significant damage. Suggest immediate retrieval attempt.

CS: Agreed. Prepare for transfer to Surgical Theater 8, movement protocol in place.

DPDx: Confirmed. [Brief pause.] Director?

CS: Yes?

DPDx: If I didn't know better, I'd swear this dead fuck is smiling.

CS: Could be a symptom of the parasite attempting to exit the damaged host. Let's keep it moving. Perhaps Matthew's got a second chance at fatherhood.

DPDx: [Muffled laughter] Yes, sir. Rolling out.

END TRANSCRIPT

BRUISED FLESH
by Craig Wallwork

THE FIRST PRESENT the old man ever bought me was a
Radio Flyer tricycle, complete with a chrome bell and double
deck rear step. Out in the sunlight, it attracted magpies
and had all the other six-year-old boys on the Farriery
Pass shielding their eyes. It was beautiful, and was my first
lesson in understanding the lengths a desperate man will
go in nurturing his own selfishness. While loosening the
bolt that secured the front wheel, my father turned to me
and said, "Try to fall on your head when you land, Jonah. A
bloody nose will make it look more realistic."

When one of his old buddies from Riversdun got
involved in a scheme selling undesirable real estate to old age
pensioners in Florida, my father wanted in. All he needed
was two thousand pounds to invest. This was way before
people caught onto what a pyramid scheme was, or how
the eight ball model worked. Under the lure of easy money
and the chance to divvy up on overdue alimony checks, he
put his name in the hat. The problem my father had was
raising the cash. He used to say he had as much luck holding
onto money as he did pussy. I once overheard my mother
tell Clara Hornthorn of the Appeal of the Women's Liberal
Association that my father was a cheap lousy bastard with
a tiny prick. Clara is now my mother's life partner so if any
validity was needed to what my father said, I guess that's it.

A week after hearing about the real estate scam in Florida, the old man borrowed a JVC GR-C1 camcorder from one of his friends, the same camcorder Marty McFly used in that movie. A five pack of VHS-C tapes, two breeze blocks and a piece of four-by-ten assured the tricycle's final moments. Setting down the breeze blocks at the foot of the Cotton Stone track, and making sure the length of plywood was angled at thirty-degrees, he pressed the record button on the camcorder and waved me down. I don't remember much about that day other than the smell of Germolene and eating a Wall's Mint Choc Cornetto on the drive to Oxenhope Royal Infirmary. But during the playback later that night, I watched myself fly like an eagle.

I had to wait until the stitches in my forehead were removed before he fed me lemon segments. He'd seen video clips where toddlers wince and screw up their faces whenever they ate something cold. I ate ice cream all the time so he knew the reaction wouldn't have impressed the television producers. He stepped it up a gear. I went through two whole lemons and one lime, all marinated in Sarson's vinegar, before he got the shot he wanted. "Jonah, we'll go into Riversdun next week and pick up a bottle of peroxide. They'll get suspicious if they keep seeing the same kid." Once he was happy the footage looked real, Dad would send the videotapes out from grandma's place. He'd then alternate it every few weeks by using the address of one of his friends at the pub. For every check received, he'd slip that person a fiver and ask if it was okay to use their address again in a couple of months. No one ever said no.

A year ago, the old man had reached a Permanent Vegetative State. The doctors tried putting him on antidepressants and then methylphendiate, but they didn't help snap him back into this world. His quack suggested moving him onto some other drug called amantadine, combined with musicokinetic therapy and social-tactile interaction. For three weeks, they laid him vertically on a trampoline and played *Gravity* by Kenny G repeatedly. If anything was going to get you walking out of that hospital, listening to that saxophone all day would have done it. But not the old man. He just lay there bouncing around that trampoline like a virgin getting banged by a fat guy. I visit him now every Tuesday, Thursday and Friday evening after my Stepping Stones Rehabilitation class. Been visiting for years. It started as a sort of requirement, you know? Even though my mother didn't wear the physical scars like me, he sure left her with enough emotional ones, and even with all that bad feeling between them both, she would drag me to see him sing a silent opera from his hospital bed twice a week. Guess she felt there was some unspoken responsibility she had to fulfill, or perhaps she thought a boy needed a father. She'd done a little research too, found out people in comas can hear stuff, you know, like the voices of people in the room. So every time we visited, I had to pull up a chair beside him and talk about school and all this other crap about my life that would probably send a person into a coma, not bring them out of one. But that was my mother, forever the bleeding heart. It was a chore, sitting there for an hour at a time; the beep beep beep of his heart monitor like some crazy soundtrack to my slowly deepening voice. I would have cut off a limb to get out of going, but that's the weird thing about routine. However tedious, it slowly becomes the one constant in your life. Whenever I was going through shit with my mother and Clara, or worrying about exams, or getting my heart torn in two by some girl, I would go and see the old man. For an hour, there was quiet. The world stopped spinning. He became a kind of sleeping priest, a mute Samaritan, and I would just blurt all kinds of stuff out at him. It didn't matter if he could hear it, or that he had no advice to give; it was just about being able to talk and get it all off my chest. Routine became my vice. That was until I hit my mid-twenties.

Falling through ceilings and down stairs most of your life has long-term side effects. Muscle damage has a tendency to develop into rheumatism when you're older. It began for me when I reached twenty-six. A shoulder injury caused by being dragged half a mile along Grange-Over-Sands by a kite during a Beaufort Scale reading of nine when I was seven years old would flare up in the night. I was getting through two packs of ibuprofen a day by the age of twenty-two. Solpadeine came into effect when the headaches started, crunching through fifty to sixty tabs and washing them down with bottles of Old Bell's. I would have continued like this but I began fucking this girl with really bad teeth who played the trumpet for some swing band in Riversdun, and to be honest, that was all that girl's mouth was good for, blowing things. But she would make me dinner and feed me laxatives when I couldn't shit out a pebble for days. Combined with the painkillers, the alcohol had pulled me from this world so I had no idea what I was doing most of the time. The small pockets of darkness that shadow your memory after drinking turned into big black holes that sucked in days, not hours. The only thing I remember about that time was when we would fuck. We didn't do it like normal folk. It was all role-play shit where I'd have to sneak into the bedroom and pretend I was robbing her, or dress up in a boiler suit and drag some piece of furniture out into the hall so she could let me in and then seduce me. One night I went to her place, climbed in through the window and put my hand over her mouth while she was sleeping. I whispered in her ear that if she made a sound I'd slit her throat. Then I pulled up her nightgown and fucked her in the ass. I served six months inside for screwing that old lady and had to attend a sex addicts class as part of my probation. To this day, I still don't know how I ended up breaking into the Whispering Pines retirement home, or how I got a hard-on, but it was the wake-up call I needed to help get off the painkillers.

I chose the outpatient program here at the Royal because it means I don't need to listen to those junkies going cold turkey in the night. It also means I can use the time before and after meets to check in on the old man, get shit off my chest, and find absolution in silence.

His doctor is an old codger who reminds me of Einstein if he had let himself go. A big grey mustache hides his lips so when he talks you have to rely on your hearing only. Every evening he shuffles into my father's room, picks up his notes from the end of the bed, scratches his head a little and then asks me how the program is going. I always tell him I'm doing fine because I know he doesn't give a shit. All he's really worried about is me stealing meds. One of the nurses told me the doctor's father was the guy who went crazy studying the cases of all those children who turned up from Black Briar Woods. It was way back in the day, but everyone in Dogmael knows the story. The nurse said the doctor's father wrote a paper about age repression, or some shit, that was published in a fancy medical journal that normal folk will never read. He then went crazy and shot his brains out. Every time my father's doctor walks in and checks his notes, I wonder if he'll write about my father and then shoot his brains out. If it was me, the sheer boredom of dealing with a cabbage would force me to hold a gun against my head.

My father would sit up most nights scribbling in a little pocket notepad about the things he could do with me, everything from simple misfortune to catastrophe. He had ideas for at least double the amount needed to raise the cash for the Florida scam. "If you want something, you have to go out there and get it," he once told me while stuffing polystyrene into his y-fronts. "Ain't nobody ever gonna bring it to you, Jonah. Now, kick me in the nuts as hard as you can." Not many people would physically abuse themselves and their child to chase a dream. Most folk would realize how immoral that is and give up, find a regular job and twenty years down the line wonder how their life may have changed. Not my father. He'd tell me most people take the safe route in life because they don't want to leave anything to chance. Life was a game of chance, he'd say. By playing things safe, you could still fuck it up: an affair, road traffic accident, cancer. Least if you took risks, you get an instant result, bad or good. Living a normal life, without trying, that really scared the shit out of him. Guess this is why he turned to the stock market.

Gordon-fucking-Gekko he was not, but the old man watched Wall Street one day and figured himself an expert in stocks and shares. He started buying the broadsheets and checking the FTSE index. One of the sots from the local pub told him he knew a guy who knew a broker who worked in London. At this stage, the alarms should have been ringing, but he believed, or chose to believe, anything that involved making money quickly. In exchange for the scar that runs across my chin, the dislocated fingers, the bloody noses and the hairline skull fractures, my father was given cash from the television company, which he then gave to strangers to invest in stocks. It took him a month, and five hundred pounds to realize that broker was duping him, if he was a broker that is. The only person who truly suffered the loss of money was me because it meant more time in front of the camera.

Every Sunday morning my mum would drop me off at his place and when she picked me up, I had a new bandage. To deflect any negligence on his part, he told her I'd bumped into the door, fallen off my bike, tripped over the rug. When the cuts got deeper, he told me to go home and drink as much cola as I could. Once I'd finished all the cola, ask for water. I had to tell my mum I felt dizzy, always before dinnertime. She took me to see the GP in Dogmael who, after Mum explained the constant thirst and dizzy spells, checked me for diabetes. The results came back negative, so they figured I had a bad ticker. The old man did his bit and attended all the referrals to cardiologists at the Royal. He would sit with my mum, biting his nails as they drained my arm to check for high levels of lipoprotein. The results were always the same. I was a fit young boy, with no reason to be suffering blackouts.

The woman from social services reminded me of a bloated aubergine. She wore thick woolen tights that gathered in pleats around a pair of black court shoes, and if there were ever an episode of Tom and Jerry that revealed the upper half of Tom's owner, then she would be it. During the cardiologist visits, one of the doctors had noticed bruising along my arm where they'd taken blood. This same doctor referred my details over to the social services, and a week later, there was a knock at my mum's door. She explained to Mum that if any child presents the three stages of bruising, red (fresh), purple (ripe), yellow (healing), all at the same time, social services has a legal right to conduct a full assessment of the household. Clara Hornthorn had moved in with us by then, and being proficient in matters of oral pleasure had developed a tongue that could make the most cutting of lawyers jealous. Accusations of discrimination based on same-sex relationships was a gambit that proved very effective in forcing the social services woman to back off and accept I was in a well-balanced and caring home. Clara's proactive leaning also helped imply the problem lay elsewhere, and perhaps she should make inquires with my father. To secure the deal, she added that it would be best to visit his house before noon, before he had time to go to the local boozer. Two social workers arrived at the old man's home one morning to find five VHS-C tapes containing varying degrees of child cruelty and neglect being copied onto VHS tapes ready to be sent to the television company.

They also found his notepad, open with a pencil drawing of a matchstick kid falling through a ceiling, and another involving a homemade swing and a small fence. Backed against the wall, instinct took over and the old man reverted to mocking that woman, calling her a fat old snooping bitch. He replayed that scene over and over to me over the phone, choosing to adopt a Deep South American drawl whenever he impersonated her. Clara was pushing for a restraining order, and I'm sure she could have convinced my mother to get one had he not told them he was going to live in Florida. The last words he ever spoke to me were over the phone: "The oranges in Florida are said to be the best in the world, Jonah. Once I get settled, I'll send a box over."

It was rumored he fell fifty feet, but from what Mum told me, I figured it was more like a hundred. The idea was simple: park his Austin Allegro on a precipice near the top of Keighley Crag, forget to apply the handbrake, and get out of the car. The videotape would show him running toward the moving car, grief stricken as it fell over the edge of the cliff. What the tape captured that day was his sleeve caught in the door, and the car dragging him over the cliff with it. It took a helicopter and five men to lift him off that hill. When they removed what was left of the car, his shirtsleeve was still stuck in the door. The doctors told Mum he had bilateral damage to the reticular formation of the midbrain. They talked her through all the machines that were keeping him breathing, and used something called the Glasgow Coma Scale to determine how far into the great beyond he'd reached. Comas don't last more than two to five weeks, but the old man was like Sleeping Beauty for five years. That coma slapped a gag on his mouth, stopped his hand from scribbling plans, and his brain from formulating them. For the first time in his life, my old man was actually there for me when I needed him. He didn't judge me when I told him

I'd smoked my first cigarette, nor did he criticize my hair or clothes. There was no pressure to go to university and get a career. And he never uttered one word of frustration when I flunked out of school and got a job selling vacuum cleaners house-to-house. He just lay on that cold hospital mattress searching for God in the ceiling. Routine got me through some hard times. Used to be I would envy my friends and the relationships they had with their fathers, all the time spent going out to football games, throwing ball, building models, all while my old man was throwing me down hills or building ramps out of weakened wood. But over time, whatever tethered them together, the pursuit to bond and all that crap, well, it got severed by monotony. Not me and the old man. The tedium of habit brought us together. The longer he stayed in that coma, the closer I felt to him. I told him about the Berlin Wall falling, and how the Americans and British were kicking ass in Kuwait. And every day his muscles weakened and tightened. The atrophy meant he was shrinking, centimeter by centimeter, and I wondered if one day I'd turn up to find him so small I could slip him into my pocket and sneak him home. By the time that junkie rock star in Seattle blew his brains out, the old man finally turned a corner and reached a PVS. To mark the occasion, Clara came to the hospital and handed me a padded envelope containing the VHS tape of him falling off the cliff. She said it was high time I let go of the past and move on.

The television company got back in touch a week ago saying they thought the clip of my father falling off the cliff was hilarious and that they hoped no one was injured during the process. Enclosed was a check for two hundred and fifty pounds, and their best wishes.

When the old man first arrived in hospital, I asked Mum why he wouldn't wake up, she told me he was dreaming of something really special and he didn't want that dream to end. I would just sit there and watch him breathing in and out, in and out, wondering if in that dream he was peeling back the rind of a Florida orange while the sun burnt his shadow into the ground. And when there were no words to share, no heartache, sadness or regret spilling from my mouth, I would close my eyes and see him splitting that orange apart, his teeth biting into its sweet flesh until it stained his shirt.

BAD, BAD, BAD BAD MEN
by Craig Davidson

"DON'T LET THE DOOR HIT YOU where the good Lord split you."

That may have been what I said, or something equally banal. Make like a tree and get out of here. Nice knowing you, fruitcake. I'm not exactly a titan of wit, besides which, I happened to be dogshit drunk.

First you take a drink, next the drink takes a drink, next the drink takes you. Don't know who said that, but I admire the sentiment. They say the first step to getting better is admitting you got a problem. I care fuckall for that, but who wants to live in denial? There comes a day where it's: screw it, fine, I'm a juicehead.

For me, that was when the mechanics of fixing a drink got so imprinted I could make one blind. Two tablespoonfuls sugar in a Collins glass, sprigs of mint, muddle, pulverized ice, bourbon to taste. The point arrives where you've made so many it's reflex-memory. You could be robot arms on an assembly line.

It's only fair to mention—really, it's a crucial corollary to all this—that by then I'd taken to drinking mint juleps. Primarily as 'bourbon to taste' could mean half a pint.

Mint-*fucking*-juleps! Ought to invest in a string tie, get me a touch of that Colonel-Sanders-Kentucky-Fried southern class.

Now the guy I'd said it to, he turns back. We—and when I say 'we,' I mean the nameless shambles I bend elbows with at this scratch-ass bar, Honey's, on Pine Street—we are rather stunned at this development. Me especially. This guy—who, I should hasten to add, was by then stalking to where I sat slumped next to a promotional cutout of Oscar De La Hoya; Oscar hawking Tekate—beer of *Aztecs!*—Oscar's skin yellowed with smoke, Oscar's eyes torched out with a Zippo, anyway, this swinging dick was not a regular. Which is why I said what I said, right? The guy was an outsider and should expect to be scorned by us regulars, who have built up our cred simply by participating in this grotesque carnival of human misery for much, much longer.

99% of the time they say: *Fuck it, what do I care what these degenerates think?* Which was the whole angle of my gambit: you gauge the chances you'll get away with it versus the possibility it'll earn you five in the eye.

Fuck me, why would I yearn to impress these assholes? It's not like we pass a peacock feather around and recite our favorite passages from Iron John. Fact is, I hated them the way you hate your own face in the mirror the next morning. But here I was lipping off a stranger in hopes it'd elicit a chuckle out of these candy-colored dildos.

"What did you say?"

I was staring at the face of a flinty Norse God. Not a shred of compassion in the guy's shark-grey eyes.

"What did I say?" I parroted back, giving him a wonky smile in hopes he'd peg me for a useless hairbag not worth bruising his knuckles over.

His punch was telegraphed from *next week.* His spine arched and his fist nearly touched his heels—like how old movie cowboys threw a punch. I'll get out the way, I said to myself. Shift my chin a smidge, or hell, slide off the stool, slip out the back door—Sayonara, shitheels!—and be halfway down the block before this guy even

I woke up on the floor. My feet were tangled up in the brass footrail. My nose all mushy, plus the taste of blood in my throat. The guy who'd cold-cocked me had taken the pains to turn me on my side so I wouldn't choke to death on my own puke—which, to give him his fair due, was a pretty sporting move. Thanks, masked stranger!

"Anyone calling the paramedics?" somebody said, without much enthusiasm.

"To the best of my knowledge," said the bartender, "he *is* the paramedics."

I snuck into the bay at Niagara Falls Memorial, hugging the wall like a safecracker. Acid-core halogens scorched my corneas as I ducked into an ambulance. After licking the head of an extra-large Q-tip I'd dug out of an Ambu-Care tackle box, I tore open a pouch of hemostat coagulant powder, dunked the Q-tip and swabbed out both nostrils. The busted capillaries fused shut—it felt like a rug burn.

I considered my face in the steel mirror above the brace kits. Blood in the chinks of my teeth. I tried to root it out with a fingernail but when that failed I unscrewed a bottle of hydrogen peroxide. It fizzed the chancre sore on my tongue.

I hunted up a baggie of Dextrose 30%—sugar water, basically, but if I mainline it into your cephalic vein it's a $200 connection fee, billed to your HMO—snipped the stint-plug with surgical shears and squeezed the warm treacle down my throat to jack some glucose into my anemic cells.

"I remember different days," I said to my reflection, and smiled. "Do you?"

Exiting the ambulance, I felt vaguely human. I showered alone, sucking down another baggie of Dextrose to quiet the keening scream in my blood. Fingers knit together, I hung off the showerhead like a prisoner in a Turkish gulag.

After donning my paramedic's whites, I found Lassiter in the cafeteria. He stood with a cook at the kitchen pass. Lassiter was tight with the cooks and janitors, the shipper-receivers. The cook was handing Lassiter a brick of leftover meatloaf.

One of the Emerg nurses had been demoted to skeleton shift. She was ragging out her Charge Nurse to a table of bored orderlies.

"Man comes in with three fingers in a handkerchief, sawed off at a construction site," she said. "Another man comes in with mild chest pains. No-fingers man gets first. Man with chest pains takes a seat. Now if that man *told* me he was taking nitrogen pills, like he's s'posed to . . . so that man's heart explodes"—in her mouth it's *esplows*—"in the waiting room and that's on *me*?"

"I heard it was on his chart," said Lassiter.

"What was on?" said the nurse, a hot coal in each eye.

"That he'd been prescribed nites."

"On a Post-it stuck to it, is all."

Lassiter said, "Right where you could see it."

"What do you even know, meat-wagon jockey?" She angled her boneless face at Lassiter. Her feeble defiance stirred pity in me. "You even know my CN? Even know who we're talking about?"

"She's the frumpy bitch with a face like a rotted hornet's nest, right? No, wait, that's somebody else, that's, that's, that's . . ." *Snap!* went Lassiter's fingers. "That's *you*, you ghastly old lesbian."

Next we were in the light-washed ambulance bay, Lassiter licking the juice from the tinfoil-wrapped brick off his fingers.

"You drive," he told me.

I cranked the wheel left, motoring north. Summer dusk in Cataract City. Down Pine Street, past the spot of my most recent humiliation. College kids colonized the patio at Unc's, sucking down ice-filled buckets of creamy cervezas. The muscles knitted at the back of my neck as tension spread across my clavicles. We passed Sharkey's, a biker bar. Last week, we'd responded to a 9-1-1 call there. A young hogger beat half to death in an initiation ritual. His scalp was covered in bloody ant hills. Lassiter pinched the kid's incisors off the floor and bounced them in his palm like a pair of hot dice.

"These aren't your milk teeth, dummy."

The kid's license said he was seventeen. The bikers leaned on blood-streaked pool cues with thick blue elastic bands cinching their goatees.

"Did they sell it as an act of deep nobility?" Lassiter asked the kid. "What fun it'll be to fetch splits of Rolling Rock for these Easy Rider fuckos. Pulling bitch position on the train."

The kid said: "I fell."

"You fell into something," Lassiter agreed. "Enjoy life with these muffins, huh?"

The bikers just blinked slow, assigning Lassiter's face to their mental Rolodex. In all likelihood Lassiter wouldn't have been so bold if he hadn't been hooped on diethyl ether. It wasn't uncommon for him to swallow pills from the Ambu-Care kit or strap the Nitrox mask over his face. A few months ago I'd even found him dipping his finger into a pouch of Pethidine powder and sucking it off—the opium-eater's version of Fun Dip. Eyes: two pissholes in the snow. "They should do something about these ants," he'd said, waving a hand round his face. "Why would God, in his infinite wisdom, grant ants *wings*?"

It was January. Flying ants aren't native to northern New York state.

And now . . . *ether.* May as well chug laudanum, or get ballsed on Doctor Pennyfeather's Wondrous Nerve Elixir. Lassiter's gone all Cider House Rules on the shit lately. The janitors had been cleaning out the hospital basement when they came across a box of paper-thin glass ampules. The little fuckers were packed in *wood*: a solid block drilled full of holes. They looked like sniper's bullets bedded in foam. They were supposed to be incinerated, but of course Lassiter cadged a whack of them.

Lassiter popped the glove box and pulled out an amp. He put it under his nose, held it in place with his upper lip. The sound of snapped glass: an ice cube fracturing in a cocktail glass. *Nice.* The air in front of the windshield went swimmy, like a stretch of desert highway.

"Ah, yes . . ." Lassiter rucked his shoulder blades into his seat, nestling in like a hamster into cedar shavings. ". . . there's the flavor."

The problem with ether is it seriously impairs an individual's fine motor skills. Which is a problem when said individual may be called upon to manually intubate a toddler or inject full-spectrum psychotherapeutics into a carotid artery.

I parked at the Niagara Reservation. Through a gap in the pines the sun set over the Falls. Quivering spears of sunlight met the spume boiling off the cataract, a billion-trillion miniature suns tumbling over and over. The sun set tortuously slow.

When we were kids, Lassiter and me, we'd ride our Schwinns down into the basin, sneak through a flap snipped in the chainlink fence and fish for rock bass in the shadow of the Rainbow Bridge. We baited our hooks with maggots: they came packed in sawdust in a styrofoam cup, same as KFC gravy comes in. We'd cast our lines into water so cold it numbed our toes. We sat on the rocks in the gloaming with the monofilament wound round our finger to sense the slightest nibble. Our faces lit by that glittering disco ball of a city on the other side of the river.

Later on Lassiter's uncle took us out in his punt-boat. He had an old crank telephone hooked to a bank of car batteries. He dangled the wires into the water and cranked the phone. "Dialing for fish," he called it. Jagged veins of stark white ripped into the black water; electricity crackled the boat's hull with Rice Krispie pops. Fish floated up, twitching. The voltage had burst their eyes. Lassiter's uncle whooped, scooping them up in a net.

Sometimes you learn a new way that's more effective, sure, but you forfeit some crucial element in the process—or maybe the process itself is the element?

The radio crackled.

. . . intersection of Third and Duggan . . . possible gunshot wound . . .

I hit the siren and stood on the gas pedal. We charged up Rainbow Road, zagging between motorists.

"GSW?" said Lassiter. "Too early for that."

Guns are late night score settlers. And knives. Occasionally hatchets. Every so often, hammers. Once, and only once, a rack of antlers off an eight-point elk.

We were first on scene. A late model Mercedes Benz was bumped up over the curb. Three college-age guys were staggering around, dazed. One had a pretty nice gash on his head. A fourth guy was on the ground.

Lassiter reached over and cupped my head in his large hands. Pulling it forward, he planted a kiss on my forehead. Ether could bring out the touchy-feely in him.

"Let's do some good," he said.

He stumbled out the passenger door. I went round back and popped the bay doors. I grabbed the Ambu-Care Kit, a few air casts, and a neck splint.

"You little fucking *MORONS*!"

I double-timed it round the ambulance. In the wash of rotating red lights I saw Lassiter, beet-faced, bellowing at the injured boy on the ground.

"You dumbshit fuck!"

Here's the thing you'll realize: as a species, we are on a termination vector. You see so many mean and petty and horrifically *stupid* things, that conclusion is unavoidable.

It becomes difficult to maintain a professional veneer. Doubly so when you're gassed to the tits on ether.

As a for-instance: one time we responded to a call in the upscale Fort Schlosser neighborhood. A bungalow encircled by meticulously-trimmed box hedges. The guy who answered Lassiter's knock was clean-shaven, with an artsy look.

"It's my boyfriend," he told us.

He led us into a wide room dominated by a white calfskin sofa and loveseat. His boyfriend stood awkwardly, with a tight smile on his face.

"Thank you for coming."

"That's our job," Lassiter told him. "Although by the look of it you could have made it into Emerg, yeah?"

The guy dropped his eyes. His body went rigid as a tremor passed through him.

"Tell them," the artsy guy said.

"*You* tell them. It was your idea."

"Okay, then—"

"It was a stupid . . ." the other guy cut in. "I have . . . there is . . . oh, for God's sake . . ."

He stared at the ceiling. At us, defiantly. "There's an electric toothbrush up my ass."

You'd be surprised how often paramedics respond to trauma of this rather specific nature. Not always electric toothbrushes, but implements of a similar physical disposition. What most people don't know is, our intestines have a kink just past the retroventrical pouch. It is even more pronounced once a man reaches early middle age, when the intestinal wall forfeits its youthful tension. When a foreign object is forcefully introduced, the sphincter muscles tighten reflexively and *force* said object into the aforementioned kink, where it can become lodged.

Paramedics colloquially refer to this kink as the 'shameful pocket,' owing to the fact that a great many dark secrets find their way into it.

"What model of toothbrush?" Lassiter asked.

"Does that really matter?" the guy asked.

"Not too much," Lassiter admitted. "The real question is: sir, do you happen to have *teeth* in your large intestine? If so, I daresay that's something Ripley's Believe It Or Not ought to be made aware of."

Of all the bizarre traumas you tend to see, an electric toothbrush up the keister actually sat on the tame side of the ledger. Lassiter drove them to Emerg. I sat in the back. They held hands—which, honestly, was nice to see. The electric toothbrush hadn't quite run out of juice. The guy whose ass it inhabited trembled fitfully whenever it snapped to life in his lower colon. The whites of his eyes quivered.

"Feeling all right?" I asked.

"Y-y-you h-h-have nuh-nuh-no ih-ih-*idea*," he said with quiet rapture.

I relate this because that's not always the way it goes. Sometimes people in the same predicament resort to some hack medical procedure—going after it with barbecue tongs or whatever—and create an anal fissure, a fistula, or even perforate the intestinal wall. They'll simply lie in bed and bleed to death. All because they can't bring themselves to dial those three digits.

As a paramedic, the one thing you want to tell those people is that ultimately, nothing is more shameful than dying of shame. But I understand that shame, part of which arises at the prospect of having to explain one's condition to the first line of response. The fear we'll show up and say:

"You had to try it, didn't you? Stick a fucking toothbrush up your fanny. Did you satisfy your curiosity, bozo?"

Me, I tend to be diplomatic, if not entirely compassionate. Lassiter . . .

"You dumbshit *fuck*!" he presently screamed at the kid laid out on the tarmac. I pieced it together. Four guys joyriding around in one of their father's Benzes, firing cat's eye marbles at bus shelters. The car hit a bump; the gun barrel dipped and a marble ricocheted off the window frame back into the interior.

"Move your hands, fuckhead!" Lassiter said to the kid. "Let me see what I'm working with here."

When Lassiter saw, he straightened up and made a defeated clucking sound. He ran his hands through his lank hair, cast me a beleaguered glance and said:

"You deal with it. I'm too fucked up."

I knelt beside the injured boy. He had one of those large, ever-weeping zits where his nostril met his cheek—the type some guys spend their entire senior years nursing. His left orbital socket was cracked clean where the zigomatic arch met the maxillary bone. One half of his cheek was shoved above the other, overlapping like patio flagstones after the ground has settled.

His eye was avulsed: this is where the eyeball has been partially ejected from the ocular vault. Some paramedics call it a 'jacket potato' injury. If you've ever squeezed a grape from its skin, you likely get the picture.

"You'll be fine," I told the boy, who was shivering like a dog in the rain. "Can you see?"

"Not really," he said.

"Anything? Colors? Even grey?"

"Yeah," he said. "Like, a broken rainbow."

"That's good. That means your retinal nerve is still attached. That's very good. Now you need to stay still while I prep you, okay?"

"Is my dad's car fucked?"

"It's fine."

"He'd kill me."

Lassiter was busy tearing a strip off the other three.

"You twisted fuckfaces!" He stalked round the Benz like a grizzly marking territory. Every so often he lunged at one of them, making them flinch. "Don't you have . . . have . . . *hobbies?*"

He lunged, then danced nimbly back, hooting.

"I got moves like Baryshnikov, baby! But this is pure *pussy-ass*, boys. Driving round in a fine aut-to-mo-*bile* shooting what? Shooting *marbles*? With a *paintball gun*?"

The Benz's motor was still running. Jarring notes poured out of the speakers. "Is that—?" Lassiter fumed.

"Is that *Godsmack*? Oh, you should all be shot." He reached through the rear window to retrieve the paintball gun. The glassy rattle of marbles in its plastic hopper. With the C02 canister resting casually on his hip, he pulled the trigger. A marble punched through the windshield.

"Okay," he said. "I can see the appeal."

"What was that?" the kid said. I rubbed zeolite moisture salve onto a strip of breathable gauze and taped it over his eye.

"Nothing," I said, and taped another strip of gauze over his working eye.

Lassiter had the boy sit on the Benz's hood while he dressed the head gash with Titebond: a non-allergenic medical contact cement used to glue split flesh together in lieu of sutures. Problem being: Lassiter was all ethered up. He'd glued the kid's wound together, yeah, but the result was . . . *Dali-esque*. He gawped at his fingers, all hopelessly glued together, then doubled over laughing.

I said, "Get the gurney, Lassy, would you?"

"I got to go to the hospital?" said the boy.

"You figure you can walk around with your eyeball hanging halfway out of your skull? You must be quite confident in your recuperative powers."

"Who's going to drive the car home?"

"You trust any of them?"

"No," he said flatly.

"Call your father?"

"No."

"Mom?"

"She doesn't live with us anymore."

Lassiter shoved the gurney out of the ambulance.

It rolled merrily away. He chased it down, kicked it around, and pushed it back—butting it directly into my spine.

"Jesus, man!"

"Sorry. Let's get Mister One-Eyed Jack loaded up."

"Come on, Lassy. Simmer down."

"Pity not the fools," he told me, and in this his voice was hard.

A second ambulance pulled up. Stubbs and Randalman got out. Stubbs puffed his chest out and strode round the scene, nitpicking with shiny ratlike eyes.

"Who the fuck Titebonded that one?" he said, indicating the kid with the glued-together face. "Looking like a plastic surgery nightmare."

"That be *me*," said Lassiter. He adopted an affected 70's-era pimp-strut, juking his shoulders and cupping his hands like steamshovel buckets—a crude but cutting imitation of Stubbs's swagger. "You got a problem, slick?"

Next they were chesting up. Stubbs took a nasty little swing and clipped Lassiter's chin. Lassiter stepped back feigning wooziness, howling with mirth. Randalman and I stepped between. Lassiter smiled, bobbing on the tips of his toes with his hands raised in the old-timey boxer's stance.

"Put your dukes up," he simpered. "Show me what you got, show me how it *huuurts* . . ."

I'll love Lassiter to the grave and had his back above all others, but here I had to side with Stubbs. After all, Lassiter was sleeping at the man's house and fucking his ex-wife.

We got the boy to the ER. The admitting doctor was a burnout case with eyes like blown fuses. He peeled the bandage off the boy's wound. Next he raked his hands down his face with sufficient force to reveal the pebbled red of his eyelids.

"I just . . ." his voice trailed off. "I just don't know."

"Well, you better figure it out," I told him.

"This boy needs an exorcist," he said.

"Are you high?"

"Listen," he said with real heat. "I'm on zero hour."

Zero hour is the final hour of an ER doctor's shift. Statistics show that over eighty percent of malpractice suits filed against ERs involve a doctor on zero hour.

"Can I do anything?"

"Can you get an eye back into a socket?" he asked, with the serious expectation that perhaps I could.

"No."

"But there's nothing to it."

"I suspect there is."

The doctor put a hand on my shoulder. His fingers pulsed like a sea anemone.

"You don't have the bottle. That's okay. They don't pay you to have the bottle, do they? Anyway, all of that was settled a long time ago."

With the adrenaline burnt off, I needed a swallow. I thumbed the combo on my locker and found the fifth of Rumpleminze. Three hard hits, the deep bob of my Adam's apple. The beauty of Rumpleminze: it's pepperminty, so you just tell everybody you'd brushed your teeth.

I leaned inside the locker, skull on the cold metal as the booze napalmed in my gut and spread in glittering wings. Every part of me that was shaking, stopped.

Back in the ambulance Lassiter was gonzo. I'm talking, nil by mouth.

"My horse is dying," he told me, eyes squeezed shut.

"Check that . . . she's dead."

His breath smelled faintly of piss and I could guess the pills he'd been chewing.

The floor between his shoes sparkled with busted ether ampules.

"I need to see Gail," he said. "Take me home."

I drove him. First of all, because he was useless to me in this state. Secondly, because I just about always did what he said. We'd drifted apart in high school. He went the way of the football team and cheerleaders with legs smooth as blue cobalt, towards some future indefinable but for its assured glory. I went the way of the smoke hole skids, riding in the back seat of Ford Topazes with my lungs hardening to pig leather. Then one day he saw me at a pep rally and must have said: *I remember liking him*. He pulled me back into his orbit and I was grateful. To this day, am. Those sorts of casual kindnesses dig a home down deep. And now he's falling apart. We both are, but him so much faster. I'm a drunk, sure, but a manageable one. I forecasted thirty, forty years of functional alcoholism—a therapeutic administration, like insulin—where I held down a job, maybe owned a dog. Now Lassiter was screwing with that. And I didn't quite know what to do. I pulled into Stubbs's driveway. The poor bastard presently hung his hat at the Passport Inn. Lassiter's fingers were still glued together. I found a tube of xylene gel, squeezed a dab into his palms. I rubbed it over his fingertips to loosen the glue. His eyelids fluttered open.

"Jesus," he said. "Your nose."

He cupped my face with one hand. The reek of industrial solvent. "You get hit or something? Why didn't you tell me?"

Sometimes I think this was why he'd taken to huffing ether: it put him back into contact with his humanity. He picked up the silver brick of meatloaf and swayed up the porch. Knocking on the front door like a visitor, not the owner.

Gail answered in a diaphanous robe.

Gail . . . Gail was immense. Voluptuous wasn't even ballparking it. Every time I saw her, one word sprang to mind: *hypertrophic*. A medical term to describe body parts that escape the bounds of normal human scale. Arm wrestlers have hypertrophic biceps. Gail was hypertrophic in manners pleasing to the male gaze. Huge, pale, vein-riven breasts. Hips that flared alarmingly from a waspish waist, gradually giving way to a massive, soft, and indubitably grippable ass. What would it be to lie with a woman of such lush *muchness*, more than was ever truly needed? You got the sense every load-bearing joint was on the cusp of rupturing from strain. The folded flesh ringing her kneecaps put me in the mind of elephants' eyes. But you could tell she hadn't always been large. More like a top-flight athlete who'd gone to seed. There remained that sense of agility, flexibility . . . of *gameness*.

Gail was *cute*. I mean to say, she had a face she may have had as a teenager. Her body inspired a tactile covetousness: you wanted it to be your hands alone on her body, your lips, your tongue, although secretly you worried it couldn't possibly be enough. She was the sort of woman men wanted to lock away—but in a good way, a respectful way—to buy her nice things and watch rented movies with in darkened rooms, to make docile and happy but never be viewed in public in her company, for to be seen with such an awesome creature would be an admission of gross and unfeasible appetites.

"Did we wake you?" Lassiter said.

Gail ran a hand through her hair. Thumbed sleep-crust from her eye and flicked it free.

"No, I'm usually up watching Oxi-Clean infomercials at three in the morning." She smiled at me. "Morning, Cyrus."

"Morning, Gail. He insisted."

"I imagine he did," she said, as Lassiter slipped past.

"I bear a gift of meatloaf!" In the kitchen, wielding a butcher knife, Lassiter hacked up the brick. Gail sat on the sofa. Her body went down in sections. Gail's dog, a beagle named Edwina, waddled over and began to lick at Gail's toenails, which were painted a glossy fire-engine red. Lassiter deposited slabs of meatloaf onto a plate and opened the fridge.

"Ketchup?"

CRAIG DAVIDSON

"We're out," Gail said.

Lassiter shut the fridge.

"Come downstairs," he said to me. "See Sissy's new digs."

He unlocked the door and flicked the stairwell light. Stubbs' basement echoed the man himself. Tools meticulously hung on a pegboard, their outlines traced in Sharpie. Boxes labeled *Christmas Lights (large)* and *Christmas Lights (med-large)*.

Lassiter yanked on strings suspended in the murk, popping lights on. Sissy was wound around a metal support stanchion. Part of her, anyway. The remainder was coiled in the unfinished ceiling: I caught flashes of dappled white-and-caramel scales threaded between the unfinished beams and tufts of pink fiberglass insulation. Her head hung in a tangle of exposed wiring.

"Hey, baby," Lassiter said, stroking the hog-nosed arrowhead of her face.

I'd been there when Lassiter bought Sissy from a rare pet dealer. A baby Burmese reticulated python. I remember her twining between my fingers like pale rope, tongue flicking at the salt on my skin. I didn't like Sissy. Frankly, I couldn't conjure any compelling reason a sane person would fancy such an un-evolved, prehistoric creature—let alone one that was now thick around as a linebacker's calf. Sissy's eyes were empty as coins. Fingernail-shaped scales stretched over cold bone and blood . . . nothing but an ice-skinned, carnivorous tube.

"You're letting her hang out down here?"

"It's only a few weeks," Lassiter said. Sissy's tongue flicked his opened palm. "I'll build a heated shed out back."

"Gail's okay with it?"

"She's sealed in down here. I plugged the ducts."

One time I'd watched Sissy eat a foetal pig. Her jaws unhinged to reveal the pink workings of her mouth: a mangle of alien contours and weird vein-ribbed bladders. Her fishhook teeth sunk into the piglet's hide—the pig had smelled like a pickle, funnily enough. I looked away after that.

Back upstairs Lassiter dashed out to the ambulance.

"He's probably checking the two-way radio," I told Gail.

"That sounds likely," she said.

She sat with Edwina on her lap. The beagle's belly was huge.

"Is she pregnant?"

"She is, little bitch." Gail scratched the dog's mudflap ears. "I don't know who, but can guess about when. Set to pop. Should've got her spayed."

"I don't think he'll be much use the rest of the shift."

"He's got that look to him, doesn't he?" she said. "You just stood idly by?"

"You know Lassy."

"Better and better each day."

She leaned back on the sofa, threw an arm over the back. This was a woman who actually *would* sleep soundly with a sixteen-foot snake in her basement. She smiled at me in a peculiar fashion that compelled me to look elsewhere. You got the sense she'd entomb herself into you. She'd certainly done so to Stubbs, who'd been stumbling around hang-dog and radish-eyed for weeks.

Lassiter came in and collapsed on the sofa. Gail shooed Edwina to the floor. She cradled Lassiter's head and pulled him in. Lassiter fell into her like a man leaping off a skyscraper.

I went to the bathroom and took a piss. Afterwards I braced my hands on either side of the bathroom mirror. My nose was a swollen root.

I watched myself get old. A recurring vision, lately. My skin went yellow and sagged round my neck. My eyes drained of color. My lips thinned and peeled back. Filigreed cracks bisected my teeth, which turned the color of faded burlap. I'd be back at Honey's soon, occupying my same bar stool beside the same wrecks. Yet I remember those nights in the basin when I'd unhooked bass from treble hooks with hands as unlined as a baby's.

"I remember different days," I said softly. "I still remember, at least."

But some nights you feel it pulling away like a ship from shore. A dwindling speck on the horizon. Gone.

Creeping back down the hall, I heard Lassiter.

"My love," he said in a confessional whisper. "My love is a tiger shut up and bellowing in concrete walls . . . you make me feel like something cut away from cancer, do you know that? My love is . . . a mongrel. You can't mate it, babe, because it doesn't bear out pure, my love is, is . . . I want to take you upstairs but only if . . . I want . . . love to . . ."

Soon he was sleeping on Gail's lap. All the shit he'd popped tonight, the inside of his skull must have been broadcasting that early-morning Indian Head.

"He's sweet," Gail said, seeing me there. "But what does it earn you?"

She eased Lassiter's skull off her lap. I followed her into the backyard. The night was warm. The boom of the Falls carried over the maples. She pulled a pack of Salems out of her robe pocket and offered me one. Our smoke curled above the fence. In the darkness the shape of her body seemed to both gain and lose something: she seemed larger, yet somehow weightless. She caught me staring, smiled slightly, and sighed in a way that spoke to some unstated inevitability.

"Why do you figure he's doing it to himself?" she said.

Most cases, you figure there has to be a reason. It's impossible to believe a man might wake up one morning and say: *Starting today, I will embark on a systematic path of self-destruction.*

"Did you see the snake?"

"You're okay with that?"

She ashed her cigarette with a practiced flick of the wrist.

"We all make our little sacrifices."

Edwina pawed the porch door. When Gail let her out she made a beeline for the bushes.

"Get out of there, you," said Gail, crossing the lawn to where the dog was nosing around after something.

There's a species of white-winged butterfly who cocoon underground. They do so communally, in holes dug for other purposes. They are the only species to do so. These butterflies only live in the Niagara peninsula. The water table is just right, and they have adapted to where they cannot exist anywhere else—a fact as sad as any I've ever heard.

When Gail stepped over their hole they burst forth, new bodies uncountable in their brilliance. They spiraled up on a warm night zephyr, coiling round her body. Their luminous wings reflected the moonlight so it appeared as though Gail were encircled by a cone of tiny, bright paper lanterns. She held her hands out, palms down, same as one does when wading into dark water. She laughed in pure startled delight. The butterflies moved together, possessed of that same hive-mind common to schools of fish, circling and ascending until they broke against the moon.

They vanished over the fence. The phosphorescent powder of their wings sparkled the air. Gail reached towards them as if to say: *take me with you*. I wished that for her. Truly, I did. Jesus, I wished it for all of us.

"Let's do something about that nose," she said after a while.

She sat me at the table. She filled a Ziploc bag with ice and stood behind me.

"Lean back."

The top of my head touched her stomach. Through all that softness I felt the persistent tension of her adductor muscles. Her hand cupped my chin. She pressed the ice to my nose hard enough to hurt, but it was a manageable hurt.

"That's better, isn't it?"

Months ago we'd gotten a call. Apartment complex

in Fallsview Heights, Love Canal district. Lassiter was tits on a bull by that point. I left him in the ambulance. My knock was answered by a rail-skinny woman. Rosacea blooms on her face, which was pinched with worry. The smell hit me like a fist. I had to crank the door against a weight of old flyers and trash to get in. Roach carcasses ground into the carpet. A half-dozen lettuce heads on the kitchen countertop were rotted to brown mush. The bathtub tub was full of cat shit. Beside it lay a girl I pegged for about ten years old.

"There's something wrong with her," the woman said.

The girl was unconscious. Her face was red and the skin under her fingernails was pale violet. I knelt on the filth-caked tiles, pressed my ear to her chest. Heartbeat and respiration weak. I stuck a finger into her mouth: gummy strings stretched between her lips. When that search yielded nothing, I figured it had to be toxic shock.

"I need to get her out of here."

The woman shook her head violently. "Just fix her here."

"*Here's* what's the matter. The mold. The cat shit. The rotting . . . *everything.*"

"It's not that." The woman smiled, as if it might compel me to see things her way.

"She's never been sick." I picked the girl up. She weighed nothing. The woman set herself in my path. "I don't give you permission—"

I shoved past. She stepped over piles of trash to block me again.

"God damn it," I said. "You want her to die?"

"I'm her *mother.* Fix her *here.* We'll stay *here.* I want—"

I kicked her in the stomach. She made a noise out of a Z-grade horror movie and slumped into a pile of newspapers. I ran out hollering for Lassiter. He came to and helped me intubate the girl. We highballed it to the hospital.

I saved a life that night. Even let myself feel good

about it for a few days. But before long it dawned that I could as easily have not. I was doing my job, and I'm pretty good at it. But you don't give your accountant a medal for filing your taxes, do you? That doesn't absolve him of being a waste in every other aspect of human existence, does it?

The truth is: I'm a garden-variety asshole. I'll happily ruin myself, but I never cleared that gap to where I'd be willing to ruin others. And that's the crucial leap. You'll never go far as a garden-variety asshole. The stakes are too low. You'll hear it said that good guys finish last, but the fact is that plenty of good guys are content in their own skin, which is immeasurable in terms of pure happiness. Then there are those who truly don't care how many spines they grind into powder—and those guys sleep the blessed sleep of the damned.

Then there are guys like me and Lassiter. We skew bad, sure, but not nearly bad enough. And nobody profits in the middle. Nobody ever has.

In the bedroom Gail was a soft marvelous monolith. She was Stonehenge and, like an ancient fear-struck druid, I wanted only to worship. She removed my clothes with practiced ease, slipping her fingers into my shirt to pop each button. There was precious little beneath her robe: panties so sheer they could be made of spider's thread and a purple brassiere with about a hundred clasps. In the darkness pale half moons shone under her breasts, the rest of her skin tanned an edible brown.

My hands felt like paws, tiny mouse paws. It seemed a very real possibility a man could become hopelessly lost in a woman such as Gail—they'd dispatch a search party and find you blissfully nestled in some wondrous grotto or delta.

"Oh, Gail," I breathed, stamping awkwardly on my trousers to free my legs. "Oh, Gail, Gail . . ." nuzzling her neck, aware of how sappy I sounded but unable to stop.

She inspired this untenable desire: a man began to wish for six arms and a half-dozen tongues to take in the full measure of her.

"Easy," she said, laughing softly. "Easy, big fella, and quietly."

We sunk onto the bed. Her breath smelled of smoke; her skin, Noxema. I grappled with her lovely breasts and laughed helplessly, the way you do at a restaurant when your desert arrives bearing a towering cone of flame.

The hound, Edwina, squatted at the edge of the bed. She made supplicating, plaintive whines.

"Do something," Gail said. "Cyrus, please."

I shooed Edwina downstairs. She went unwillingly, her belly swaying.

Back in bed Gail guided my head down until it resided between her legs. Oh so arid down there—a ghost-town gulch. She gripped my hair *sternly*, as a rider grips the reins of a dressage mount. Her free hand slid under my chin, centering me.

"Stick your tongue out," she said. "Flex it, now. Make it hard."

Gail moved her hips slightly, flexing her gluteal muscles, rubbing herself on my tongue. I wanted to caress her but my elbows were trapped under her thighs. She emitted soft songlike noises. My tongue hurt from the constant clenching.

"What are you doing?" she said, when I took a moment to moisten it. "Not now."

Her rocking became vigorous. A violent claustrophobia overtook me. Her body tensed, relaxed, tensed again, went slack. She rolled my skull onto her thigh.

I clambered up to the pillows. She lay facing the opposite direction. I kissed her neck. She ruffled my hair absently, as if I were a child or a dog.

"That was great," she said.

The depths of her insincerity sucked the air from my lungs.

"I'm glad."

"Really, fantastic."

"He doesn't deserve you, Gail."

I had no proof that this was true. I didn't know what Gail was worth, really, valuations of that sort being difficult. It just seemed the thing to say.

"You're simple, Cyrus."

She stated this as a known fact. The sun is hot. Water's wet.

"You're pretty much harmless, I guess, but your view of the world is simple. And also, you're a drunk."

She got out of bed. After a while it seemed silly not to do the same. I gargled with Listerine and found her downstairs eating meatloaf. Lassiter remained kayoed on the sofa.

"Where do you keep it?"

Gail nodded to the cabinet. The ice she'd pressed to my nose was on the counter, barely melted. I iced a glass and hit it with a healthy splash of Comrade Popov's potato vodka—econo-jug-size. And *I* was a juicehead? I topped it with OJ and asked if Gail wanted anything.

"Can you make a Buttery Nipple?" she said, with a coy smile.

In that moment I saw an obese ungenerous slag with a tramp pedicure spilled over a cheap Ikea kitchen chair shoveling cold meatloaf into her yapper. Gail caught my look and nodded, as if she saw the same thing.

"Give me whatever you're having," she said.

I fixed her one and sat opposite. Before long I heard them. The squeals. The thin, febrile squeals.

I took my drink and tiptoed past Lassiter, down the hallway to the basement door. Which was open. Just a smidgen. Just a crack.

I flicked the stairwell light and walked down the steps.

The prehistoric smell of snake—the way dinosaurs must have smelled. The squeals were much louder down here.

"Cyrus?" said Gail from very, very far away. "What is it?"

I groped for the nearest white string and popped on a light. The glass slipped from my hand and it shattered.

Sissy was eating Edwina. The snake had unhinged her floating jawbone to engulf the hound's head and brisket. Tucked tight to its body, the dog's paws clenched spasmodically. The squeals hadn't been coming from Edwina, though. They came from the embryonic creatures she was still giving birth to while being devoured. Laying about the dusty concrete were a quartet—and in short order, a quintet—of slick, dark, egg-sized puppies.

I ran over and started kicking the snake in the head. As I only had socks on, there was only so much damage I could do. Kicking Sissy in the face, jaw, the . . . what, *neck? Elbow?* Only so many parts to a snake.

I booted furiously but Sissy didn't let go of the dog. A snake's teeth point inwards, so by the time it reached this stage they were pretty much committed. Sissy looked at me—I believe so, anyway, a snake's eyes being no more expressive than drops of molten steel—with a forlorn expression, as if to say: *What the fuck you kicking for? This is the sort of shit I do, baby.*

Gail stood at the foot of the stairs stifling a scream.

"Get me something," I said. "*Fast.*"

She hightailed it to the tool-board. I stepped on Sissy's neck, or whatever you call the spot where her skull gave way to the acidic conveyor belt that was her body—stomping with my heel like a man trying to kick-start a motorcycle. While I put the boots to Sissy another slick dark egg squeezed out of Edwina. The dog's paws weren't twitching anymore—they were stiff, as though a tremendous current were passing through them.

Gail handed me a hacksaw. Well, okay.

I straddled Sissy, cinched my knees tight to the brilliant cylinder of her body—a beautiful snake, as far as that went—positioned the blade behind the point where her jaw thinned and raked the blade across her scales.

Sissy's tail whipped up and tagged me on the shoulder, throwing me off-balance. Gail leapt on the snake and pinned it to the floor. What a woman! Our combined weight was well in excess of Sissy's, but the snake was pretty much all muscle, and deep in the lizard cortex of her brain she must have realized we were bent on her extermination.

"Go!" Gail said. "*Cut!*"

I bore down and muscled the blade across Sissy's neck. Blood buzz-sawed out of the gash, accompanied by a high hiss, like air let out of a bicycle tire. Sissy bucked frantically. I scissored my legs round her, wrenching my free arm underneath. Her skin was chilled industrial plastic coated in Teflon. My fingers snagged in the sideways 'V' of her mouth: dog fur coated in warm lube. The sluggish *bap* of Edwina's heart.

I dug my fingers into the cold bone of Sissy's skull and inhaled the dry reptilian stink of snake: a pile of rotting leaves. Taste of snake blood: cheap Chinese wine. My elbow pistoned. The blade sunk deep. A sound not unlike the rip of old lawn chair webbing. We both rolled aside as the snake lashed crazily, tearing her own head off. Sissy's body coiled round itself the way a nightcrawler winds itself round a fishhook. The snake's lung—a ten-foot-long bladder all wormed with veins—slipped out of her chest cavity like a gigantic condom.

"Oh, no," Gail said. "Oh, no, no, *no.*"

Awful, watching anything die. So rarely does it occur with much dignity at all. Sissy's muscles released. Her tail thumped the ground, raising plumes of dust. A pint can of Rust-Oleum paint disgorged from her stomach and rolled across the floor.

Edwina's snout protruded through the ragged hole in Sissy's neck. I'd inadvertently sawed her nose off.

"Is she dead?"

"Of course she's dead," I told Gail. "I sawed her . . . her fucking head off."

"I mean Edwina."

"I'm sorry. She's dead. Suffocated."

My fingers were so tight-clenched I had to use my opposite hand to pry them off the hacksaw handle. The puppies issued fitful mewls. Their slick bodies were picking up dust. One was latched onto Edwina's nipple, sucking.

I dropped them into the pockets of Gail's robe, like two kids stealing crab-apples. Her robe was torn down one side, her hair tousled, jewels of blood on her feet. Never had I beheld any woman so purely magnetic.

Upstairs, Lassiter remained dead to the world. This was best.

"We need whole milk." Gail cupped her hands under her robe pockets. Pulled them tight to her stomach. "Warm milk . . . I have an eyedropper somewhere."

Walking to the 24-hour Piggly Wiggly, I couldn't stop thinking about that can of Rust-Oleum. Time was, Lassiter would never have forgotten to feed Sissy. Now she was living in a basement, swallowing paint cans in the dark.

The store was empty, halogen lights buzzing. I grabbed a gallon of milk from the cooler. Only then did it dawn I was covered in blood. At least I was wearing my uniform.

The cashier was a ratty-haired scab with partially-lidded eyes. Pale blue tattoos braided from the sleeves of his orange uniform.

"That snake blood?" he asked, waving the milk over the scanner.

"Yes . . . snake."

"I figured snake. That, or lizard."

He bagged my milk with the same half-lidded gaze, then became deeply absorbed in the crispy-burnies rotating on the frankfurter rollers.

When I got back Gail had swaddled the puppies in terrycloth towels. When she took the milk from me, she kissed the side of my mouth. She poured milk into a saucepot and warmed it on a burner. I fixed another drink and gazed at the puppies. So small, but everything was there. Paws like tiny hands.

I couldn't say what woke Lassiter. Perhaps, in ascending to a higher plane of existence, Sissy's soul paused momentarily at his ear to hiss:

... *sssss—avenge me!—sssss* ...

He sat up, stiff-backed, a vampire out of its coffin. He looked at us, smiled faintly, rubbed a hand over his sleep-puffed face and then, without saying a word, he stood and went downstairs.

The moment stretched forever. Then Lassiter let go a shriek like a man who'd just suffered a hole punched through the dead center of his heart.

Things tended to get very distinct in moments such as these. A pristine clarity settled. A butterfly perched on the patio screen. Its wings opening and closing. Lassiter's shoes thundering up the steps. Gail sliding behind me, her fingertips light on my hip.

That butcher knife stabbed into the cutting board. The shine down its blade a stem of fine white fire.

It's like this: the world is always spinning. But you don't necessarily feel it move, do you? Until one day it stops dead on its axis and puts it to you: Well, my son, how bad are you? How bad are you, *really*?

THREE THEORIES ON THE MURDER OF JOHN WILY

by J David Osborne

THERE WERE THREE FIGHTS, two broken plates, a miscarriage and a bathtub full of moonshine at the wake of "Little" John Wily. They didn't call it a "wake." They weren't really sure what to call it, so they just called it a "reception," like it should have had invitations printed in cursive on whalebone.

John's dad took it the worst. Started just after the funeral, at the beginning of the reception. He'd dusted off a slide projector he'd found wedged between a four wheeler and a toolbox in the garage and set it in the living room. Projected on a tarp that his father had stretched to cover the bay windows, the red-faced and snuffling crowd had been subjected to photos of the recently departed as a child: smiling and squinting under the sun, in a bathing suit, by the pool. Sitting in his underwear, enraptured by the television. Holding a fish. Holding a deer. On the four wheeler now gathering dust.

The police had closed the book on John's case, not officially, of course, because officially it was only three days after the murder, after an unknown gunman torched John's car and left him in a clearing in the middle of Pocahontas, Oklahoma, with a belly full of buckshot. But it was as good as closed: tire tracks had been analyzed, the clearing had been combed by latex-gloved hands, and witnesses, most of

223

them floating in and out of a haze of methamphetamines, had been questioned. Nothing turned up. No one was going to pay for John's murder. When John's dad came around the station for the next few weeks, around five every day after he got off work (because you can't just stop, can you?), the detective, a balding man with a paunch and an affinity for Japanese-themed tattoos, would roll up his sleeves, revealing bright orange koi and white-faced geisha girls, and he'd thumb through a coffee-stained manila folder, turning the pages, humoring the weathered man holding his leather face in his hands. Then he'd set the folder down and shake his head and listen as the old man rambled and cursed.

Time passed and so did John's dad.

Though no one was ever officially indicted for the murder, John Wily was from a small town, and small towns talk. His death wormed its way into every conversation, between talk of the weather and whether or not the Pocahontas Bulls had any shot at state and what Mrs. Rita thought about the lawn ornaments crowding her next door neighbor's lawn (she hated them). By the time the talk had reached folks like that, though, the reality of the situation had dwindled, and the conversation was usually short, something like, "Did you hear about the Wily boy," followed by a "Yep" followed by, "It was drugs, they say," followed by a "Yep."

You'd find the good gossip downtown, where the streets stop having names or numbers, where grass and power lines fight for dominance, and where every person takes fifteen minutes to answer the door. If you were to sit down with them, in their living rooms, with their grooved couches and scratched endtables, if you were to offer them something and they were to put it in a pipe or tinfoil or a lightbulb and inhale and you had the patience to sit back and wait for their brains to come back from Shangri La, they might give you a few theories on what happened to

"Little" John Wily. Theories might be different, sure, but they'd all start out the same:

"John Wily was a fucking asshole."

Theory 1: The Angry Father-in-Law

John Wily met his wife, Angela, at the Shady Pines apartment complex pool. He had just dived into the water with his cell phone in his pocket. He cursed the dead thing and threw it in a trash can by the Coke machine and put a dollar in and that's when he saw her. He pressed the wrong button but didn't care. He sat in the pool chair and smacked his best friend Tamer Reynolds in the arm and pointed. They said "damn" under their breath and watched her take her shirt off and rub the oil around her sunflower bikini, over her fishbelly skin.

Tamer jumped in the pool and John skipped over the hot white concrete to where Angela either was or wasn't looking at him from behind big insectoid sunglasses. He opened his mouth, the words spinning like a slot machine in his head, each one slowly coming to a halt to form the perfect first phrase, that pickup line that would set the alarm off and all the red lights and have him lugging his big bucket of quarters up to the change girl, but before he could muster the oxygen, Angela said:

"I'm gay."

And this forced him to regroup. He played with the strings on his swim trunks. He ran his hand through his buzzed hair. He fingered the cross on his neck. Then it came to him, bright and clear like it was from God. He got closer, till he could count the rivulets of sweat squeezing around the faint hairs on her belly, and said, "Why are you gay? I could lick it better than any dyke, swear it."

Had she chosen to hit him, or mace him, it would not have been John Wily's first time. He spent the better part of sixteen spraying himself with mace, every day, usually just after breakfast, with the intention of immunizing himself.

Though it didn't make him immune to mace, it did force him to wear glasses, which he refused to do most days, instead choosing to squint and fumble and nearly kill himself on the highway. Still, when he said things like what he said to Angela, and when he was inevitably maced, he insisted that it didn't hurt too bad, that he was used to it.

Angela, however, had a rather fucked up background. She was from a family whose claim to fame was two appearances on national television, first as contestants on Family Feud (they lost) and second on Cops (her uncle asked an undercover cop to "beat his bishop"). Her father, a bearded construction worker with six teeth and about as many IQ points, beat her and worse on the regular, and her mother was too busy collecting Star Trek memorabilia to care. So whether it was the permissive environment or the years of incest, Angela found John Wily to be cute rather than creepy, interesting rather than radioactive.

Angela's father was not happy with the two dating. John, for all his pervy talk, turned out to be a fairly traditional courter, taking Angela out for dinner and ice cream and for rides in his dad's canoe. His dad, for his part, loved Angela almost immediately, and set about to showing embarrassing home movies which John smiled and sat through because even though he wanted to run away from the grainy footage of him putting macaroni in his pants, the magnetism of Angela's off-white smile and the smell of her cherry blossom perfume kept him firmly rooted to the vinyl of his father's couch, staring at her, watching the blue reflect in the wetness of her eyes and wanting to kiss her and be alone.

The first time John Wily met Angela's father he offered John a beer, which John accepted. The two cracked their tabs and talked for a few moments, back and forth, John looking at the pictures of Angela and her siblings as children on the wall, and once Angela's dad had the information he needed, i.e. that John didn't have a job and didn't plan on getting one, the judgment was passed, and he showed John Wily his shotgun and told him not to see his daughter anymore.

The threat was not taken lightly. Angela's uncle, the same one caught on film asking for a handjob, had gone to jail for life recently for shooting his own son in the back of the head. Spilled his brains all over a box of Cheerios, the kid face down in his breakfast, for what, once again, no one is sure.

Assuming that crazy ran in the family, John went to the pawn shop with the painting of the frog on the bricks and pointed through the smudged glass at a tiny twenty-five nestled in a coffin of foam. He failed his background check and the hairy man of indeterminate origin behind the counter told him "Congratulations, you passed," and took his crumpled dollar bills. John left the pawn shop and called Angela and told her to pack her bags.

The last night in her room, toeing the crumpled McDonalds wrappers and tissues and magazines across the sticky hardwood floor, Angela hugged her yellow pillow and cried. She touched faded Polaroids she'd taped to her wall. She opened old toy boxes and board games and read through old diaries. She stood over her father's snoring body for seventeen minutes, playing with her hands and eyeing the K-bar he kept on his endtable. After she stuffed her last pair of jeans into a pink backpack she closed her door and took a deep breath. Her hand inches from the door, she turned back into the foyer and marched into her father's room and threw her arms around the old man's neck. She hugged him and cried and in his sleep he patted her on the back and told her to go back to bed.

When he woke up that morning her father tried to call her, once or twice, but she wouldn't pick up her cell phone. He called AT&T and had her removed from his phone plan. He went to work and tuned cars. He went to the range and unloaded. He drove to John Wily's apartment complex and drank malt liquor from a brown bag. He watched the young man drive up, walk to his door, disappear. He repeated this routine for several weeks. He was fuming with an odd mixture of confusion, hatred, and jealousy that is usually reserved for young lovers. And we all know how impetuous young lovers can be.

Theory 2: The Cold-Blooded Killer

Tamer and Little John started selling meth as soon as they dropped out of high school. The money was good and they made a pact with themselves, lying in the back of Tamer's green pickup, droning and mumbling in a cloud of potsmoke, never to use the stuff, to become victims, flunkies. And they didn't. They sold a lot, Tamer more so than John, and they became the most popular folks in "that" part of town, but they never once touched their lips to a pipe. Once, after selling to a particularly eager group of addicts, John was not able to escape before the tweakers lit up, the smoke swirling in the glass of the lightbulb like magic in a crystal ball, their eyeballs white with ecstasy. The smoke floated and the room became hazy, and he ran out the door and sucked in the night air, the smell of wet dirt and diesel, and his head was spinning and he was sure that he'd gotten a contact high. He ran full speed down the road to Tamer's house, where his best friend cooked him pierogies and calmed him down and convinced him to keep selling, that they were partners and he needed him.

There was one thing that John could not be convinced of, and that was selling to black people. He wouldn't speak to them, barely even look at them. He approached Tamer one sunny day, fingering the cross on his neck, and nodded his head at the two black children handing his friend two twenties stained with blue ink:

"What are you doing?"

"Selling."

He squinted his mace-induced squint and said, "Meth is a white man's drug."

Tamer sighed. "With that attitude, it always will be." He patted the kids on the back. "Enjoy, guys."

They pedaled away on their bicycles.

Little John Wily's racism potentially got him killed on a cool day in late autumn. He was at the convenience store picking up the usual: Red Bull for him and water for Angela, who was coming down off of a wicked meth binge (she had no equivalent abstinence pact regarding meth, a habit that was a holdover from her other, slightly more fucked-up existence pre-John).

He got distracted in the candy aisle, trying desperately to decide whether he wanted the peanut butter cups or the almond bar, and when he looked up at the counter, his place had been taken by a muscular young black man in a white T-shirt and jeans. The young man was listening to his CD player and halfheartedly making conversation with the clerk when John Wily reached him, the candy bar dilemma forgotten, and shoved the pack of gum and the Dr. Pepper off of the galvanized metal counter. The soda bounced and fizzed wickedly inside the plastic. The gum clattered into the corner. John Wily looked deeply into the black man's eyes and said, through clenched teeth. "Always me before you. *Always.*"

The young man plucked the headphone buds from his ears and inclined his head towards Wily's mouth. "Come again?"

Wily reiterated his maxim.

Now, in the great karmic wheel, the magic forces of comeuppance occasionally work in our favor. We all want to see shit like this punished, but the sad fact of the matter is that a good man calls the police, leaving it up to a bad man to lay down a righteous ass whipping. Such was the case with John Wily: Tom Miles was not a good man. At that moment, in fact, he had a whore in his car, a raven-haired former video-store clerk named Mary, upon whom he had bestowed a purple shiner hours earlier, for running down the street, banging on doors, attempting to stop cars, begging someone, anyone, to save her. He would kill her later in cold blood, pinning her down and injecting her with enough heroin to flatten a moose. But that day, through no fault of his own, Tom Miles did the right thing: he dragged John Wily to the back of the store, which doubled as a bait shop, and began drowning him in the minnow tank.

Wily was saved by the clerk and his steel bat, with which he delivered a swift blow to Tom Miles' legs. The pimp stumbled away, cursing and holding his thigh, and John Wily caught his breath and dried himself with paper towels from the bathroom's automated dispenser.

People say Tom Miles might have come back for Little John. The evidence is solid: the clerk ended up dead a week later, and when Tom was eventually arrested, it was for a triple murder. He'd driven a father, mother, and daughter into the middle of nowhere, shot them, and torched their car. They call that, I believe, a modus operandi.

Theory 3: The Best Friend

The night Tamer Reynolds met John Wily, they stole street signs and lights from a railroad crossing. Tamer dropped the first set, the giant amber bulbs shattering on the asphalt, so John got the second pair, handing them down gently, hooting loud at the moon. They were inseparable. They drank and harassed women at strip clubs. They smoked pot and sold meth. They kept their mouths shut both times the cops kicked in the door, neither of them eyeballing the hidden panel in the floorboards.

They raised hell. They rigged a taser to a car battery and pressed the coils to the fiberglass of sedans, leaving big black burns in the sides of Chevys and Toyotas. The fuses fried, they'd be free to slim jim the lock open and steal the money or food or TVs that rich people tended to leave in their cars.

The meth dealing was easy. The tweakers showed

up, handed them the money, left with their stuff. They didn't worry about police surveillance. Tamer had friends in very high places, or low, depending on whether you were talking status or morality. Big men in dark sunglasses would show up and joke around for a few hours with him, just shooting the shit, and John would sit in his leather recliner, smoking a cigarette and laughing when appropriate.

John's problem was that he was an idiot. He shacked up with Angela, the two of them spending all day screwing and watching courtroom reality shows, and soon he was getting crazy ideas. Angela was happy in and out of her meth haze, and she loved John enough that sometimes she'd let him hold her for hours. But John was sure something was wrong, as though he were in tune to some cosmic disturbance that no one else could tap into. Angela told him he was crazy.

He asked Tamer to ask his connections if he could front him eight grand worth of product. Tamer asked and was approved immediately; his credit with the rednecks was good.

John sold all eight thousand of it, and quickly. Almost doubled his profit. Then he refused to pay the money back. He didn't buy a bus ticket, didn't think about catching a plane. He simply dropped the money into a bank account (it took him a while, but he found a bank that would have him) and sat on it. And wouldn't budge.

Tamer came around and tried to talk sense into him. The rednecks were pissed. The rednecks were gonna kill him. John shook his head no, he wasn't going to give the money back yet. He'd pay them, he promised. But the money was his for now, until he and Angela could get a better life. He'd make a down payment on a house. He'd buy a car. They'd start a life, there in Pocahontas, and those rednecks would just have to wait. "Besides," he said. "They ain't gonna kill me. I been to that guy's house. He loves me! We shot the shit for hours."

The redneck who loved John Wily sent two men to empty several hundred rounds of ammunition from an M-16 into his apartment. He also sent two men to see Tamer, whom they informed had to "take responsibility" for his friend's debt, or face the consequences. The consequences were hinted at with a broken toe and some work done to his face. Tamer showed up at John's door, bloody and yelling through cracked teeth, but John wouldn't be swayed. That shoulder-shrug mentality, that he didn't care what happened to his best friend, broke Tamer Reynold's heart.

What happened next occurred within a day or so of John's death. He woke up that morning by himself and poured a bowl of cereal. He opened his front door to have a cigarette (because Angela didn't want the house smelling like smoke) and nearly tripped over a small package from UPS. He opened it on his couch, still smoking his cigarette, and removed the videotape from inside.

He pressed play. The footage came on, grainy. He saw Tamer, saw his ugly bruises looking grayer in the camera light. The camera spun, and there was Angela, sitting in a chair, playing with her hands. The camera rocked and then was still, making a slight noise as it slid into a tripod.

The voice sounded forced, like a Shakespearean actor forced to do Z-grade sci-fi. "So it's been a while since you've had what you need, right, baby?"

Angela nodded and bit her lower lip.

"John hasn't had any in . . . jeez, nearly a week, yeah?"

She scratched at her arm and looked away.

"So you need it?" The way he said it, it was like he was hoping she would say "no."

She nodded again. Her eyes were glassy, and John Wily thought of the first time he'd seen them like that.

"How bad do you need it?" Tamer had gotten closer. Standing over her. Casting a shadow.

She only thought for a second before she began to

undo Tamer's belt buckle. He wiggled a baggie of crystals in her face and told her to be a good girl.

John kicked his TV over and ran out the door.

He was dead the next day.

Angela went back to her father, who held her close and took her out to play a game of miniature golf. They were mostly quiet and he kept score with a dull pencil and that night he tucked her in and told her he was happy that she was home. When she woke up and checked her newly reinstated cell phone, amidst the texts asking where she'd been and what she was up to she saw one from Tamer, and she felt the butterflies of young love in her stomach, and when she opened it and read it she vomited into the toilet and spent the morning on the cool tile, crying.

When she doubled over at John Wily's wake it was Tamer that held her by the shoulders, Tamer who called the ambulance. It was the first sign of emotion he'd shown all day. He'd sat stoic through the slideshow, numb from the rush of emotion and Vicodin.

He'd decided against breaking into Wily's place and destroying the tape on the off chance there were police watching the apartment. Instead he split his time praying that the cops wouldn't find it and praying that God might bring Wily back. He sat in his apartment in the dark. He deleted Wily's number from his phone. He deleted all the pictures of his friend from his hard drive. He couldn't eat.

He worked his jaw and blinked in the dust kicked up by the ambulance. The funeral guests went back inside the house, dead set on finishing the moonshine in the bathtub. He sat on the porch and wrung his hands. The tall grass crept up to the edge of the yard. Bird chimes clanged in the hot yellow air. He got up and unlocked his car.

The silhouette of Tom Miles watched him from his

Honda. He stepped out into the oppressive heat and hobbled toward the skinny boy walking to his car. Tom had at the very least done a little research, asked around those same neighborhoods you're asking. At the most he'd coaxed the information out of John Wily at the end of a sawed-off shotgun, and it was with the butt of that same shotgun that he broke two of Tamer Reynolds ribs. He kicked the boy's legs out from under him and dragged him to the Honda.

He laid the shotgun across his lap and listened to his CD player, only taking the buds out when he needed directions to Tamer's apartment. As the town of Pocahontas disappeared in the distance, the two men stared at the road ahead of them. One of them had loved John Wily and the other couldn't have cared less, but one of them was certainly responsible for his death. No one is sure who it was to this day, but they do know one thing: that was the day that Tom Miles became involved in the meth trade.

THE ROAD LESTER TOOK
by Stephen Graham Jones

Not only was it not Lester's night, but it hadn't even been his year, really. What he was doing was hiding from the private investigator his insurance company had tailing him. Where he was hiding was deep in a Friday night, in the farthest corner of his friend Wayne's basement. Why he was hiding was because he was supposed to be wracked with pain, unable to place one foot in front of the other, the medication stripping his concentration so that all he was good for anymore was daytime television.

The reason it wasn't his night tonight was Johnny, the new guy, who'd served enough weekends in county that he knew every way a hand of five card draw could fall.

Lester pushed his last two Vicodin into the pharmacy in the middle of the table, seeing Wayne's nickel bag. Wayne had lifted it from his son Wayne Jr.'s sock drawer stash. Wayne had a pair of tens; Lester had seen them already, half on accident, half because Wayne didn't care.

"So?" he said, to Johnny.

Johnny tongued his lower lip out slow, like a lizard would if he were a man, then shrugged, pulled something up out of his shirt. It was on a dirty string around his neck. A glass vial, rubber stopper. White inside.

"Shit," Delbert said, and folded.

Johnny smiled, threaded it over the back of his head, guiding his thin ponytail underneath.

"Break in case of emergency," he hissed, and nestled it onto the pillow Wayne's nickel bag was.

Wayne dumped his cards as well, tried to push himself back from the table in his folding chair but it had rubber feet, and the drama was lost.

Johnny never looked away from Lester.

"That your pretty wife calling?" Johnny said, tilting his head to the world above.

"Crying for more . . ." Lester said, studying his full house for the four thousandth time.

"Set of lungs like that—" Johnny said, his smile thin.

Lester nodded, knew Johnny was trying to get him thinking about his wife Janice's new, insurance-money breasts instead of the game.

"It's good shit?" Lester said, about the glass vial in the pot.

"It's baby aspirin," Johnny said, shrugging. "Confectioner's sugar."

Lester smiled, looked to his cards again, then made a show of looking to his side of the table. His empty bank.

"Linda's phone number," he said finally, to match Johnny's bid.

"Linda?" Johnny said, one side of his face drawn up in doubt.

"I'd take that," Delbert said, in all seriousness. "I'd take that and bend it over—"

"Linda who?" Johnny said, and Wayne filled in, with "Lovelace, practically," then explained: Linda was the main reason Lester had almost gotten divorced from Janice four years ago. Her and the snake tattoo curling around her right breast, so blue you could even see it through a bra, if she ever wore one.

Johnny nodded, packed his cards on the table.

"She's a sure thing?" he said, to Lester.

Lester nodded. Johnny smiled, looked off at nothing then came back, said that was too much. He didn't want to take advantage, being the new guy and all.

"What then?" Lester said.

Johnny shrugged, fanned his cards out again, closed them up into a stack.

"I just want to see them," he said.

"Them?" Wayne said, nodding down to Lester's cards.

Johnny shook his head no, was still staring at Lester.

"Them," he said, again, and Lester heard, understood. Shook his head no.

Johnny was talking about Janice's new breasts.

" . . . like hide in the closet?" Wayne said, over his beer.

"Thinking more like a . . . video excursion," Johnny said.

"Bull shit," Lester told him, making it into two separate words.

"Hey," Johnny said, opening his hands over the pile, to take it, "doesn't matter to me, man."

"You can't just buy it like that," Delbert whined. "This is supposed to be a friendly game, J."

"Small wager between gentlemen . . ." Johnny finished, the pads of his fingers to the vial, now. And everything under it.

"No," Lester said finally, his hand on Johnny's now.

Johnny nodded, had never been expecting anything else.

"It doesn't matter," Lester said, to Delbert, flashing his cards over. "He's not gonna win."

"Yeah," Johnny said, "I mean, shit. You three are probably running a game on me anyway."

Wayne shook his head but didn't say anything, just swirled his beer in the bottle, drained it.

Lester swallowed, looked at his cards again, one more time, then said fuck it, laid them down, face-up.

Delbert whistled, smiled his crooked smile, and then Johnny did what all the Johnnies of the world had been doing to Lester since he was fourteen, and one of them had married his mother: laid down a full house of his own, king high to Lester's two jacks.

"Shit, she's gonna kill you," Wayne said through his teeth, to Lester.

Lester was just staring at the cards.

"Can we watch it too?" Delbert stage-whispered to Johnny, and they touched fists softly over the table, and then the big joke of the night was later, after the Vicodin had been quartered up, Wayne Jr.'s pot still in the air, Janice calling on the phone at the end of every hour. The joke was Johnny, holding a cup of coffee under his face for the warmth—he was on shift at seven—then lifting the vial from his shirt again, emptying it into his mug.

It had been sugar all along.

Lester watched it all through a haze, then Wayne was talking through the narrow window at the top of the room, telling Lester that the coast was clear of private eye eyes, he could walk home now if he ran. Lester smiled a sleepy-feeling smile, nodded, and saluted Johnny with two fingers launched off his forehead.

"SP or extended?" he called back from the stairs.

Johnny smiled with his eyes closed, held his fist down like he was jacking off, and said SP. Because it paused better.

Two soaps into the afternoon, an hour away from the talk show Lester liked, Janice called from work.

"Still beautiful?" Lester said.

"He was up here," Janice said back.

"Dick Man?"

Dick Man was their private eye. For a while he'd been LTD man, but then he got an Impala from some p.i. motorpool.

"He didn't talk to you, did he?" Lester asked.

"Lester, please."

"What was he doing, then?"

"Coffee. Pie. It wasn't on accident, though."

"Nothing he does is on accident."

"He's got a new toy, L. He kept it right there on the table by his water. One of those big lenses for his camera. He says he can see through a wall with it."

"So he did talk to you."

On her end, Janice exhaled, said Lester's name one more time, then hung up.

Lester stood looking at the phone too long, then took it with him to the window. The Impala was three houses down, in front of Wayne's old Ford van. Dick Man raised his coffee cup to Lester and Lester let the curtains fall back between them.

Except for the insurance checks and prescription meds, he might as well be in jail. He smiled, shook his head, and the phone rang in his hand. He dropped it like it was alive, his foot trying to kick it back up to him before he could tell it not to. The yellow battery pack crashed out the back, slid under the couch, leaving Lester to scramble for the bedroom phone. He made it on the sixth ring, fell back into the mattress.

"Lester," he said into the receiver, winded.

"I know," Johnny said back. Behind him somebody was wet-sanding a car, it sounded like. That high-pitched whine, grey water slinging all around the shop.

"What?" Lester said. "How'd you get my number?"

"We're friends, remember? Anyway. Just wondering, y'know. What was on the old boob tube . . ."

"Fuck you," Lester spat.

"Hey," Johnny said, in a way that Lester could see the smile he was smiling around the receiver. "You're not—not backing out here, are you?"

Lester stared at the dried-up moth bodies collected in the smoky white globe of their ceiling light. His and Janice's.

"Tonight," he said. "I asked her. She's cool with it."

"Perfection," Johnny said, dragging the word out, and Lester dial-toned him.

Twelve hours, now.

Lester got one beer from the fridge and drank it, staring at the sink for an answer.

The school bus usually rumbled through just shy of four o'clock. Lester was through with the six pack he'd promised himself he wasn't going to drink by then. It helped with his coordination, though. The way he needed it to help.

He levered himself out the door, shut it behind him with the rubber foot of an aluminum crutch.

He'd brushed his teeth for three minutes, the longest ever, maybe.

Instead of crossing the packed dirt of his front yard—the most direct route to the Impala, which had been inching forward with the shade of Wayne's tree all afternoon—Lester poled down the cracked sidewalk, made a production of everything involved in a left turn. In four ugly minutes, he was to Dick Man, tapping on his passenger side glass.

"Lester," Dick Man said.

"I need your help," Lester said.

"Say the word, my man."

"Our landlord, there"—the house, Janice's name on the lease—"he won't spray for roaches unless we establish roaches, if you know what I mean."

Dick Man nodded, leaned forward over the wheel, to study the house.

"Bring him a jar," he said.

"He says I could have got them anywhere."

"What are you paying per month?"

Lester looked off, at the bus's complicated door,

opening to spill kids back into the neighborhood.

"Too much," he said, finally. "But ... I mean. Immobile like I am and all. Shit. This is embarrassing. They're like, fucking—crawling on my leg sometimes, y'know? I mean, if I get like infected or something ... I could be here for months, I guess."

Dick Man angled his head over, in appreciation, compassion, something like that.

"And you need me to—what?"

"Nothing," Lester said. "Just—I don't want to get you in trouble. Conflict of interest, or assignment, whatever."

"What?"

"If I can just borrow your camera for the night?"

Dick Man looked down to it, its white telephoto lens heavier than the camera itself.

He smiled, patted the lens, said, "Les, boy . . ." but Lester was already shaking his head no.

"Shit, not that," he said. "Just like a . . . you've got a video unit in there, right? Just an old one, man. Like, with the big tape and everything."

Dick Man was still looking to his telephoto lens.

"For roaches?" he said.

"I won't get it dirty," Lester said, "c'mon."

The bus rumbled away, shaking every dish in every cabinet in the neighborhood, and, finally, Dick Man nodded, said, "What's a videocamera between friends, right?"

Lester nodded, met him at the trunk.

The video camera was in a black plastic case, like the drills some of the contractors carried to and from work.

"Sure?" Lester said, and Dick Man nodded, hefted it up to Lester, and Lester took it, held it with the fingers of his right hand, down where his crutch handle was. It stuck out like a wing.

"Got it?" Dick Man said, his eyes the eyes of a used car salesman, suddenly.

Lester shook his head no.

"You do deliveries?" he said, smiling as if embarrassed.

Dick Man looked down to his car, the camera there. Said, "Sorry, this one—Chevrolets, y'know? She doesn't lock. One of these miscreants"—the kids—"could walk away with everything I own."

"I'm just there," Lester said, pointing three houses down with his chin.

"Fast little boogers," Dick Man said, and Lester nodded, agreed, and tried hard not to hear the shutter falling behind him as he made his way down the sidewalk: Dick Man, documenting how the subject could, it seemed, carry a thirty-pound camera case. At least.

In the house again, Lester started on six-pack number two, and called Delbert, asked if his brother still worked the door down at the Foxx.

"That's at night," Delbert said, still half-asleep.

"That's not my question," Lester said back. "I just need his number."

"Cell or home?"

"Both."

The Foxx was The Foxx Lounge. It had had three x's in it for about a month when it opened, but some zoning law had killed the last x.

Delbert's brother answered his cell on the fourth ring.

"Dink," Lester said. "It's me, Les."

"Caller ID says Janice Markson, Lester-san."

"Yeah, well. It's me, Dink."

"Okay, it's you."

"Good. Now I was just wondering, kind of, if any of the girls up there make, like, house calls?"

"Like an escort, you mean?"

"Just for a few minutes. A lap dance."

"What about Janet?"

"Janice." Lester looked down to the talk show at his knees, a man's mouth moving and moving, no sound coming out. "She's at work, now, Dink. I that stupid?"

Beat, beat: Dink thinking.

"We open in forty minutes, Les. Shit."

Lester explained Dick Man to him. How when you can't go to the lap dance, your only choice is to bring the lap dance to you, get it?

"I don't know," Dink said, when Lester was done. "How much you talking?"

"That's just it," Lester said. "I don't really—shit. It's the end of the month, Dink. And it's not like I'm exactly working, either."

"Les—"

"I don't even . . . all I want her to do is take her top off. Just for about twenty seconds."

"For free?"

Lester breathed out through his nose, closed his eyes.

"I've got some medicine from workman's comp," Lester said. "It's good shit."

"Back medicine?"

"Vicodin."

"I don't care if it's—"

"Dink, please. I'm in a jam."

"Get a magazine, man."

"I can't go to the store," Lester said. "And—you think Janice is going to buy one for me?"

Dink laughed, said, "Twenty seconds?"

"Fuck you, Dinkman."

Tamara was there in fifteen minutes, said it was on the way. Lester opened the door, watched her breasts enter, then the rest of her.

She was perfect.

"So my man says you have something," she said, not turning her back to him.

Lester nodded, punched the pharmacy number into

the cordless. He'd had to lick the contact points on the battery to make them work again.

The pharmacy's system was automated. Lester entered the number from his old pill bottle, let Tamara listen: his prescription was ready.

"You just have to pick it up," Lester said.

"Bullshit," Tamara said, turning for the door. "I don't know what Dink told you, but—"

Lester stepped in front of her, trying not to lose her eyes.

"This isn't what you think," he said. "The Vicodin's really there. Anybody with my name can pick it up. And I'm not wanting anything special here."

Tamara stared at him, then shook her head slowly, side to side.

"Where?" she said, finally. "I don't have time for this."

Lester smiled, looked to the clock: 5:52.

"You still have a few minutes, right?" he said.

Tamara nodded, shrugged, and, when she wouldn't go into the bedroom with him, he went there himself, came back with Janice's sleep shirt, the pink one with faded red cuffs. And the video camera.

"What is this?" Tamara asked. "D didn't say you were a freak."

"I'm not," Lester said. "Just—like this," and, like that, it only took four minutes.

Janice got home two hours later.

"Dick Man," she said, closing the door behind her.

"I know," Lester said, from the couch.

He was still thinking about Tamara. More than he'd meant to.

They ate tacos Lester cooked. The shells kept breaking, until it was funny. He put his in a bowl, finally, let it be the taco salad it wanted to be.

"I didn't tell you," Janice said, putting some more frozen cheese shreds onto her taco, "that new guy down the street, Jimmy—"

"Johnny."

"Whatever. His whole body shop came in after lunch today."

Lester pretended to just be looking at his taco.

"Popular place," he said, the obvious thing.

Janice laughed through her nose, took a bite.

"I stopped for your pills," she said.

Lester quit chewing, looked over his broken shell at her. She shrugged, smiling, hiding something.

"What?" Lester said, then, impulsively, "They weren't ready."

Janice stopped chewing, looked at him across the table.

"You already got them," she said, suddenly bored with the subject. "I had to go in, though, the drive-in was all fucked—"

"Drive-through."

"Yeah—what'd I say?"

"Doesn't matter. You were saying something else anyway."

Again, the smile. Then, "They should put warning labels on these."

Lester smiled, looked down to her hands, whatever she was holding. It was just the taco, though. But her hands were wrong, too, not close enough together. Framing her new breasts.

"What do you mean?" he said, tracking back up to her face.

"What do you think?" she said, taking a bite, smiling around it.

"I don't know," Lester said. "Janice, really, God. I don't know."

"Think, L."

"I can't—the meds."

Janice set her taco down, took his left hand in both of hers.

"They have pregnancy tests there," she said, her eyes wet now, and Lester swallowed everything in his mouth, saw a little him in the yard with him, on crutches like the old man; Janice, her breasts flotation devices practically; and Uncle Dick Man, snapping pictures of every precious fucking moment.

"Well?" Janice said, still holding his hand, and Lester nodded, made himself smile, and knew the only pills in the world that could soften this were the pills he had just given away.

Three weeks later, Johnny and Wayne and Delbert were still talking about what they thought were Janice's perfectly tanned breasts. Wayne Jr. had even stolen the tape from the VCR in the basement, taken it to school once and forever, entered it into legend.

On his side of the card table, Lester was arranging his cards from biggest to smallest, then back again. When he'd peed fifteen minutes ago, he'd still been able to smell Tamara on him, and had apologized again to the Janice in his head.

It was just a one-time thing, though. Every time Janice was at work.

Dick Man had to know all about it.

And it wasn't his fault anyway, Lester's. Janice wasn't supposed to ever get pregnant. Nobody was, by him.

Now he was having to think about names, though. Wayne of course thought Lester Jr. was the way to go, Delbert was all for Robert for some reason he wouldn't go into, and Johnny's contribution was less a name, more a visual meditation on Janice, leaking pale blue milk through a tight cotton shirt.

Lester liked Bent, or Bint; he'd heard it on a show once, and it had stuck.

Janice said none of their names mattered, because the baby was going to be a girl, like her momma.

Lester fingered a tablet from his bank, held it close enough to see.

"Not speed, is it?" he said to Wayne.

Wayne had lost fifty of the tablets three hands ago.

"I don't know what they are," Wayne said, cocking his head to the side. "I just know Junior Boy was selling them for five a pop."

"'Was,'" Delbert echoed, the key word.

Johnny smiled, took two cards, completing another royal flush probably, and Lester shrugged, let the pill dissolve on his tongue. It was bitter, chalky, meant to be swallowed, or ground up.

He'd promised himself he wasn't going to bet Tamara's number tonight, or anything free from her, was just going to hide in this one little pill, in this one little basement, and never have to be a dad.

But, too, he kept saying it in his head, just loud enough—Bent, Bint, Bint—and making promises to himself, to Bint: that he would never steal any of his stashes; that he wouldn't even have to have stashes. That he was going to be faithful to his mother for him, Bint. Not make her cry. That he wasn't going to play cards for dope anymore. That he was going to go back to work, set a good example.

And then the pill exploded wetly behind his eyes, washing the cards monochrome, and he smiled, looked around at Wayne—Wayne Sr.—Delbert, Johnny, Johnny Hood, as they were calling him now, since he'd got fired for folding one in half at the end of the day last week. It wasn't his fault—it was a 1982 Chevy pick-up, for Chrissake, with a hood like a wet piece of paper—but still, he wasn't employed anymore. And the terms of his probation were specific about that.

In ten minutes, Johnny Hood had all the pills and baggies in the room, was kicked back on the old couch Wayne's wife made him keep downstairs.

Lester nodded off with whatever was in his blood, came to again with Johnny Hood still exactly the same. Meaning either he'd blinked, or slept through a whole nother cycle of drinking, peeing, and smoking.

It didn't matter.

"Wayne Bo," he said, his words slurring under each other.

Wayne was shuffling the cards over and over at the table. They were twelve years old again.

"Good shit, yeah?" Wayne called over.

"Fucking A," Lester said, pushing himself into some kind of standing position. Lifting his head to the small window that opened onto the street.

Wayne nodded, rose, did his recon.

"Past his bedtime, I guess," he said, about Dick Man, and Lester nodded, pulled himself hand over hand up the stairs, said something hopefully good to Wayne's wife, sitting on the couch, balancing a plastic cup of wine to her lips, then slipped out into the night, let it swallow him.

The first pole he pushed off of, heading home, it turned out to be a bush, and he fell through, laughed his way up again, and stumbled out to the sidewalk, suddenly both aware of his need to swallow and intensely paranoid about the whole concept of swallowing. What a design flaw it was.

He didn't recognize Dick Man until he put his hand on the passenger side fender and their eyes locked over the long hood.

It wasn't the Impala anymore, but the LTD. And Wayne had been looking for the Impala. Lester smiled, nodded, opened the door to explain this to Dick Man.

"Lester," Dick Man said, loud and clear, as if he

were recording this, and Lester nodded some more, finally swallowed, and passed out.

When he woke again it was a different day. Daytime, anyway. And not his neighborhood.

The LTD was pulled into an assigned slot, in a parking lot shadowed by a huge granite building.

Dick Man was looking up at the mirrored windows.

"Know where we are?" he said, without ever looking around at Lester.

"There," Lester said, rubbing his right eye too hard.

Dick Man nodded, smiled. 'There' was Hell—the insurance company's headquarters. The sign was tomb-stoned between the parking lot and the building. Suits going in and out like ants.

Lester closed his eyes against it all.

"You don't have to do this," he said.

"I get paid to do this," Dick Man said back.

"What?" Lester said.

"What what?"

"What do you get paid?"

"Half of what you still have coming to you."

"Commission?"

"Percentage."

Lester pulled his lips back from his teeth. Just to see if they still would, mainly. And to give him time to think: if Dick Man wasn't open for business, here, he would have already carried Lester in, deposited him on some mahogany desk. Turned in his tapes, his logbooks, his report.

"This can't be the only thing you do," he said, finally.

"What do you mean, Lester?"

"I mean—shit. I've got two weeks left, full pay. Half of that's four hundred, before taxes. You don't pay liability on two cars on that."

"Maybe I'm independently wealthy."

"Yeah. And maybe I can't walk without crutches."

For this, Lester looked over. Dick Man was smiling a thin smile, nodding.

"This is the part where I beg, right?" Lester said.

Dick Man shrugged.

"It do any good?" Lester asked.

"Depends," Dick Man said.

"Depends," Lester said, tasting it, then just shook his head, asked it: "What do you want?"

Dick Man pushed his lower lip out, as if he hadn't had all night to think about it, but then Lester cut him off: "—that's better than four hundred dollars, I mean. But not too much better."

Dick Man tapped his hands on the dash like a rimshot, shrugged.

"What do you got, Lester?"

He was Johnny Hood, practically. The world was Johnny Hood.

Lester stared at the keyhole in the glove compartment for just long enough, then said it to himself again, that this couldn't be the only thing Dick Man did, right?

"What else?" he said, leading.

"Usual," Dick Man said. "Cheating wives, little repo action now and then. Skip tracing . . . 'other' . . ."

Lester nodded, had expected the other, but knew better than to ask. But the skip tracing. He smiled. It was in the right family.

"Say I—" he started, "what do you get if you catch somebody, like, y'know, a criminal-type, breaking probation?"

"How?"

"You'll find it on him, maybe."

"Maybe?"

"For sure."

"I'm listening."

Lester smiled, told the invincible Dick Man about Johnny Hood's rounds for the last week, strolling around with pocketfuls of poker winnings, selling here, there, to Wayne Jr.'s customer base when he could find them. Always making time to catch lunch down at Rita's.

"Why there?" Dick Man said.

"Twelve o'clock," Lester said back.

"Doesn't your wife work there?"

"It's just a place."

Dick Man nodded, smiled, and said, "What else, Lester?"

"What else? That's all, man. Shit. What you think I'm made of here?"

Dick Man kept smiling and popped the glove compartment. It opened onto Lester's lap. Black and white glossies of Tamara, coming, Tamara, going. Tamara Tamara Tamara, leading with her breasts.

Lester just stared at the photos.

"Blackmail?" he said, quietly.

"Not quite," Dick Man said. "I don't want anything for her. I just want her, sabe?"

Lester looked up, to a security guard behind the glass doors of the building. Watching them.

"I'm not—I can't—" he started, and Dick Man circled his thigh in his thick hand, and Lester nodded, told him how Tamara used to be a model, how all you had to do was point a camera at her, pretty much, and her clothes would just start jumping off her.

" A camera," Dick Man said, raising his, the ponderous lens scraping the dash, "like this?" and Lester nodded, looked away. Just wanted to go home.

Four days later, Johnny Hood was gone, and the game in Wayne's basement took on sane dimensions again. Mostly just Wayne Jr.'s various stashes trading hands.

Lester was going back to work in one Monday. One Monday more.

It had been a good run, anyway. A good vacation.

To make it fun, they played with two decks at once—four jokers—and then just split up the dope at the end of the night. On the way up the stairs, Lester turned around, caught the dime bag Wayne was looping up to him.

"What?" he said.

"Piss tests," Wayne said, shrugging.

Lester nodded, held the bag out to Delbert, who shook his head no too, for no reason Lester could make sense of. He felt like crying, for some reason. Walked all the way to the end of the block and counted cars driving by until he got to one hundred—though one of them was a repeat—then looped back to Janice.

"Early," she said, when he opened the door.

Lester shrugged, twisted the deadbolt behind him.

On the floor in front of the television were all their old tapes. Janice had been crying.

Lester sat down by her, looked to the screen. It was rewinding.

"We're—Lester," she started. "Me, I mean. Marce at work says I'm going to have get them removed. So I can lactate properly. Because they can like, like leak into the milk. Poison the baby."

Lester put his arm around her, tried not look down at the top slopes of her breasts, not to think about the underswell.

"It's okay," he said. "I'm going back to work. I'll ask for some overtime, maybe."

"It doesn't—taking them out's a lot easier than putting them in. It's just, you liked them so much, right?"

"I like you," Lester said, in a way that almost didn't feel like a lie, and she stopped the rewind, snuggled close. "What's this?" he said.

Janice laughed through her nose. "I want to see what I used to look like," she said. "B-cup Janice, yeah?"

Lester smiled, felt a sudden stab of fear for some reason but fought it, told himself he was just addicted to her new breasts, how when she lay on her back they hardly even spread.

But then she hit play.

It was their old wedding tape, from six years ago. Lester nodded, remembered thinking not long ago of Delbert, his best man. The mustache he'd grown for six months for the ceremony, then shaved at the last minute.

And then he remembered why he'd thought of Delbert's mustache not long ago.

"What?" Janice said, feeling him stiffen, but he couldn't get it fast enough, could only hear his own voice through the speakers, reciting everything the preacher said, and then it was too late: the tracking on the tape shuddered, the recording shifting from Extended Play to Short Play. Because SP paused better.

The next scene was neck down, Janice's night shirt. The television set itself just to the right.

This was the back-up copy, the personal copy.

Janice's shirt, rising, pulling taut over the nipples then over, Tamara's breasts bouncing into the frame, standing at attention.

Janice beside him, covering her chest, pulling her feet up onto the couch. Lester shaking his head no, but not looking away from the screen, either.

What he wound up trading Janice, in apology, so she wouldn't divorce him, was every birthing class they could sign up for.

The Friday before his first day back to work, they were there with all the other expectant couples. The instructor put his hand to the light switch, said something about the glow in the room, how they didn't even need lights, and most of the husbands knew that was their cue to clap.

Lester tried to keep up, to get his hands into that paternal kind of rhythm, but had enough of Wayne Jr.'s stash in him that it took some effort. But he was there, at least, for Janice. That was what mattered. And that Janice was finally saying she believed him, about Tamara. That the recording had just been him being a good husband, protecting his wife's honor. That he had done it for her. Because he loved her.

Now he was just waiting for Dick Man to show back up, with a stack of prints for sale.

But fuck it.

Brent. It was what Janice had finally conceded, was part of their new deal; Bint wasn't a real name to her anyway, not like it was for Lester. He still said it in his head, though. His lips moving with it sometimes.

For the birthing class, Janice had worn a halter top, no bra. She only had her breasts for two more weeks now. Lester told her it didn't matter, that she could be his nature girl. They could start eating vegetables, even.

They got to the birthing class ten minutes late, just in time for the tired joke. Had to sneak in just as the lights were going down for the projector. Moving up each side of the rows of chairs were nurse trainees like deacons. They were passing out barf bags.

Lester took one, looked into it, then up to the screen.

This was his life. He shook his head, held Janice's hand, and the movie flickered on. First the date—three years ago this month—then a gurney-level view of a maternity ward rushing by.

Janice's hand tightened on Lester's, and he tried to match what she was feeling with everything he was. It was different, though; she was thinking about Brent, or Brianne, and he was still stuck on Dick Man, his stack of photos.

Stuck on how ready Dick Man had been to deal with him, how that was probably how he made his real living: letting people skate. For a price.

Most people, anyway. Johnny Hood still hadn't turned back up for cards, or at Rita's for lunch, or the chain-link fence by the high school.

Lester wanted to blame him for everything that had gone wrong, but couldn't talk about it with Wayne or Delbert, either. Because they probably had bench warrants on them for something too.

He laughed with his lips closed.

"You watching?" Janice said without looking over, and Lester nodded, let her fingers twine into his. Her voice was full of everything it should be full of. Brimming over.

The girl on screen was in the delivery room now, masked doctors swarming around her like aliens, the fetal heartbeat drumming into the background.

"—so exciting," another mother-to-be said behind them, and somebody two rows up started crying, quietly.

Lester watched them, these people he looked like probably, these people who were supposed to be like him, and thought of the sonogram Janice was going to be getting on VHS as well. How it would look with a stripper's inflatable breasts recorded over it.

He laughed, covered his mouth. Blamed it on the stuff in his system. That he shouldn't have taken so much.

For the rest of the movie, he focused hard on a small white dot of intense light at the lower left of the screen. A chip in the projector's lens, maybe. The woman giving birth screaming, clenching, breathing.

This was exactly what Wayne had said it was going to be.

Lester looked at his dot of white, held Janice's hand, and waited for it to be over, but then she was talking to him, saying his name over and over. And crying.

It was the baby. Lester could hear it.

Without meaning to, he looked up to the baby, the boy, still slathered in the yellow and red of another world. The mother, reaching up for him, drawing him close, pulling her gown aside, over her right breast. A blue coil there for a flash, pale against the white skin. Not a milk vein, but a snake.

Lester felt something give deep inside him. Like a Christmas ornament in space, falling in on itself, no sound. He felt his lips going like he was reaching down with them for a straw.

He was trying to breathe again.

Her name was Linda, the mother on-screen. Linda, no husband, no coach, just her. Linda, from four years ago, and this movie was a year later, almost. Nine months. And maybe you got to deliver for free if you let somebody video-tape it for a class.

Her name was Linda, and—his son.

Bint. So small on-screen. So delicate. So loud, and mad, a teenager already.

Lester said it out loud, just once—Bint—then someone stood into the dust-filled beam of light, his lanky shadow sharp on the screen.

Johnny Hood.

Lester swallowed, made himself swallow, his eyes watering from the effort, the heat welling up inside of him.

Johnny Hood winked at him with the whole side of his leathery face, his steel trap criminal mind planted deep in that blue snake tat, the one Lester had tried to trade him once—the sure thing—and then he did the last thing Lester would have ever expected: flashed his wolf smile past him, to Janice, who stiffened beside Lester, clung to his arm like she was afraid. Like she didn't want this.

"No," she said, maybe.

"What?" Lester whispered loud, between the two of them, suddenly aware of the fifteen minute breaks Janice got twice a day, but Johnny just shrugged, fingershot both of them, then sloped back out into the world, his hands in his pockets, his shoulders rounded. Lester didn't say anything, and neither did Janice, until they were driving home. Missing their street, having to dogleg back around.

"Is it—" she started, then closed her eyes, started again: " . . . a paper towel tube, right?"

The paper towel tube was how their instructor had said to baby proof their house: if it'll fit through, then it's a choking hazard.

Lester found her hand on the seat between them, took it without looking down.

"We can just tie everything from the ceiling maybe," he said, and she scooted closer, onto the hump, and told him that would be perfect, yes, please, and Lester held her shoulder as he made the next left turn, so she wouldn't slip away, and had no clue anymore what street they were on. Just that it was smooth. That he could drive it all night if he needed to.

MY GERMAN DAUGHTER
by Nic Young

You were heavier than I expected, and the room felt bigger than it was. Kelly and the nurse watched my every move. I tried to see our faces in yours, but you were buried in cotton. You stirred and I handed you to the nurse. Kelly's eyes fluttered and closed. I stood there, waiting for the faith that when I reached for the door I'd feel the cold surface of the handle.

Kelly's words are gone but I remember the sour, metallic taste that spilled into my mouth before I hung up the phone. I stared at the ceiling and listened to my parents move through the house. The sunlight turned orange then faded behind the growing shadows of spring flowers. My stomach felt hollow. It burned whenever my father's footsteps rose and fell past the door.

"Dad?"

I buried my head in my pillow.

He entered and I stared at the neat crease of his trousers.

"Yes, my boy?"

"Remember when you asked if Kelly and I were sleeping together?"

"Yes."

"I lied. We were. We used a condom but it didn't work." Another lie.

Kelly and Megan sat on a bench outside our classroom. The seam of Kelly's dark jeans turned a strained, aching white at her thighs. Folds of floral maternity-wear enveloped her arm where it cradled her bulging stomach. Megan's fingers rested on top. She yanked her hand away, and they squealed with laughter. Kelly saw me and froze, then looked away at the ground. I wanted to talk to her, to ask her what she needed, but Megan stared me off. She took Kelly's hand and leaned in close to whisper some substitute for the support I couldn't give.

A thin woman with brittle eyes and a forced smile met us on the porch of a house that was no longer a home. A sign above us read Choices. The woman shook Kelly's hand.

"Hi, I'm Ms. Emslie. It's nice to meet you, Kelly. Please, come in. It's cold out here."

Ms. Emslie nodded to me, then ushered us inside and showed us to a small, pastel-colored room packed with dated furniture. She fussed Kelly into one of a pair of faded sofa chairs, and I took the other.

Ms. Emslie straightened, finally satisfied that Kelly was comfortable.

"I'll be right back. Just going to fetch us some tea."

She looked at me and shut her eyes in a single, extended blink, then shook her head and left the room, closing the door behind her. I stuffed my hands into the front pocket of my hooded sweater. It was the first time Kelly and I had been left alone together since before that phone call. I dodged eye contact and turned to examine a watercolor painting of a sunset behind us.

"How have you been?" I asked, still staring at the painting.

"I'm okay." She laughed into her lap. "Getting big now."

"And you're managing?"

"I guess. Everyone at school has been really nice. I expected them to hate me or something."

I turned to her and nodded.

Kelly looked at me. "And you?"

The door opened and Ms. Emslie came in with a tray bearing biscuits and a single cup of tea. She put it down and started to sit in the remaining couch, but stopped and glanced around the room. She left and came back with a high-back wooden chair, which she set down next to Kelly.

"You'll be meeting a lovely young couple from Germany. They're unable to have children of their own. The man is an engineer, and his wife used to be a model. She'll be a stay-at-home mom. They've got two dogs and a big garden."

She smiled and handed Kelly the cup of tea.

I passed the German couple on my way into the maternity ward. A white hospital gown dwarfed Kelly's tiny frame, and the knowing, rounded features of a mother seemed to clash with her youth. She held a newborn baby girl. Her own mother stood by her bed, either allowing herself or presenting for Kelly a grim smile. She left when I entered.

Kelly sat up and I remembered how my father had said that holding me for the first time was the most powerful experience of his life.

She slurred her words.

"Do you want to hold her?"

WHAT WAS THERE INSIDE THE CHILD

by Blake Butler

I was going to tell you now what was found there on the air inside the child

how when the child's soft child skin became exploded, the ideas or items stored in the child's innards splashed against the night in liquid cloth

I was going to tell you all about this and then I wasn't and now I am going to again

how the child's ex-flesh laid upon the air we'd all been breathing in skeins of ruptured blood and tendon, wadded cells and other shit that for years had made the child's skin go kaboom

the cause of the explosion not being something I have the will to outline here and now in fear of god

a god who may by now also have exploded

or turned to blackness

or to ash

as how most evenings, and in this writing, I can not see even just my hand right there before my face

except in swift moments among the globes of soft explode-
light, cold and gloaming over all

a kind of light that for years had been only found in certain
types of horses, in the meat inside their minds

I was going to speak aloud about this child

ours

one of the hundreds we'd seen bursting in the magicworks
of mud and longing

slung through our nearing streets and cul-de-sacs among a
cavalcade of lathering and awful gloss

the skies in throes over all children, for their fresh flesh, for
where they had not yet become sore

their bodies quick in precognition of the coming moment,
gloaming, their hands straight up over their heads, postures
flattened into erect as if being stretched or slightly thawed

and their eyes

the way the lashes would molt to bright white, and the skin
around their holes would fill with blood, growing so dark
around the edges that all and any other light seemed sucked
down or turning hard, like little combs or keys or jewels
someone could wear pinned to a shirt or in their hair

and how the skin around the neck and chest would turn
translucent and there would be a slight decreasing of the
child's size

a tautening around the kneecaps and at the earlobes and
armpits, shriveling as if parched or quickening in years

Though some children

in their uncoming

would not even blink or itch at all

there would be nothing there about them that seemed changing, until their heads and skin and sight burst into flues, fleshy human banners than flew upon the screaming human air as if in pleasure

as if something on the air was being formed as the explode-light scratched at our eyes

dressing the face of the earth around us in marbled scabs and hazy patches and large pastures in which nothing could be seen

Through most of these explodings I'd hid my face and held my head between my hands

And though I could not keep the sound of the skin ripping from out of me, the throttled milliseconds as the lungs sprayed waste, I could for sure keep myself all hours inside, fortified against the night

swearing never again to step foot into the nothing where even cows had grown demon-sized teeth inside their heads

and how the grass was spurting acid

and money barfing from the light

how I could teach my sagging body to let me live off of the fluff out from the sofa, suck the sweet out of the ink, gnawing my own hair and tongue and knuckles in the meantime, in the idea that surely soon this would all bend

the evenings soon would return silent and I could sleep again in minor light

but this child

this is me telling

this one I'd held for years in hours, already old

he who'd lived inside me for such stinging time and time regardless

who'd therein eaten of my body and swaddled up a body of his own

(I could not control which cells of mine inside my body he had taken and which he'd left for me to grow old with, made of, alone)

he who then had taken those soft sections in him and stretched them fleshing over bones

years in rooms where I could not see what he was doing, what he would make of what he had made of parts of us

how hid in those nights I could sometimes feel among the evenings the ache of his insertions, his destroy

sitting up still in the bed where he'd been made there with my whole chest hardened into bone

knowing without knowing

what he knew then and then knew

The child's first layer on the air was made of such light that it made the light already trundled on the air go curved

slowing out around the edges of my vision, flexed, so that in this light here I saw the sky under the sky

the sky with our names printed on it, peeling

the sky with bodies hung from it in troves, fat pock-marked purses of slopping bodies, divided in their drooping into colored groups

colors not of how the skin had been in living, but the current state of their decay

some of the bodies in cluster like enormous fruit, globes glistened, picked apart by gobs of geese, and gnats grow fat off of the black-blistered ankles, so distending

I felt hungry in the child's light, I could not help it

I felt like breathing money, meat, so badly

I could hardly therein stand

From the child's first layer burped the next one, a job of old fat that poured upon the room of air

columns wobbling in the child's breeze, each tied to some exploded center in him, clubbed with wart

Sat in the fat among the burstflesh the child had all these visions nuzzled hid, rendered in him in the shapes of items from our house

things I had long written off as discarded or sucked under or eaten or misplaced:

—the bit of hair I'd scalped off the child's head as soon as he could grow it, nut-brown and slick, a lock I'd needed to remember to remember, or in reclaiming, *a lock he'd sucked into himself from out of me*

—the key to the black box under a false board in my closet, for which I'd combed the house a hundred thousand times, fraught with such heat in my seeking that I could no longer now even recall what that black box itself contained

—a node of bone that'd killed our only cat by choking, its gristle still somewhat rubbed into the grain

—a bullet I might inside the night had dreamt to use and use and use soon on someone again already gone

All our other crap in wrappers and uncoming sunk too deep in the bloodseam and flesh for me to read:

the pictures of me enraptured at the child's center's center, thrown in poses I had never known I'd held;

my mother's pads of skin that'd come off her in her thinking;

the lizards in my sleep

hair in my mouth

From out of this, under so much junk, the child's third and thickest layer sprayed

mud on the air so hard and fast then that air was mud too, and so was I

every color in one color

so much mud I could not think

and everyone was looking

all the flesh turned cinder, bone

blood was pouring out my blood, from the rafters

all you were was old

Among the mud I sensed the scent of something burning—
the lick of wet flames enmassed and eating where they'd ate

ash of ash and ashes' ashes

in this too I drank the drink

I could taste so much of where the child had been, his skin a
book of stink

—the mesh of all he'd ever eaten, smushed and buttered
into cells, or stored in doors and tiny ovens, in skins that
separated what was inside him and what out—destroyed—
the teems of beef and sauce and blubber; the chocolate, the
rice; the mass packaged cellophanes of colored cereal and
meat shanks frozen into crème; the butter, nubs and chutney;
muscles; things that had grown out of the ground; the water,
blood; the oil

—the stink of my own liquids, having all throughout me
aged, and transferred to the child among such purring, the
smelting of our air so tightly wound we could not sit still—
how in the house the walls were always nearer than they'd
been just before, I knew—how I could feel this—and yet I
would get up every day—I would walk into the folding of the
air, a lidless throng so crushed and neverending it had no
color and no sound

—the stink as well of what had come into me to make the
child there and what had been about that other body then—

the mosaics of cells stuffed therein fused or scrabbled against mine, so hard I could hardly see which was which and what was gone

—the smoke he'd sucked out of pipes and heirlooms and from other people turning into air; and the slur of sounds where they'd drummed, disrupted; shit he'd meant to shit out and yet had not and shit he'd shit out and breathed back in; and click of glue; and sunning; and the old air suffered in his sleep; the crush of voices; the slapped saliva; the rip of every hour, every day

There was so much there clapped inside the child

I could not breathe him in, not another inch then, even those I'd once infested, mine

something offset in the smell sound

something rapping at my guts

my backbone pruned

and popping through my slowly softing body—sod

the skin around my scalp and shoulders curling up—a crown

the gifts unwrapping back into you, overlapping

you would have died soon anyway

I would have died soon too, even beyond this

the black door buried in our guts

a door leading into a long hallway

a hall long as our lives

that hall into a hall again

that hall into a room full of black doors

Yes, I could see it in the child there

A black door

under the confetti of his brains

scored with the clawmarks of the birds and bugs his lungs had harbored

swathed up in a drumming sound

The door's cold frame throttled blackened, winking with the smell of awful milk

milk I'd given to him

I could smell me in there still somewhere too

though I had changed

I could not name how or when or where

There against the door set in his sternum, destroyed

I pressed my head against the clot

the door with no knob, no knocker, no small hole

The door's face was fleshy, warm

The welcome mat stitched with symbols that made my body
want to sleep

I was drooling on my torso

Where the drool hit it made cream

cream in oceans, combing

below that I was creaming too

spurting from my sore spots, unnoticed on me until here
now in the screaming, in such strobing robes of wrecked
childlight

For a second then I could not blink

I could not stop the air from where the child had been before
he went exploded goosing down into my lungs

into the dry alveoli in there, nesting, making more doors

doors in doors

the curd of child burped back through me, filling spaces
where once for a while it'd been

the child's voice slapping at me, from the insides from
the slue

begging new to thrust into me glowing

I could not pull my face back off the door

its flat face stuck and snuck flush to my cheek meat, kissing
slow coils down through my pores

Through the door I heard the air becoming thicker, clustered in bubbles at my face

slathering in packets, my meat embroidered

sucking all my body's weight up through my body to my head

my so soft mother head, dividing

my heat, my limbs, my lust—devised

And overhead the sky increasing, already having sucked its surface clean

the splattered remnants of my gone child shucked and buckled, drank in and on itself

and underneath, the light-horizon, torched with tunnels of new smoke and shriek, shit burst in replicate commotion of young explosion spreading through and through the gone

soft bodies blurting out a scrim of black so long and wide it could not be measured

opening the doors

SEED

by Gayle Towell

GREY-PINK WITH DARK VEINS running through it, two black dots for eyes, little webbed flippers, and a residual tail stub all curled in like a lima bean. An embryo. A baby seed. What was supposed to be an infant in seven months now sits in the palm of my hand. A surprise find rescued from soaked underwear and rinsed off in the bathroom sink.

I turn it over and run my finger down the C-curve of its back. It's all perfectly intact. No neural tube defects. It looks like the pictures in the baby books. Tiny and rubbery like a wet gummy bear. I wasn't expecting to find it in the mess and now I don't know what to do with it. Flush it? Throw it in the trash?

Tim will be home late tonight. He doesn't know and I can't tell him over the phone. This little sea creature in my hand, all I can think to do is keep it there, incubate it in my palm. I can't put it down yet.

My eyes burn hot as I work to clean myself up one-handed. Tears roll down my cheeks, down my chin, down my neck and I can't stop them, and I don't even care about the heavy molten lead feeling in my abdomen. Somehow I feel stupid for being pregnant in the first place. I crawl into bed and curl like a lima bean around my little lima bean.

In the middle of the night the bedside lamp comes on and Tim curls quietly behind me.

I whisper, "I'm not pregnant anymore," and unveil the embryo still in my palm. It smells of warm blood.

He says nothing but I can feel his body stiffen and I can tell by his breath on my neck that his mouth hangs open. He places his hand under mine. An embryo in a hand in a hand. A bean curled around a bean curled around a bean.

The next morning we're out in our yard. A tiny bean in a tiny box in a tiny hole. A baby seed planted beneath a rosebush.

THEY TAKE YOU

by Kyle Minor

THEY TAKE YOU at night.

Or, they take you early in the morning.

They take you from school, tell you to leave your backpack at your desk.

They take you without warning, or they give you forty-five minutes to say goodbye.

They take you with the clothes on your back. They take you with your father's blessing. They take you young. They take you unwilling. They might take you alone.

They took me from a birthday party, three elders in business suits. I was bent over candy just fallen from the piñata. Hannah Rae had broken the piñata. They took her, too, on her birthday. She was twelve. Her mother had just announced Pin the Tail on the Donkey. She was holding a blindfold in her hand. My pockets were full with Junior Mints and Tootsie Rolls. Out the window behind us the mountains rose toward the sky. My father stood, watching. They shook his hand.

I am Hiram's fifth wife. Judith, Edith, Emma, Jolene, and me, Leah, I'm fifth. And Hannah Rae, she's sixth. They took us to the temple, and Walker Getty, the President, said repeat after me. *I take thee, Hiram. To love and to serve. In sickness and in health. Till death we do part.* The other wives stood as bridesmaids. Edith is a friend of my mother. Hiram slipped a ring on my fourth finger and shoved his tongue in my mouth. He grabbed my shoulder, hard, so I'd know not to move. Walker Getty said how since God ordained our true love, no man could tear it asunder.

Then I got in line to be a bridesmaid for Hannah Rae. Edith put her arm around me and pulled me close, which felt safe and good. She leaned down and whispered in my ear. "Remember this," she said. "You're fifth. I'm second. You'll do as I say from here on." Then she smiled and gave me a long hug, which felt ugly. At the altar, Walker Getty told Hiram he could kiss his bride, and he shoved his tongue into Hannah Rae's mouth. When she tried to pull away he grabbed her by the hair and pulled her to him to finish his kiss.

Walker Getty led us to the candle with thirteen flames, which he said symbolized our family. Twelve small candles circled and bowed to one large flame. Hiram lit the large flame with a butane lighter, and one by one we wives lit one small candle with his big candle. Six candles stayed unlit, Walker Getty said, until the Lord saw fit to bless Hiram with more.

Judith got us ready for the consummation. She leaned over us and dabbed our necks with perfume. Her skin was loose and pale. Her breath smelled of garlic, and her body of cornhusker's lotion. She told Hannah Rae that she must serve me, since she was sixth. She said I must choose who saw Hiram first, since I was fifth. I chose Hannah Rae.

I waited in the kitchen. Judith asked if I'd like a sandwich, and I said yes. She said I'd have to make it myself, and one for her, too. She scolded me for being slow.

I couldn't find the bread because I didn't know to look in the refrigerator. From the other side of the house I heard Hannah Rae scream. I heard the sound of flesh striking flesh, a sound I knew from my father's rages. Hiram shouted at her to be quiet, but still I heard her wailing. Judith scolded me for putting too much mayonnaise on her sandwich.

When it was my turn Judith escorted me to Hiram's room. We passed Hannah Rae's new room. She was lying on a twin mattress on the floor, sobbing and curled into a ball. Judith closed the door as we passed and clucked her disapproval.

I remember these things: He said I love you. He was still wearing his shirt, and his tie. He was heavy. I hurt. It bled. When he got going he said fuck me, fuck me, fuck me, fuck me, sweet Jesus! He liked to lick the sweat from my forehead. His tongue was rough and scratchy. He grabbed my hip bones with his hands and shook me up and down. He said I was his favorite. He said he only had eyes for me. He said he didn't care if the others knew. He said he had made me a woman. He said we should do this more often. He cradled me in his arms like a baby and sang me a lullaby. He kissed my cheek softly and fondled my breast. Then he did it to me again. He said darling, darling. He said precious, precious. When he was done I went into my new room and threw up all over the floor. Edith came in with a wastebucket and a Brillo pad and some soap, and said, "Get scrubbing."

They take you to the thrift store. They give you ten dollars to shop for maternity clothes. They take you after hours to the office of Elder Byrum, a medical doctor. He spreads cold gel across your stomach and probes with a metal wand. He shows you an image, a black-and-white lizard with tiny human hands. He places your feet in stirrups and shoves his wrinkled knuckles inside you. He wraps a tape measure around your belly. He pokes and prods. He says praise God. He asks about Hiram. He gives you thick brown vitamins and writes on a yellow chart. He tousles your hair and calls you little momma.

They take all the girls to the ammunition chamber. They say this is a twenty-two, this is a forty-five, this is a Glock, this is a three-fifty-seven Magnum. They show you the knives, the daggers, the Samurai swords. They kneel you down in a long line, press the shotgun shells to your palms, speak of when they come to get us, and yes they are coming. We are in the world but not of it. They take you to the test range and teach you to fire into paper shaped like a man. They say, "Semiautomatic, praise Jesus."

They take you to the tabernacle on Sunday. They tell you to walk in a single file line behind your husband, then veer off toward the balcony to sit with the other wives. The men sit up front. Only men are allowed entry to the area behind the veil, the Holy of Holies. Men are priests. Women are for childbearing. Mornings, you puke. Rhododendron grows beneath the skylight. Walker Getty says God is loving and wrathful, too. He tells the story of a great exodus from Egypt and into the promised land. Next to you, Hannah Rae is smiling. She only smiles now. Walker Getty says true happiness can only be found in submission. Look at Hannah Rae, they say. She is truly happy.

Daddy used to tell stories about the world beyond the mountains. There, he said, people do not share things in common, but they hoard selfishly. They are consumed by covetousness. They think they possess things, but their things possess them. They call themselves consumers. Wives sleep with the husbands of other women. Sexual immorality is rampant. Women dance naked on tabletops for money. There is no regard for God. Children do not honor their mothers and fathers. The races cohabit and interbreed and produce bastard mongrel children. Gangs of teenagers drive through neighborhoods and blanket them with automatic gunfire. We are in hiding, he said. The world hates us. If they find us they will try to kill us, because we follow the ways of God.

Jolene is haunted by the mountains. Jolene is Hiram's fourth wife. She rises every morning at four o'clock to pray. I've seen her through the window. She wanders to the edge of the valley and becomes a tiny speck beneath the old redwood. I've seen her weeping there, perhaps because Hiram loves her less than the rest of us, perhaps because of the long scars that run the length of her left cheek. As a child she pulled a pot of boiling water from the stove and ruined her beauty. Hannah Rae's mother said she was cursed for her disobedience, that Jolene was a stubborn and willful girl.

Some mornings a blue haze ascends from the tallest peaks, then settles and disappears as the sun rises. I've seen Jolene's eyes follow the dimming haze until her head is sunken to the ground. She is eighteen and has borne no children. I can feel mine kicking inside my skin.

Tuesday morning Hannah Rae rose early and scrambled eggs and fried bacon. She brought trays to our beds and plates of eggs and bacon and glasses of milk. She filled mop pails with soap and water and washed our feet as we ate. She kissed us each on the cheek. She whispered in my ear: "I love you, Leah." She dried our feet with good towels, and when we had finished eating she took our trays away and washed them in the kitchen sink.

They found Hannah Rae Tuesday evening. Jolene found her first. She was hanging in the closet, swinging limp from Hiram's black belt. Her left eye had popped loose from the socket, and her swollen tongue rested against her chin. Elliot, her brown teddy bear, lay at her feet. She had been holding him when she kicked the footstool away. Her lips were upturned, her teeth showing. She was still smiling.

They took her to Elder Jeffers, the coroner. They drained her blood and pumped her with fluids. They lay her in an open pine box, on a flatbed truck, and paraded her through the streets. They assembled us, all the people of God, on the lawn of the tabernacle. Walker Getty said that some sins were graver than others. He said murder and disobedience were worst of all, and that Hannah Rae had chosen by these deeds to separate herself from the congregation of the saints. He said she had chosen the way of death, and so eternal death and separation would be her lot. He said as she'd turned her back on us, so we must turn our backs to her.

And so we did, all of us, turned as one, away from Hannah Rae and toward the tabernacle. As I turned I caught a glimpse of my mother and father, their hands to their hearts. We sang a hymn and waited for Elder Jeffers to drive her away to an unmarked grave in the mountains. Hiram touched each of us, all the wives, on the head, and spoke a quiet blessing. A yellow butterfly hovered above a blade of grass at my feet. We finished singing. Our ears filled with silence. When we turned again, she was gone.

I pushed and pushed. I threw up on the delivery table. I said, "I don't want to have this baby." I said, "Get it out, it's hurting me." I said, "I hate this baby." I said, "I love this baby."

It came out blue and bloody. Elder Byrum turned it

upside down and slapped its back. He stuck his finger in its mouth. He called for oxygen and got it breathing.

He said, "It's a beautiful baby boy."

Hiram rushed in and grabbed it and named it. He prophesied, saying, "I name you Moses, for you will lead our people out of Egypt." He kissed my mouth and called me blessed. He took Moses from the delivery room, holding him high for everyone to see.

We took him to the tabernacle. We dressed him in white garments. We sprinkled his head with water and stood together as a family, Hiram and all the wives and children. Walker Getty said how God giveth and God taketh away. Moses wailed, and Walker Getty said how the sound of a boy child was a balm to the heart of the Lord.

Moses sleeps with me in my bed. When he cries I comfort him and let him drink from my breast. His skin is smooth, the softest skin on earth. His eyes are a piercing blue. Sometimes he looks into my eyes and I think maybe Hiram was right in his prophecy. Maybe Moses, my Moses, is the chosen one Walker Getty speaks about. Moses, so soft, so warm, so beautiful.

In the mornings I sling him to my front. I sing to him as I do my chores, as I clean the kitchens and bathrooms in the mornings, and tend to the garden in the afternoons. I sing: *Bye-oh, baby-oh, my own baby-oh.* He touches the long part of my neck, the part Hiram likes. He does not like to fall asleep, and he fights and fights and cries until he is exhausted and closes his eyes and beats my breast with his tiny fists. I have seen the way the other mothers look at him. He is a special boy. They know.

I woke at four in the morning. Jolene was standing over my bed, holding my winter coat. She said, "Come pray with me." Moses was still sleeping. I wrapped the sling around my shoulders and cradled him in it. She wrapped the coat around my shoulders and said to be very quiet.

She took me to the edge of the valley. She cleared a dry patch of ground and we crouched low and stared out at the mountains. I watched her lips move. She made no sound. She blinked, and a teardrop made a line down her cheek.

She shuddered with cold. Her lips stopped moving, and I asked her what she was praying. "For strength," she said. "For courage."

She looked at me and then I knew. She planned to run. She planned to cross the mountains. She planned to take me with her.

I stared at her. The tear had frozen along her scar.

I could have let her take me. I could have run with her then. I could have left Moses bundled in the bed. I could have taken him with me.

I thought of the words of the prophecy. I thought how Moses might one day take me, take all of us, over those mountains. I thought of leaving him, and I felt very wicked. I thought of leaving with him, I thought of leaving Hiram, and I felt very selfish. My boy. My man.

I took the holster. I took three bullets. I took the forty-five. I slung Moses to my chest and took him up the mountain Jolene was climbing. I called, "Jolene! Jolene!" I took my time climbing to her. I took a deep breath and then I took the gun from the holster. I raised it toward her face and then I took her face off. I took her by the feet and dragged her. I took the lid off the closed-up water well. I took her by the shoulders and dropped her in, head-first. I took off the holster and dropped it in the well, and then the forty-five.

I covered the mess with rocks and covered the rocks with snow.

I took Moses to the laundry room and washed my arms and hands and washed my clothes. I took him to the kitchen and peeled the potatoes while Hiram sounded the alarm. I took him to the wash room while they formed the search parties. I washed and rinsed the floors while the elders asked their questions. I killed the chicken and made the broth when the word came down that she had run off. I put Moses in his high chair and fed him his chicken soup. I took him to the tabernacle lawn, where they laid the empty casket. Walker Getty said, "Here lies wickedness. Here lies Jolene. May we never speak of her again." We turned our backs. We sang a hymn.

THE REDEMPTION OF GARVEY FLINT

by Vincent Louis Carrella

THERE IS A MOMENT in the midst of a severe beating in which the world fades, and sound dies out, and a man, finding himself upon the threshold of death, slips into a dream and sees things from another time and place altogether. In Garvey Flint's case he could see horses. That was the strange thing about the beating. That was his dream. Horses. As the violence rained down upon him, blow after blow, closed fists and boot heels, the dull whap of a pipe, between the flashes of light, between the thunder, he could see the eyes of the stallion they called Bowdun, and he could see that roan colt who drowned in the rains. He could see Snowdancer, the alabaster mare. All the horses his father once owned came back to him. All the horses that burned.

They beat him back to a place he swore he'd never go again. It's strange what hard violence will do to a man's thinking. It'll bring back those long forgotten places. It will run a man out of his refuge. It'll make him face himself. His daddy always said that a good beating was a good thing for a good man gone bad. And so it was for Garvey Flint, who had left home at the age of sixteen after giving his father the beating he had prophesied for his son. He left him in the corral that morning, bleeding from both his ears, and he set the barn ablaze with the horses all locked inside.

He could hear them, kicking at their gates and screaming like the drowning souls of Wormwood. And until this day, that's all he could remember. That sound. Those screams. The dying pleas of a dozen good horses.

On this occasion Bill Gurns was the author of his misery. Garvey owed him four-thousand dollars in gambling debts, bar-tabs and whores on credit. But it was more than just money that fueled the wrath of Bill Gurns, and Garvey could see that in his eyes, which were as blue as the topaz cufflinks he was famous for. The eyes of Bill Gurns had a way of peeling a man open, and when he was angry the tiny veins would swell up in the whites of them and he'd take on the fevered look of a man burning with sepsis. He had two of his men hold Garvey back by the arms and he stared into his eyes for a long, hard minute and in that short span of time Garvey could see every wrong, every wound, every violation that had been inflicted upon Gurns—from the day he was born and left to die swaddled in a burlap sack to this very morning when he kicked in Garvey's door to find him astraddle Patsy Murphy, who they called Fat Pat, and who Gurns could hardly give away except to the drunkest of the ne'er-do-wells who came nightly to the brothels of Nashville, which he purchased, one by one, until he united them all into a kingdom of great profit and infamous reputation.

The two men designated for this duty beat him slowly and they work in shifts, sometimes holding him down, sometimes hitting him and sometimes leaving the room altogether to take a drink or to relieve themselves in one of the tar-paper jakes out behind the brothel where the night's customers had deposited the spent portions of their revelry. But Gurns himself never leaves the room. He never takes his eyes off Flint, who lies now slumped between the two men, men who normally work the door but who are earning an extra five dollars for this special service. One is named Fred. The other is Mack Stilton, who likes Garvey and who's played cards with him on many occasions, and who likes him all the better for his infamous losing streaks and rash bluffs. Mack considers such prolonged beatings to be torture pure and simple. Especially the end, for they all end the same: in a ritual that has become known as *the baptism.*

Gurns leans back on his chair and swirls the ice at the bottom of his glass. There's no whiskey left, but there's still the flavor of the liquor on the ice and Gurns sucks the cubes to savor the residual taste of oak.

How 'bout that brother of yours? he says. He's got some money.

Garvey blinks to clear the blood from his eyes. He slumps forward but the two men keep him on his knees.

Let him go, Gurns says. And the men obey, releasing Garvey's arms and allowing him to fall to the floor.

You go home to your brother, Gurns says. I hear he's a man of God, and a man of means. You get what you can and you come back here. I'll give you seven days. You understand, Garvey? I know he lives in Leatherwood. And I know people in Leatherwood who still owe me.

Garvey nods and tries to look at Gurns but he can't lift his head. He reaches out with his hand, to prop himself up on his arm but he falls over. He tries again, but fails to raise himself from the floor. The man named Fred pushes him over with the sole of his boot and Garvey rolls onto his back. He stares up at Gurns, his eyes rolling.

Go on home, Garvey, Gurns says. Use that famous charm of yours. Brother to brother. Play that hand. That's a powerful hole-card. That's an ace.

Gurns tilts his glass back and lets the ice fall into his mouth. He spits a cube onto Garvey's belly.

This here's your last chance, Garvey, he says. Your last.

Garvey's head spins. His face is just inches away from the sole of Gurns' python boot and Gurns takes advantage of its proximity. He inserts the steel tip of the boot into Garvey's ear and applies gentle pressure.

I'll do it, Garvey says.

I don't want to kill you, Garvey. It's bad business to kill one's best customers.

Gurns places his glass down on the table and stands.

Baptize him, he says.

Behind the brothel is a narrow pathway of thick black mud where a thousand boot prints are filled with oily water. Garvey Flint can hear the sound of the men breathing. He can hear the sucking sound of their boots in the mud. The spatter of their boots is a hollow, familiar sound that reminds him of the horses and the cold Tennessee mountain mornings of his boyhood when he'd lead Bowdun out for exercise, and then the mares with their colts, none of whom he was permitted to ride.

The men drag him through the mud and he can smell it, the black earth, the manure. It begins to rain. He can't feel his legs but he can feel the cool drops on his face as they lay him down before the jakes. They prop open the door and the smell hits him like a blast from the bowels of a gut-shot deer. His eyes water and he can feel himself about to retch. The enclosures are narrow and hard for a man to sit in, let alone two men, yet for this event the chamber must somehow accommodate three. This takes skill, and strength, and practice. They must grab him a certain way in order to make it work. They must find the best holds, and since each man's body is unique, they must find them by feel. They grasp at his ankles and his wrists. But Garvey is lost in that other time and cannot feel anything. He's back with the horses.

He sees a torrent of rushing water. He sees a creek swollen with rain, brown as tobacco juice and roiling like the day of damnation. He can see the water coming down through the dry creek bed, a flash flood snapping trees and sweeping before it huge stones that groan and rumble like thunder. The men find good purchase on the sinewy limbs of Garvey Flint and in one quick motion, he is heaved up and inverted and dropped. The floodwaters swirl. All Garvey can see is the dark water and his body is sucked under and swept over stones and stumps and taken downstream. He thrashes and kicks and finally comes up for air and he sees the mares, lying on their sides, spinning and floating and dead to a horse, and he finds that he is holding onto a thing that he thought was a log but turns out to be a bloated colt. He is breathing, coughing up water, but breathing, and above him now he can see a circle of light. Stilton Mack throws him down a rope.

Garvey Flint walks the center of the Dutch turnpike. He is three days out of Nashville and still caked with the dried remnants of his baptism. He walks slowly toward the town of Leatherwood, and he walks with a limp, carefully choosing each step he takes so as to avoid the sharp stones on this road. He has long since abandoned his shoes. On this road he had once walked as a child to the Little Sparrow Schoolhouse. On this road, bareback like a renegade Cherokee boy, away from the Flint farm, up from Solomon creek, bound for the hilltop meadows on stolen horses he did ride. On this road he had run from the fire. On this road, he was the wind.

And as the wind does return, so does Garvey Flint. He comes down the road toward the familiar white farmhouse. He can see its roof through the trees. He sees the tiny cabin in the lee of the hill where the old woman used to live, and might still live for all he knows. It is her he fears the most. For his brother is among the best of Christians, and will receive him without judgment. The old woman is of a different mind altogether. They say she can see straight through to a man's heart. They say that she can look into your eyes and tell you the exact date of your death. She cannot be lied to, she cannot be deceived. And he knows this to be true.

She stands beside a flowering Dogwood tree in her nightclothes and at first he takes her for a ghost. She is hardly four foot tall and she is barefoot in the wet grass. Around her head is tied a kerchief of faded pink linen. Around her neck there hangs a large brass key on a string. She holds a cob-pipe in the corner of her mouth and puffs on it. Smoke swirls above her. Garvey stops in the road. The smell of her tobacco carries him back in time. She was there with his momma, on the day he was born. She was there to deliver Charles too, when Garvey was just four years old and was sent out for water and for fresh linens to soak up the blood. She had that pipe in her mouth on that day too, and when he came back with the bucket and the torn sheets, feeling proud of himself for being able to help her, she told him he was too late. His momma died while he was gone. She took the bucket and used it to wash the blood from the floor. And now she's looking at him the same way she did on the day he came in through the door when he was four years old, her eyes with that faraway look she gets when she's seeing beyond the moment, into a place of certainties and simple truths. She takes the pipe from her mouth and taps the bowl on her thigh.

I always said you'd come back, Garvey Flint, she says. And come back you did, as the child you was.

I won't be staying, he says.

I always said you'd come back.

She watches him walk on up the road and over the small rise to where the house sits among the small willows and the oaks that grow beside the creek. She watches him until he is gone.

Charles Flint is a strong man with long, sinewy arms and hair dark as crow's feathers. His eyes are equally black and when they fix themselves upon a task they widen and bulge and shine like obsidian stones. The eyes of Charles Flint take full part in all his endeavors. He uses them the same way he uses his hands. He uses them to pry, and lift and move that which he wishes to change or destroy. His eyes, like the axe he holds above his head now, are tools. In the moment just before the axe falls, Charles Flint splits the wood with his eyes. Thus the motion of the axe, the swing itself, the passage of the blade through the dry oak, is mere formality. He is already eyeing the next hunk of wood. He sees it in the pile, calling out to him, showing its weak spot. Charles Flint is so intent upon this task that he does not see his brother coming up the hill behind him. Nor does he hear him, until he calls out his name.

Charles.

At first he does not turn. He does not lay down the axe. He simply cocks his head and listens, as if the call of some bird, rare to these parts, had caught his ear.

Charles.

He lays the axe beside the woodpile and wipes his face with a rag. And then he turns to acknowledge the call he had long expected.

It's me, Garvey says. I got myself into some trouble, brother. Bad trouble.

The eyes of Charles Flint widen again. The eyes of Charles Flint glisten. It has been too long since Garvey has seen those eyes. And they have changed. To a stranger they would look mad, they would look wild. But to Garvey, who remembers how his younger brother would stare this way at a butterfly alight upon a flower, they are simply the eyes of a man who sees the face of God in all that he beholds.

I need help, Charles.

Charles steps closer to his brother and fixes his eyes upon the bone just below his left eye where there is a swollen patch of violet colored flesh. He does not see the dirt and the filth which covers his brother's face, he does not see his bare feet or his torn clothing. He sees only that patch of bruised flesh just below his eye. Thus the motion of his arm, his swing, the impact of his closed fist upon that tender bone occurs mechanically, as does the backward spiral of Garvey Flint. The second blow does not land under his jaw, as he had planned, but smashes into his throat right at the thyroid. The third manages to clip his ear. And that's all it takes is three. One for the Father, one for the Son and one for the Holy Ghost.

Garvey Flint is down again, clutching at his neck like a man poisoned with lye. Charles Flint wipes his hand with the rag. He stands above his brother. This is a moment he had rehearsed as a boy, with a flour sack in the rebuilt barn, with a bag of oats, with a bale of hay. His legs became strong from the mock beatings. His diction became stronger too. And years later, when Charles Flint would one day tell the story of how he became known as the most eloquent Holiness man ever to conduct a backwoods tent revival in the state of Tennessee, he would say that it was the sins of his brother Garvey that fueled his passion for scripture, and his life in pursuit of the Lord.

Charles watches his brother clutching at himself, he watches him struggle to breathe. There, lying on the ground amidst the splinters of oak, is a man he has never known. And he sees now that his clothing is in tatters. He sees that his feet are bare. He sees the black soles of his brother's feet and his ankles and he remembers how he'd interlock his fingers, as a boy, and kneel, and provide for him a stirrup with his hands, lifting him onto the back of Bowdun in the night so that he could ride under the moon. He remembers how Garvey's feet were always so cold.

What has thou done? he says. The voice of thy brother's blood crieth unto me from the ground.

He kneels in the wood chips and he places one arm beneath Garvey's legs, and the other behind his neck, and he lifts him.

It's all right now, Garvey, he says. You're home, and I will not strike you again, nor will I let another man ever strike you again.

He carries Garvey up to the house. He has grown into a big man and Charles holds him with all of his strength. Garvey looks up into his brother's eyes and finds that they are closed. He can hear the wind in the willow trees, and he can smell all the new horses in the barn. The barn. It is rebuilt and larger than it had been before, but it stands upon the same ground. Inside he can hear the horses nickering in their stalls. And that is a sound he has prayed to hear again. Every night for fifteen long years.

BLOOD ATONEMENT
by DeLeon DeMicoli

For the life of the flesh is in the blood, and I have given it to you on the altar to make atonement for your souls; for it is the blood by reason of the life that makes atonement.

—Leviticus 17:11

The man stepped into an empty bar.

"We're closed for the night," said the bartender.

The man relaxed into a stool. "How about a cold one for the ride home?" The man dug in his pocket and threw a few crumpled up Georgies onto the bar.

The bartender grimaced. "No booze afterhours, sonny, and don't give me no growl about it either 'cause I've heard it all before."

The man slapped down a few more notes onto the counter like he was raising the poker pot.

The bartender stood tall with his arms crossed like he'd seen on television when he watched George Reeves, hoping the man would fold.

But the man remained seated. "Be a pal. I've had a helluva day, I tell ya."

The bartender kept an owl's stare on the man and slid open the cooler. He pulled out a cold one and placed it on the counter.

The man picked up the ice cold beer and took a long, hard gaze at the bottle like it was the Hope diamond before guzzling it down in one gulp. After, he set the bottle down on the bar and wiped his mouth with the back of his hand. He reached into his coat pocket and pulled out a gun. "Now hand over the money."

The bartender raised his arms. He stared at the barrel of the revolver as if it was a growling dog.

The man lifted himself off his stool and leaned over. He yanked out the gun the bartender had taped underneath the counter and placed it inside his coat pocket.

The bartender pointed to the end of the bar. "The money's in the register. Take it all, just don't shoot me. I have a wife and child."

"I don't want the money in the register. Leave that chump change for the two-bit suckers. I want the money in the safe."

"The safe's in the office. I'll give you whatever you want." The bartender slid across the back bar to a door that led to the office.

"Hold it there, partner."

The bartender stopped dead in his tracks, his arms jolted up.

"I don't want the rolled up coins and petty cash you got in the safe in the office. I want the money you keep in the safe behind the painting." The man pointed the barrel at the bartender's head. "Open that safe."

"How did . . ."

The driveway bell at the gas station across the street rang twice in the distance as a car pulled up to the pump. The neon sign hanging in the front window of the bar blinked in schizophrenic pulses.

The bartender felt uneasy in his skin as if the inner coating of his flesh was lined with coarse wool. No one knew about that safe, not even his wife. But that was the least of his worries. If the man knew about the safe, what else did he know? And did he tell anyone? No one knew the secrets the bartender kept. The type of secrets that got you two Jack Bennys for the price of one or an all night thigh-hugger if cold hard cash was in hand. He never confided in his friends, neighbors, or pastor. He sinned to keep his sins hidden, or so he thought.

There were many late nights when Missy let that soda bottle figure breathe on the couch in the back office. The bartender stared at her like she was a cherry car. Sometimes she let him take photographs.

The bartender wanted Missy to stay longer, but time was money and he had to pay extra. When he refused, she got angry. But he didn't care about some floozy. What was she going to do, go to the cops? Not likely.

The bartender turned around and grabbed the gilded edges of the gold frame and pulled it open. The safe was recessed in the brick wall.

The bartender told his customers the portrait was of an ancestor that was a duchess. The truth was the painting had been hanging on the wall long before the bartender purchased the tavern.

The bartender opened the safe. Photographs rested on top of the stacks of hundred dollar bills.

"She's a whore and will always be a whore," he said.

Bright flashes lit up the room. Glass bottles exploded like a carnival game. The bartender's life trickled down the floor drain along with his sins.

"Nobody calls my girl a whore," the man said, and ran out of the bar.

The man was sleeping one off. He was woken up by banging on the door. His head rose off the floor. A string of saliva dangled at the corner of his mouth. He placed both hands on the side of his head, suctioning them against his ears to make the high-pitched siren he thought he heard fade.

The door was kicked off its hinges. Two officers appeared with their guns drawn. The man used his hand to cover his eyes from the bright sunlight.

There were crumpled up beer cans surrounding the man and an empty bottle of booze knocked over on the ground.

The officers put their pistols away and knelt over the man and got him to his feet. They held onto his arms and shoulders until he had the strength to stand on his own.

"You have the right to remain silent . . . blah, blah, blah," was all the man heard as he was dragged outside.

His rundown bungalow faced a scrap metal yard. Living amongst the broken down machinery and abandoned cars was a junkyard dog. It jumped up on its hind legs and into the fence, barking terror threats at the police cruiser.

"Shut that damn mutt up!" The man made an attempt to approach the dog, but the officers had a good grip on his arms. They placed him inside the cruiser. He stared at the dog as it barked and showed its teeth. Drool dripped from the corners of its sweaty mouth.

"Shut up, you stupid mutt."

"Quiet down back there," said an officer.

The man wished he would've done one last thing after returning from the bar, and that was to shoot that damn mutt and put it down for good. Then he would've been able to get a better night's rest.

The prosecutor called on his witness. A young man approached the stand wearing a suit borrowed from his father's closet. It hung wide and loose on his still growing frame. He made a brief pass at the defendant, but the man was unable to recognize him.

The bailiff appeared with the good book in his hand. The young boy rested his shaky palm on top of it.

"You swear to tell the truth, the whole truth, and nothin' but the truth so help you God?"

"I aim to, yes, sir."

The bailiff returned to his post. The counselor rose to his feet. "State your name and what your current occupation is for the record."

"My name is Henry Cole and I'm currently employed as a gas station attendant over there on Laurel and Beech. Been that way for a good two years or so."

"And can you tell the jury what you saw that night, young Henry?"

"Yes, sir, I can."

That night Henry was seated inside the gas station reading a Doc Savage yarn from off the magazine rack. A car drove up to the pumps. The service bell rang. Henry stepped outside and filled up the man's gas tank.

When the car drove off he heard multiple pops that sounded like a pack of black cats exploding in a garbage can. When he turned around he saw the man exit the bar, run to his car, and fish tail it out of the parking lot.

"Who is 'the man' you are referring to, Henry?"

Henry pointed at the man seated across the courtroom.

"Henry, please explain to the jury what you did next."

Henry hid behind the gas pump until the man's car disappeared into the night. Then he got up and ran across the street. When he walked into the bar he found the bartender dead. He also discovered a safe hidden behind a painting and when he looked inside it was empty.

"Thank you for your testimony, Henry."

Henry nodded.

"No further questions, your honor." The prosecutor sat back down.

The judge looked over at the public defender. "Counselor, your witness."

The man's attorney was hidden behind stacks of folders that pertained to sorry chaps that couldn't afford proper representation. The public defender was an overworked man and didn't know one defendant from the next. They all seemed to blur into one stupid criminal he tried, day after day, to set free.

The public defender rose from his chair. He looked over the man's file. "I have no questions, your honor."

The man turned to his lawyer in awe. He stood up on his own behalf. "I'd like to ask the boy some questions if that'd be all right with you, judge."

The judge turned to the stenographer. "Let the record show I heard the defendant's request and have denied him the opportunity to question the young man."

The stenographer typed feverishly.

The judge turned to Henry. "You may step down, son."

The man watched Henry approach the door. Henry stopped at the last row of benches and assisted a woman to her feet. The woman wore a black shawl and cat-eye sunglasses and it appeared she was trying to conceal her identity, but she wasn't fooling anyone, especially the man.

Missy handed the man a disposable razor. "Shave my legs, sweetie?"

She kicked out her leg and placed it on the rim of the tub. Water dripped onto the cracked bathroom tiles.

The man dipped the blade into the warm water, then scraped the blade across his cheek to make sure it was sharp.

"You know, sweetie, I was never meant to do the nine-to-five grind like the average Dick and Jane. I have ambitions and dreams like those classy dames I'm always reading about at the grocery store, ya know?"

The man was shaving her inner thigh, carefully

pressing the blade against her supple skin. It sounded like fine sandpaper polishing a stone.

"Now, sweetie, you know I love you, right?"

The man washed off the tiny hairs. Steam rose over the bathtub.

"And I hate to be a burden," she continued, "but someone owes me some money. I wouldn't bother to bring it up if it was just a few Georgies, but it's actually a lot of money and I believe the bartender is tryin' to put one over on me."

The man worked over her knee and down to her calf muscle, concentrating on the right amount of pressure to use so he wouldn't cut her.

"But you know me, sweetie. I don't jump off the handle over foolish things. You know if I didn't think it was important I wouldn't bring it up. But it is, at least to me. And I think for principles' sake it should be important to you too."

The man felt like a doctor, shaving the area and prepping it before surgery. He saw it done once before at the hospital when he was a teenager and his brother broke his leg after falling out of the crab apple tree in front of their home.

"Will you do it, sweetie?"

He knew if he didn't she'd find someone else who would. He had no choice, or at least that was how he saw it.

He cleaned the blade and began shaving her other leg.

The bulls appeared by the man's side. "It's time."

The man stood up and turned around. He was handcuffed and led out of his cell.

The man knew Missy was there that night waiting with Henry at the gas station. Their plan was to sneak up on the man, kill him, and steal the bartender's money. Then place the loaded gun in the man's hand and place another gun in the bartender's hand and let the cops sort out the rest. What they didn't anticipate was the man walking out with nothing. When he drove off, Missy realized they had to come up with a new plan, so that was what they did, or so the man thought.

The man was led to an abandoned warehouse that once served as the prison's death house back in the 1920s. Twenty-four cells once housed men on death row. Some claimed they could hear inmates scream as they fried on the electric chair. But nothing was confirmed.

At the end of the warehouse was a large curtain serving as a partition. On the other side was a chair surrounded by sand bags. The area was brightly lit by two camera spotlights. Reporters stood at the end of the partition and wrote in small notepads.

The bulls placed the man in the chair. They grabbed the leather straps and locked in his arms, legs, and chest. Two straps secured his shoulders. One last strap was placed over his forehead. The man took in several breaths and his eyes grew as he stared at the wall in front of him that had gun ports carved into it. Five officers stood behind each gun port and held onto .30-caliber Winchester rifles. One of the rifles had a blank bullet loaded inside the chamber. The officers did not know which gun it was.

"Any last words, son?" The warden was a big thick cut of concrete with a very well trimmed moustache.

The man tried to move his head to look at the warden but couldn't do so. "Let's do it."

The reporters scribbled in their notepads.

The warden nodded. He turned around and snapped his fingers to grab an officer's attention. The reporters quietly walked off into the shadows. The officer flagged his arms out and looked like he was directing cattle into the byre as he led the reporters outside.

A pastor appeared from out of the same shadows and stood next to the man. He held onto a worn copy of the Bible. "Would you like a specific passage read, my son?"

Sweat slowly slid down from the man's hairline and collected into the leather strap. "Not one in particular, pastor. I reckon whatever passage you see fit to read for the circumstance is fine by me."

The pastor nodded. He began to read aloud. The officers removed their hats. The warden bowed his head. When the pastor said "Amen" so did the men in the room.

"God be with you," were the last words said to the man.

An officer approached the man and placed a black hood over his head. Another officer affixed a cloth bullseye over the man's heart.

The warden nodded to the officers behind the gun ports. They took their positions aiming their rifles at the man. The warden had instructions on when the men should fire.

"Five, four, three, two . . ."

The officers fired their rifles. It sounded like the ten second warning claps you heard during a boxing match to signal the end of the round.

The man's forearms tensed. His fingers gripped the arms of the chair. His head shook frantically as the bullets pierced the bullseye.

After a few seconds his arms went limp. His head dropped into his chest. A pool of blood began to soak through his blue jump suit.

A medic approached the man once the smoke from the rifles cleared. He placed the end of the stethoscope against the man's chest. He looked over at the warden and nodded.

THE LIBERATION OF EDWARD KELLOR

by Anthony David Jacques

THE MOON IS FULL ON THE HORIZON, full and dancing along the top of every gentle wave. Three feet above the low tide mark the rug doesn't move.

The hands of the watch glide silently over the Greek key pattern in red and gold. The time reads 10:52 a.m. His silent protest these seven years, but no one ever looked that close. She always made sure he wore the watch because she bought it to make him appear distinguished.

The rock he sits on is half submerged and worn smooth, and he takes off his shoes. His jacket lies crumpled behind them and he has to fight the compulsion to fold it in half and then in half again. Stepping out onto the darker sand the ocean water wells up from within each successive footprint.

The moon is full in every watery footprint and in the distance the seagulls sleep along the pier. His slacks are getting wet and losing their crease. The waves wash over his path once, twice, and the third time it's like he was never there.

The sand washes from underneath his feet and he imagines some of it swirling up and settling into the cuff, and when he looks over, the waves have reached the end of the rug. He imagines the waves are slowly pulling the fabric down, washing the sand from underneath with each regress. He imagines little granules creeping in between the fibers.

The reverse image of the red and gold key pattern is soaking up the seawater. The pattern that matches the drapes and offsets the couch and loveseat. Matches the pattern beneath the pretentious Roman numerals on the face of the watch.

There are no clouds tonight. The sky is deep and infinite and the wet sand glistens like the stars and with his bare feet he's standing on top of the universe.

He glances up to the road every few minutes, but nothing changes. No one comes out at night in the winter.

His calves feel strange with every icy wave that pulls away and while he's still thinking about this, the rug starts to move. Are his knots straight and evenly spaced? Are they tight? And he hates himself for thinking it, but he wonders, maybe he should have cleaned the rug one last time.

When he tries to step up and out of the sand he falters. His palm hits the wet beach and then the water rushes up past his wrist, over the watch. He waits for another wave to rinse off the excess sand, then walks back to the rock. The watch is not waterproof so there's water under the face.

His feet are close enough that if he wanted to, he could prop them up on the rug and recline in the space between two shoulder high boulders. But he can't.

No feet on the furniture. No shoes on the rug. No beer in the formal living room. Then no beer in the house, so why don't we get a refrigerator for the garage? Those pants need to be ironed and where's your watch?

You look ridiculous.

The rug moves again as the lower half begins to slump downward where the sand is disappearing beneath, and it sounds like a seagull at first but the pier is to the west and none of the birds are stirring. The sound is too close and he needs some distance.

When he gets back from the car the water is three-quarters of the way up the rug and the knots still look solid. But there is noticeable movement.

He thinks about how he's never had a flat tire, though he's helped change one or two like a Good Samaritan, but never with his own tire iron. It smells like the grease on the scissor jack and the rubber of the spare tire, and the weight feels good in his hand. Solid. Significant.

He raises his arm and in that perfect nothing moment, the space between lifting up and crashing down, the moon and every last star reflects full and bright in the face of the watch.

The rug gives under the weight of the tire iron, and he bears down with all his strength once, twice, and the third time he finds the muffled, hollow crack he's looking for. He imagines that the red and gold key pattern is turning mostly red now, but it looks perfectly black in the moonlight, and the black spreads slowly as the waves reach higher.

Now it's quiet again except for the waves, that insatiable chorus of ghosts, and he imagines the ocean washing her away bit by bit. He sits on the rock and folds his jacket, sets his shoes neatly in front and then he waits for the tide and eventually the sun.

When the rug is just peeking out of the highest waves, he takes off his watch. It's stopped. He sets it between the shoes, parallel to the soles. He imagines the rug laid open and the corner medallions soaking up the seawater, the red and gold key pattern bleeding into the inner labyrinth.

He thinks about her skull.

Edward throws the watch into the ocean and sits back down on the smooth rock. When the people do show up the rug is still there, peeking out of the water every few seconds and beginning to bob with the ebb and flow.

Someone screams. When the people come back again, he does what they tell him. He puts his hands behind his head and he feels his naked wrist and it's worn smooth. He kneels, and it makes him smile that he won't have to iron these pants, and he thinks about the stupid fish staring at the red and gold key pattern of that dead watch.

ACT OF CONTRITION
by Craig Clevenger

SHE FLARED IN THE DARK like some wild animal's lone eye in my headlights. White sweatshirt and ragged sunbleached hair, a ghost with her thumb to the road. I slowed to the right and stopped just ahead of her. My tires straddled the broken black edge where the dirt shoulder dropped below the asphalt, the car sloping passengerwise like a sinking boat. Its lopsided timing shuddered through the wheel and into my arms. I nursed the gas, nudged the idle back to its center and kept the engine alive. My brake lights bathed the hitcher in blood then she turned white again, stopped at my passenger side and looked back down the road. Maybe somebody else would stop. But she bent to the window and her eyes said she was long past working those odds or any other. Her sunburn ran deep, patches of skin flaking from her face. Lower lip split open and dried to a hardened hairline of blood.

How far you going? she asked.

I named some place. I lied.

Okay. She climbed in and pulled at the door but it pulled back.

Try again. Hinge is real stubborn.

She did. On her third pull I saw headlights in my mirror, a diesel rig snailing around the one-lane curve to my back. Her door was still open when I punched the gas.

With no shoulder grade to the road I reckoned maybe six-inches of crumbling curb beneath my chassis. I torqued left onto the highway and scraped my oil pan across a yard of jagged blacktop. A sound I heard through my teeth.

Crystal was fifteen and she was my cousin. She wore jean shorts frayed at the top of her thighs, snug like she'd cut off the legs last summer before she started looking the way she did. The way she cocked her hip and bent to scratch her bare foot or chewed a lock of hair tickling her face, oblivious to herself. She caught me looking at her once and I froze, squeezed out a smile with my mouth full of cold meatloaf. She gave no read at all, just picked up the remote and turned her back to me. She caught me a few times after that but never got creeped or let on that she did. But her spell broke anytime she opened her mouth. She was just a kid again, wanting help with a bicycle flat or a ride to the mall.

I pray every day. Crews on the job site got quiet when I came around. Work was drying up and the scarce jobs were going to friends of foremen and subcontractors first. I had to give up my place. I prayed for help. My aunt and uncle had a room and there was lots of development out where they lived. They let me slide on rent, long as I built a new railing for their deck and kept an eye on Crystal from time to time. I prayed more.

The grid went down during a heat wave so the job cut us loose early. I collapsed on the couch with a cold beer and some solitude. It was August, there was no school. My aunt and uncle were gone for the weekend. I heard the back door open and close and there stood Crystal, bronzed from her afternoons in the backyard and smelling like coconut, wearing a two-piece I could ball into my fist. She looked taller in the doorway. Legs and gold hair meeting at her hips where a more modest suit had cast a shadow of pale winter skin. She drifted toward me, strips of wet light shining from her skin and I saw her every movement in quarter time.

Got any more of those? She didn't sound like a kid this time.

No. These are my last six. Sorry.

She didn't whine or plead like she did when I turned down certain movie rentals or enforced her bedtime.

I'll help myself, she said, and stuck her tongue out. She left the room, catwalk-style and I followed the curve of her waist, the shoelace knots at her hips and the stretch of bright yellow fabric in between sliding into itself with each step. A minute passed, slow and hot. I heard the hiss of a bottle cap crimping open.

I shot to the kitchen and she tucked the bottle behind her and ran so I chased her and grabbed her before she could pour it on me and had to pin her and she wouldn't stop laughing and the beer foamed all over both of us.

I knocked that clip out of my head.

I grabbed her wrist and squeezed until the bottle hit the kitchen floor, beer foaming around the shards of brown glass. I can't remember what I said but I may have held her wrist too hard. Crystal locked herself in her room. She didn't come out and I didn't knock. At 4:30 the next morning I slipped a hundred bucks under her door with a note that said her parents would be home after the weekend. Then I left for good.

The hitcher looked older up close, hard years beneath the sun damage.

Got no radio? She spoke slowly, words from a morphine drip.

Radio works fine, was all I said.

She didn't touch the radio. No one ever does. I'm okay with just the humming road but most people need

313

noise, the talk shows and morning deejays. They need the ad jingles, something they can hum silently to help forget their forty hours every week. She sat frozen with her hands folded in her lap, gearing up to do whatever the ride or a few bucks called for, her body flying solo while she looked away from somewhere inside her head. I didn't want anything. The silence was enough for me, like a sleeping guard dog between us.

Crystal and her backyard tanning routine were seven-hundred miles away. I filled my tank, then blinked and found myself staring into the open back hatch of my car. A stray socket wrench, hot to the touch. A ballpoint pen with no cap, a few pennies and bits of dog kibble though I've never owned a dog. I loaded up the provisions I couldn't recall buying moments earlier. Two gallons of drinking water, a dozen granola bars and a canvas knapsack. I had a thin recollection of the air conditioner and the bored liquor store clerk, but they could have been from another stop on a different day. Whatever was clipping the time from my waking activity was getting greedy. I used to zone out for a few seconds, maybe a minute or two. Then the stretches of time got longer and longer. I'd be parked at a job site with my keys in my lap and the half-hour commute wiped clean from my morning. Lately I'd practically been leaving my body.

Hey. Can you spare any change?

Straight black hair and pale skin. She was a year older than Crystal, judging by her curves, and dressed for the heat. Gossamer skirt rippling high on her legs and a babydoll top with pink script across her breasts that I couldn't read without staring so I didn't. She was too clean to be homeless and too young to be panhandling.

Do you have fifty cents?

Sorry, I said. Can't help you.

What's your name?

The thin silver chain around her waist looked like a wire of sunlight. The cold free-fall rush blew through me and I reckoned every wrong twist of backstory before my keys hit the ground. There was a stepfather or stepbrother in the scene. She didn't know where to get help but she was learning the angles, and I could be one of them. She came through the heat, twisting a rubber band between her fingers. Her flip-flops slapped the soles of her feet but the way her hips moved made everything else quiet.

Ezekiel, I said.

For real?

Yeah.

Sounds like a Bible name.

It is.

But you don't have any money?

None to spare. I didn't look below her neck. And I didn't look around. If I wasn't doing anything wrong then it didn't matter who saw me.

Someone peeled out of the gas station and set my pulse loose like a racing dog. A matte-black Nova with a bondo patch on the driver's door screamed through the intersection. I picked up my keys and when I stood up she'd found another mark, a middle-aged business man with a map spread across his steering wheel. Her hazy skirt rode on the current of heat, flaring up to her hips in slow motion. Pale crescents of skin flexed at the tops of her thighs. The skirt settled around her again, like something cast off and drifting to the bottom of a swimming pool.

The hitcher's fingers danced nervously on her lap and tickled the edge of my vision. They went still if I looked at them straight on. Maybe she was playing with me. Maybe she was thinking this ride was her last, that I had a rag for her mouth and a shovel in my trunk. The highway was empty one second and the next I was bearing down on a five-hundred pound elk standing on the dotted yellow divide. I hit the brakes and we swerved. The elk bolted. Big enough to take out my front end and kill us both but it darted like a squirrel, so quick I wasn't sure I'd really seen it.

The fuck was that? The hitcher had braced herself against the dashboard, elbows locked and eyes wide but she wasn't asking about the elk. The accusation was silent but clear. Maybe I hadn't seen anything.

Keep your hands still, I said. It's distracting. I was parked right where the phantom elk had been, crossways in the dead middle of the highway, a broadside collision set to go.

You fucking crazy?

You got a problem then walk, I said, then hit the ignition.

I've been good my whole life, walking that barren firebreak between feeling the rush of caving to temptation but still having the strength to resist. A girl came to my hotel room once, after I called an ad in the paper. Somewhere in west Texas. She took off her clothes and asked me what I wanted. I said I didn't know. Then she opened my door and a guy was waiting there, big guy with a tattoo on his shaved head and lots of earrings. He held out a badge but not for very long. Said he could arrest me or fine me on the spot. I asked him how much the fine was and the girl laughed. Another hitcher had offered to thank me for the ride. I stopped at a liquor store and gave her money for condoms and beer and when she got out I drove away. It was always the same. I never did anything wrong but I never stopped thinking about those things I never did.

I'd lied to that girl in the parking lot. My name wasn't Ezekiel, not yet. That was up to God.

When the girl and the big guy left, she'd stuck her business card in my Bible. The big guy laughed when she did that. The glossy pink card had a picture of her chest and a phone number. It was marking the Book of Ezekiel.

I knew a sign when I saw it.

It's easier to hear God in the desert. Fewer obstructions, so God's got a halfway decent view, plus a man's got fewer things clouding his own sight. Jesus, John the Baptist, all of them, the desert was where they heard God loudest and clearest, where they had their showdown with the Devil. I'd been driving around the desert for weeks since I'd left Crystal's house. Driving and praying, waiting for God to show me where to stop.

We hit the truck lot after midnight. A row of fueling bays the size of a city block with a cashier's booth in the middle, a coffee shop, a cheap motel on either side and a couple dozen eighteen-wheelers. Two hours since I'd picked her up and I don't think she blinked the entire trip, at least not since the elk that I may or may not have imagined, that may or may not have nearly killed us.

This is good, she said. Right here.

The cashier's booth was lit up like daylight. I could almost read the newspaper headlines from the far edge of the lot.

Just stop right here, she said.

Let me get you closer. No sense in you walking through a parking lot this size in the dark. You want the coffee shop or just that little convenience store?

Let me out of this goddamned car.

I stopped. Probably a couple hundred yards out on a stretch of empty asphalt. She'd been so docile until now and I was nervous. I hadn't done anything wrong. Her bag strap had caught under the seat. She was fighting with it and cursing under her breath, louder and louder. She flung the door open and jumped out. Then she screamed. She hugged herself and closed her eyes and screamed as loud as she could. She stomped her feet and beat her fists against her head then pointed at my car and screamed for help.

I couldn't lift my hands or move and I felt hot all over.

She screamed that I'd tried to kill her and then she ran toward the coffee shop.

The dome light came on in a nearby semi. I reached over and closed the door and drove away as fast as I could, found the nearest onramp and doubled back toward where I'd just driven from. It didn't matter which way I went as long as I kept driving. I prayed for forgiveness, told God I was sorry, that I was ready and just needed a sign. I passed the truck lot on my left, kept to the speed limit and watched for square headlights in my mirror. After a while I was back where I'd first picked her up. At the next juncture I took the unfamiliar road.

She was the last one. No more inhaling the vapor in Hell's vestibule. I promised God, no more.

I loved cowboy movies when I was a kid. Ford, Peckinpah, Leone. But I had a weakness for the second-rate gunfighter films with cowboys and Indians and cattle barons and railroads. They hotwired the classics then stripped them down in some B-movie chop shop and recycled the good parts as their own. Like when the hero walked into a saloon for the first time and everything stopped. The music went quiet, folks would stare for a minute and then go back to their whiskey or cards. But everyone had to look at the good guy.

My Sunday school teacher had taught us about life in the Holy Land. She wanted to make the Bible real for us. She taught us about the desert, how the heat wave we once had was nothing compared to life in the Middle East. We learned how they had to preserve food and how risky it was to travel. It took the Israelites forty years to make it to the Holy Land. They only survived because of miracles. John the Baptist ate insects. I'd been driving through the American desert for weeks, where all of those frontier towns from the cowboy movies used to be. The pile of maps and guidebooks in my glovebox agreed on the highways and major roads and most of the big dots but little else. The small towns and the little roads, especially the dirt ones, never matched up. They couldn't agree on exactly where the desert began, or the exact annual rainfall or average temperature. We know as much about the desert now as those people in the ghost towns did. It's hard to make a deep map of a territory that can kill you in a matter of hours.

Someone showed up in one of those Old West towns by himself, no railroad or wagon train, of course people were going to stare. Because he was supposed to be dead. That's how you knew who the good guy was.

I passed three more elk that night. No close calls but their electric Roswell eyes hovering in the dark startled me every time. It was four in the morning when I found a rest stop with an RV slumbering in the lot and four other cars parked as far apart as they could manage. A stretch of grass with picnic benches, fire pits and a brick hut split into restrooms, its curbside face a mottled black and white mural like a blown-up newspaper photograph. The collage of leaflets came into focus once I was up close.

Missing
Have You Seen Me?
Missing
Missing Since—
Last Seen On—
Missing
Missing
Missing

Young teenagers and children. Mostly Caucasian, mostly female, last seen wearing anything and everything from the Junior Miss Department.

The bathroom smelled like an outhouse and had almost as little light. The floor was wet. I held my breath long enough to take a leak then went back to my car. I passed a station wagon with expired tags and a coat hanger twisted around the loose muffler. One of its back windows covered with duct tape and a garbage bag. I locked my doors, let my seat back as far as it could go and draped a T-shirt over my eyes. Before long there came a tentative knock, the way someone knocks to see if you're awake without disturbing you if you aren't. Definitely not a cop. I sat up and saw the face fogging up my window, hands cupped around his eyes to see through the dark. If he'd needed money, gas or a jump start he wouldn't have been smiling the way he was. I gave up on sleeping, started my car and he made the looping pantomime signal for me to roll down my window. I couldn't exactly race my engine, but he got the message that I was driving off and the placement of his foot didn't worry me.

The high desert had too many elk and too much plant life. Too many places to hide or disappear. And it was full of people hiding or disappearing. If you walked out of nowhere into a room full of strangers nobody would give you a second look. The high desert was no place for a prophet.

By 10:00 that morning it was ninety-five degrees. Nothing on either side of the road but bleached sand and brittle shrubs as far as I could see. The mountains ahead of me hadn't changed size since sunrise. An hour later my temperature gauge was reaching for the red and the bottle of water in my passenger seat was hot to the touch. I turned on the heat and rolled down my windows and the needle eased back. I drove on, eyeing the mountains and the needle but neither one moved. At the stroke of noon my dashboard blacked out and smoke billowed from my hood. I coasted to the shoulder and once the hissing and smoking stopped, I stepped out and just stood there in the desert. Heat like nothing I'd learned about in Sunday school, silence like I'd never felt in church. A short distance off the road and I'd be standing where no human being had ever walked. It was like being on Mars. A place where a man finds redemption beneath the unyielding sun that burns away his sins and what is left of that man becomes a prophet.

I opened the map and found my place, a scratch of north-south highway hardly worth printing. The nearest town of Jackdaw Flats lay forty miles due west on a faint pencil mark of road roughly parallel to mine, with neither a direct route nor an inch of shade in between. I emptied the hot bottle of water over my head then cloaked myself in a beach towel. John the Baptist didn't wear sunblock. I packed the granola bars and my Bible into the canvas knapsack, slung it over my shoulder then took up a gallon water jug in each hand. There hadn't been anyone else on the road all morning. I crossed the highway without looking, stopped at the edge of the road and prayed. The triple-digit temperatures would drop below freezing after dark. There were definitely diamondbacks, possibly coyotes and the narrow chance of a flash flood. I could be in Jackdaw Flats by morning.

When I come in from the desert, everyone will stare at me. And my name will be Ezekiel.

SAY YES TO PLEASURE
by Richard Thomas

THIS IS WHAT IT MEANS TO BE A SLAVE, living in fear, of discovery. The easy way out would be to kill myself, to end my suffering and pain. But I won't allow it. There is a retribution coming, at her hands, I think. In that freedom, in that release, there will be redemption. It won't make things better for her, won't bring him back, but there will be justice in the spilling of my blood, so for now, I live between the lines.

The rain outside washes away the litter, the sidewalks clean if for only a moment. Discarded soda cans and plastic bags are blown into the crevices, covered in dirt and grime. Lying on my bed I am a crumpled up, discarded tissue, knees pulled up in the fetal position, my back to the windows that rattle in their frames, the streaks of grey water cleansing the earth. I belong out there, in the cold, the rain, but no baptism in the tears of God will alleviate my sins. My hands are numb, curled into claws, clenching the wool blanket to my chin, never able to warm myself, always empty, always cold.

She's coming over soon, and the mask will go back on. It has to. This will play out the way it's supposed to play out, for maximum impact. Without love there can be no hate, so I build up that stockpile, show her the world is not random violence and chaos, not cold and calculating, willing disaster, offering up failure. In other words, I lie.

"How was work?" I ask.

"The usual," she says. "Drunks, jerks, and the occasional dine and dash."

Veronica works at a diner down the street. It's contemporary retro, a shiny new place made to look like it's been around forever.

We sit at the small kitchen table in my apartment eating french fries that she brought home, reheated in the oven, sprinkled with sea salt and parmesan cheese. In ten minutes I'll force myself to get up and vomit the food into the toilet. I'm not allowed that simple pleasure.

Two cups of coffee sit in chipped ceramic mugs, the faded simple shapes as bland and common as I could find, utilitarian, and yet there is an appeal to the simple lines.

She used to smile when I said she was mousy. Now it feels too predatory to say. She stares at the swirling liquid, often retreating into herself, eyes dull and unresponsive, a fraction of what she used to be. It's expected when dealing with death, with loss, when a part of you is taken away. Her son's ghost haunts our streets, but I avert my eyes at his ethereal presence. Her skin is so white it is almost translucent, her small breasts hidden under a long sleeve shirt, a faded pink T-shirt on top of that, grease stains and a splotch of something tacky and dark that I keep telling myself is only ketchup. She hides away her femininity when she goes to work, to keep the wolves away. The boys in this part of town don't hesitate to leer, wool hats pulled down over their foreheads, goatees and stubble, work boots and attitude spilling over. I picture those perfect little breasts, pale and trembling, pink nipples taut, revealing her desire. She buries it as deeply as I bury my secret, and when it's dark outside, dark inside, she lets it out, embraces it, tears on the pillow afterwards, as I hold her in my arms.

"Shower?" I ask.

"Yeah, I better. I stink."

"I'll clean up," I say.

"Thanks."

In the bedroom, I rub her back, and know this isn't for me. It's for her. She sleeps in one of my old grey shirts, and nothing else. It hangs down to her knees, but I run my hand up her thigh lifting her shirt, and hold her, rubbing, hold her tighter, breathing. Lavender and a hint of grease, vanilla and talcum powder and salt on my tongue. There's silence in the room, always this vacuum, broken by the creak of a bed spring, the rush of traffic in the distance, one street over, more rain, and the constant rattle of the window frame.

It's the rocking of a boat on a trembling lake. We drift, and we don't talk, we don't make ourselves larger than we are. It's as base and rudimentary as we can be. It's the need of one animal to be taken, and the other to take. She always gasps when I enter her, as if startled. And that's not far from the truth. We're always startled, jumping at a loud noise, twitching, unable to be still. And yet, the urgency with which she pushes back at me, wanting me deeper, fusing our flesh to each other, this one moment of beauty in our lives, it's always hidden under a cloud of despair. Even when we finish together, her nails digging into my arm, calling out to higher powers, asking for forgiveness, asking to be seen, even then it leaves me empty. I assume she's equally raw.

She sighs, and I don't ask where she is. I know. She's thinking of him, her boy. It's where her mind always wanders when there is pleasure, when she relaxes. Against all will. When she says yes to the pleasure, she says yes to the pain. I slide my hand around her waist, and no matter what she does, I'm always willing, always ready. She reaches back and grabs my thigh, the need in that one gesture, to be whole, it washes over me, and I'm too scared to deny her.

The buildings fly past me and my eyes are anywhere but on the road. A slice of cold air cuts at my face, the city black and blue. Cigarette smoke fills the cabin, my hand searching for another light. Turning the wheel as I lean over, head ducked below the dash, a wave of panic washes over me. There's no way I'm keeping this car on the road. I straighten up and everything is fine. It was only a little drift, a bit of panic. The music gets louder, hands banging on the steering wheel, head bobbing up and down and now I do need another smoke. The cigarettes only appear when the edges get dull, whispering in a stranger's ear, asking for a favor. That sharp stab in the lungs balances the dull stupor that blankets me. Flashes of green leather bar stools, pints of amber lined up on tables, the jukebox crowded with musical genius, the pool cues snapping, dollar bills dropped on the sticky bar, eyes caressing tight jeans, and tattoos on the small of a back, descending down into pink lace panties, a sly grin returned. I'm anywhere but here.

I lean in to click the flame, cupping my hands, leaning over, and this time, I drift too far. There is a shear of metal, a crack of glass, a groan that's machine, or maybe it's me, a jolt, a bounce, and I'm back on the road, never stopping. The cigarette has fallen in my lap, burning a hole through my jeans. I'm slapping at my thighs, the car swerves again, and my eyes find the mirror, and the wreckage behind me. Bent and fractured bumpers lean out into the street, side panels dented and scratched, plastic scattered over the pavement, and one woman leaning over, a lump at her feet, her dark, stringy hair falling into her eyes. I keep moving, away, everything getting smaller. There's a shriek filling my ears, but it can't be true. I hear it anyway. I hear it every day of my life.

The car will be stolen, I make sure of that. Hosed down in a do-it-yourself car wash for seventy-five cents, there's little to betray my violence. My freedom comes cheap. And as I wander the streets over the next several months, unable to sleep, unable to eat, wasting away, the streets become my home. I'm the undead, shambling across the pothole-ridden road for something, anything to give my life meaning. I need someplace to go to keep me from coming unhinged, but unaware of my destination, the want I had minutes before, I become lost in a tornado of disjointed thoughts. My gut rolls over in disgust, back alleys filled with my vomit, my wrists scarred with scabbed over slashes, I'm unable to break through to the darkness that awaits me. I'm a coward in so many ways. I stand in the rain, allowing it to seep through my coat, my flesh no longer my own. Every flashing light that passes by is a beacon to my demise. Every siren song that pierces my thoughts is a call to make it right. When I see her standing in the diner, hands on her hips, dead weight behind her eyes, her face slack, I realize there is one thing I can do. I can bring her back to life.

I give her the truth on an ordinary day. It's the release she's been praying for. I hand her the gun and the phone. I ask her to decide. With a shaky hand and eyes filled with fire, she does.

THE WEIGHT OF CONSCIOUSNESS
by Tim Beverstock

MIDDAY 12 P.M.

You're gone. Not among the discarded clothes piled next to the bed. Used condoms. Jim Beam bottles heaped near me. I can't hear your voice among the chrome pipes and car sirens. Shouts of neighbors' arguments. I know you haven't left here. I rummage among the clothes. Patting pockets. A lighter and bent cigarettes fall into my palm. Next to the blister that wasn't there last night. I probe the surface. Soft and yielding. The size of a quarter. I pick up my shirt. See the chunk missing from under the arm. Feel the matching throb in my side. My shoulder muscles ache like twin forks. Conduct my disorientation like lightning. I continue the search elsewhere. Narrow hallway greets me. Thick with fermentation. Both bulbs blown. Floor sticky under my feet. I haven't emptied the trash in days. The kitchen reveals more bottles. Empty pizza boxes. Sink overflowing with dishes. A bloody handprint and a knife. A trail on the floor. Like a junkie I follow the drips down the hallway. Stop outside the bathroom door. Listen. I can't hear you breathing. The seconds tick like sands in an hourglass. I knock a sharp staccato. Feel the echo bounce back. Push the door open without an answer. Find you curled round the toilet. Clad in your underwear. Protecting yourself. I shiver. See the open window. Goosebumps on your leg. I reach down. Feel skin cold to the touch. The blood pools from the center of you. Like a scarlet well for me to drown in. I black out.

AFTERNOON 4 P.M.

I stand in front of the bathroom mirror. Knuckles bleeding white. My right bigger than my left. Like it hit something. The blister has burst. My hand bathed in warm glycerine. I put the lid of the toilet down. Sit with my head in my hands. Lungs full of tar and the weight of diminished returns. I refuse to look down and acknowledge you. I'm spiraling. The day before. Drunk and home early. Too much to take. You left me sitting in my chair. Jim and Johnny for company. Still entertaining me when you came home. Early evening. Not happy. I come back to now. Open my eyes between slatted fingers. You haven't moved from your spot. I cover you up and leave. Find the cigarettes by the bed. Smoke alone. A fly rattles the window. Caught in a web. Sun filtered through sulphur tint. We're trapped together. The nicotine subdues the pounding in my head. The memory refuses to return. Stubborn like its owner. I light another cigarette. Formulate a plan of attack. I boil coffee until the ring sends up smoke signals. Drink a cup full of tar. My limbs become energized. Under the bed I find the last object you touched. Cold steel kisses my hand. Shields me. Images burst in camera flashes across my retina. I remember. More drinking, spilled wine. Me yelling. You yelling louder. A slap. You fall against the bench. Pull the knife from the drawer. Falling over and over. Like me now. On hands and knees I pass out by the door. Grasping with both hands. The gun wasn't this heavy when I bought it.

Consciousness

DUSK 8 P.M.

Come to lying on the floor outside the bedroom. Warm copper on my tongue. Carpet rubbing sandpaper across my cheek. My head throbs like a beaten heart. My first instinct was wrong. The holes in you came from bullets. Not a blade. I crawl back into my room. Sit up against the bed. Sniff the gun barrel. Residue of powder round the rim. My sweat matching yours on the trigger. Flashback to last night. I'm watching you from the doorway. Bent over my nightstand. Writing. I interrupt the note. Your hand in the drawer. Our yelling cancels each other out. The gun shaking in your hands. I'm pressed close to your body. Taste aluminum on your breath. Feel the bullet discharge. Wear a hole beneath my arm. A chunk from the doorframe. My hand on yours. Hot metal sears my palm. I gasp and drop. Barrel angled upwards. Two clean shots. A scream. Not my own. The sounds of running. Bathroom door slammed. Crying. Not my tears.

MIDNIGHT 12 A.M.

The gun twirls round my finger. I lie on the bed. Shoulders pinned back. Silhouetted by a solitary bulb. I hold up the photo of us. Pulled from my wallet. I love the way you lean into me. Your smile. On our anniversary. How did we stray so far. I pick up a bottle. Throw it against the wall. See my guilt reflected back in the shards of glass. I run my hand over the fragments. Don't wince when I feel them bite. Can't start over.

DAWN 4 A.M.

I sit at the table. Old T-shirt wrapped around my hand. Note in front of me. Read in disbelief. Pen marks slash my psyche. I shred the paper. Words fall to the ground like bullets. Last night was a warning. Next time you would leave. Yet the bag in the closet is new. Packed and ready. Proof that you lied to me. Another chance lost. I pick up the whiskey bottle and clear two mouthfuls. Wince as the liquid scrapes my throat. Soothe with the last cigarette. I can't believe you went for the gun. I wouldn't have hurt you. I'm guilty of not seeing until too late. I want your forgiveness. Even in the bathroom I still can't look at you. Tears fall into the sink like melted snow. Bleached to white heat. Consume my vision. All I know.

MORNING 8 A.M.

I phoned the cops. The least I could do for us. They will be here soon. This won't wait. I pick up the gun. Slide the chamber round with my thumb. Squeeze. An empty click. Repeat. Primed. Press the barrel to my temple. Pull the trigger. Explode.

IF YOU LOVE ME

by Doc O'Donnell

IF YOU LOVE ME, she says, you'll do this.

She hands me a razor blade.

A cigarette dangles from my lip, ash spilling onto my lap. I stub it out because I'm not smoking it. Distracting myself. My lips feel empty and I find myself reaching for another cigarette but stop.

Beads of sweat bubble over my forehead and slide into my eyes.

Her bunny sleeps on her lap. Fur so white it looks like it would burn to touch. She puckers and its red eyes flick open. She folds down its floppy ears, kisses it and sits it on the bed. It watches me from behind crumpled sheets and I try to avoid direct eye contact.

My hands are still, but I shudder from the inside out. The anticipation sets off a stampede in my heart. I hold my forearm where I plan to cut, and I breathe in the deepest breath. I imagine my flesh falling open as though it isn't strong at all, just pretending to be. A chill creeps over my skin in the shape of the scar-to-be and gives me goosebumps. I rub the skin, trying to warm it. But it stays cold, regrettably cold.

The gold flecks in her green eyes flicker like tiny fires. Brilliant embers setting the Amazon ablaze. It means she wants me to start. I push back her dark bangs and lean in to kiss her, but she shies away. I wait for her to wink and tell me it's all a joke.

She doesn't wink.

The regret I will later feel when I meet a different girl envelopes me.

Who's Suzannah? the girl will ask.

And I'll mumble, trying to forget that part of my life and wishing I could cut off my arm.

But something inside of me is begging to be loved, to be wanted, to be needed—maybe even begging to be owned.

I tell myself I can wear long sleeves. I suck in a deep breath, holding it, clenching my teeth.

And I drag the blade down my arm.

The fire in her eyes spreads to her face and she smiles, without teeth. A strange kind of smile. Scary.

The cut isn't very deep. A surface scratch, at best. The thought of breaking open my own skin is terrifying. Blood dribbles out pathetically. It isn't open enough for blood to spill out—yet.

I dig the blade in deeper on the second letter and the fire leaps into my arm. The blade feels heated. The blood still isn't offensive. I apply more pressure with each letter, and by the end of her violently long name the blood flows out thick. Dark and sadistic. My sanity escapes through my open flesh, but I don't care anymore. I don't need to. She does.

She doesn't have my name engraved down her arm though.

My skin is open in the shape of *Suzannah* but, to me, it looks more like a mistake I wasn't meant to make.

I light a cigarette and draw back longer than normal. My lungs stretch and slap against my raging heart. I ash into the wound and it pops like crackling candy on a tongue. My head spins. I lie back. My arm dangles over the side of the bed. I have pins and needles in my hand. I clench and unclench my fist. Sharp tingles swarm.

We collect my blood in a schooner—her idea.

Blood trickles down my arm, running off my fingertips into the glass. It coagulates quicker than I expect. She pinches out one of the clumps and holds it out for her fucking bunny. She's feeding me to him. I'm hers now. And I'm nothing but rabbit food. The bunny sniffs at the blob and tests it with a flick of its tongue. It decides against me and scurries under the sheets. She drops the blood back into the glass and wipes her fingers on my jeans.

Smoke falls from my mouth. It moves through her hideous name like early morning fog through an empty park. I try to kiss her but she shies away. Again. Embers from the last fire flicker in her cruel, black eyes, waiting for a breeze to spread them to a fresh patch of greenery. She pinches the cigarette from my fingers and takes a long drag before stubbing it out.

If you love me, she says, you'll do this.

She hands me a nicotine patch.

TOUCH
by Pela Via

'We can't,' you said.

'Oh. Okay.'

'I'm sorry.'

'Don't apologize,' I said. 'We can just touch.'

'I hate this.'

'Shh.'

You tinkered with my breasts, drawing circles with your finger around my nipples.

You said, 'So light,' and emphasized the long i in *light*.

'What does that mean? Is that bad?'

'No. Just pale. They're the color of ballet shoes.'

'In thirteen years you've never said they were pale.'

'Mmm. Because men don't state the obvious.'

I considered this. Goosebumps on my skin followed the trail of your finger. I whispered, 'I thought that was all you stated.'

You didn't laugh at my jokes then.

Instead you looked up at me, and when you said, 'Only when you're driving,' I believed you wanted me to smile at you.

So I did.

I pulled your hand away and bit your forefinger.

'Ouch. I liked that,' you said.

I dropped your hand onto my stomach and laughed when it crawled like a tarantula back up my chest.

'Men don't critique breasts the way you're thinking,' you said. 'It's like reviewing a baby. You can't criticize a very young child? Same with tits.'

'Breasts.'

'I thought I was allowed to say tits.'

'When we're making love.'

'Right. The dirty talk clause. That's useless to me now.'

You sighed and I waited.

You said, 'No, breasts are nature's most perfect creation.'

'Nature's? Not God's?'

With or without humor—I've always wondered—you said, 'If God existed, he would have commanded that breasts be sheared off.'

You had fallen asleep there, your cheek smashed against my skin. It was late in the night and I felt like talking. Your comments were often severe in those days. Pregnant and fatalistic. The words infuriated me when I replayed them in my mind. Your disease created a pressure in me that could go nowhere, do nothing. It was a thing I had no license to hate.

'Your remark about God—wake up—only works if the god we know to be real had in fact existed. Wake up.'

'What? Why— Fine. Leave me alone. I don't care about God. Sleep.' You wiped the shared sweat from your cheek then palmed my breast and pretended to sleep.

Your hand was warm and my body wanted more. I didn't want you to know. I shuddered and tried to kill the thought.

'You do though,' I said. 'You must. Are you bitter because he doesn't exist, or because he does and he's cruel?'

'Liz.'

'What.'

'I love you.'

There was an urgency to your voice, a wakefulness that has always haunted me.

'So much,' you said. 'I could be happy if you were the only person left on earth with me.'

'No. Honey. You're forgetting Wes.'

'I'm not.' You wiped your face again and contemplated your answer. 'He's different. He owns a part of me, of us, but it's like my soul leaves my body to love him. Inside me, what I need to be whole and human . . .' Your voice trailed off and I prayed you'd go back to sleep.

After long terrible moments you said, 'When we were first married I worried I loved you too much. Even before that. The day I met you. All I wanted in the world was to touch your hair.'

'Shh. You don't love me that much. You probably have another family in Cabo. It's all lies.'

It wasn't, and you didn't acknowledge me anyway. But I had nothing else to say.

I could barely form the thoughts, but the words were there. My devotion to you, all the tepid nights of touching when I wanted to be fucking, that wasn't love. It was a heartbreaking obligation to some part of us I could no longer touch.

We never learned to lock our door. All the years we did secret things in quiet rooms, we never learned our lesson. I've always wondered what that said about us.

We were teenagers the first time it happened. In your bedroom while your family was at church, your body over me, your hand in my panties and your clothes on the floor. I heard him approaching. Ominous Sunday shoes hit the wood floor in a crescendo. But I couldn't be bothered. I was close. The door flew open and I didn't think to cover myself.

'Jesus Christ, Israel.'

I had never heard him use strong language, so I stared, sideways from the bed as I waited for him to go on.

'What's wrong with you? You have no shame?'

I wanted to laugh. But I felt the static rage in your body. So I held you. Your eyes still closed, face calm. Your blood was lava.

I cleared my throat, without a thought to what I might say next. 'Mr. Kaufman?'

His eyes popped forward from his face.

'*You* don't speak to me. And would you cover yourself? For Christ's sake.'

I pulled the sheet over both our bodies.

'I want you out of my home, Elizabeth. There was a time my son was stronger than this.'

Together we listened to the sound of his shoes falling on stair steps. The front door slammed shut and you asked me if I believed in God.

'I don't know.'

'I used to believe in loving fathers, more than omnipotent gods.'

You rested your cheek on my shoulder. 'I have neither,' you said.

'I know.'

It happened again, the morning after you fell asleep on my chest. I brought you your pills then opened your pants. 'Before the meds take effect. Let's just try.'

You frowned but I persisted. I had you in my mouth when I heard the clumsy kick at the door. I flipped over, wiped my face and covered you with a sheet, in one motion, as we were both assaulted by running legs and punchy fat arms. My body was a bridge as he climbed to his daddy.

'Who is this brown bear stomping on me?' I said.

'It's Wessey!'

I glanced up at you. Your eyes were new, like you had won a prize.

He threw himself onto you, bouncing and twisting. I watched and laughed. He giggled and made strange sounds for no reason. His hair was pure boiling chocolate, so shiny then, and eyes so deeply brown. You once compared them to discarded motor oil—these are the things I remember.

'Dada!'

'Yes?'

'Mama say— Dada! Dada!' You were staring right at him, inches from his face.

'What?'

'Momma say yester-night Dada say I have cookie? Okay, Dada? Okay?'

'Mommy said Daddy would let you have a cookie?'

'Huh.' He nodded his head. So vigorous it wobbled.

'Okay,' you said. 'I do whatever your mother wants.'

You never looked at me when I helped you. I took your arm and helped you balance, and we walked together in the long succession of baby steps that led from the bed to the bathroom.

I loved you in a strange way when I assisted you. My affection was endless and fierce, begging to be challenged; I could have slapped you. But you weren't playful then. If I was ever irritated by helping you, it was because you refused to see the humor in Parkinson's.

I hid this though. Your dignity was a bully.

You asked for different pills that morning.

'But you don't normally have these . . .'

'Because they impair my speech. Hand them to me.'

'But—'

'They impair my speech but they improve mobility. I want them today because I'll be alone with Wes. I'll need to be able to move.'

'Oh. I just didn't think these were the ones that . . .'

I didn't finish. Whatever I said then didn't matter.

Alone at the beach, I didn't think about you. I spent the afternoon sprawled on the sand, and I thought about what your disease threatened to steal from me. I thought about never making love again. It was too much. I cried into my towel and swore to myself I couldn't do it. I couldn't give up sex. The alternatives sickened me. The idea of reaching for you, for your flaccid body—

Driving away from the ocean, I turned onto our street as blue and red lights flashed onto our house. My hands twitched and my throat ached as I parked behind an ambulance. I have no memory of getting from my car into the house, but I know there were words repeating in my head.

What had you done.

You killed me that day. Have you ever had to hold your mouth with both hands?

They wouldn't let me see you then. They covered you with a sheet and all I wanted was to touch your body.

The house stayed dark after that, all browns and greys and whispered tones. Your dad had the pink eyes of a rabbit, though I never saw him cry. I watched him kneel on Wesley's lion rug and lower his head to the floor. His grief settled in his bones like cement. He doesn't go to church anymore.

Wesley only acknowledges you when he's angry, as though his rage is his sole source of confidence.

When he was five I heard him tell his best friend to please not touch him. 'It hurts my skin,' he said. 'Like you have claws.' I asked him about it when I put him to bed that night. He said, 'You too, Momma. I love you. But it's you too.' He doesn't remember the way you rubbed his back before he went to sleep each night. I've asked him.

His eyes get still.

He's discovered sex and I'm concerned. He loves sex and he bristles when I hug him.

I have to hate you some days.

Other days I wonder why God can't make himself exist.

Alone in my bed, I have a recurring dream in which you kiss me on the forehead and laugh below my ear and we touch.

LOVE

by JR Harlan

"CUT ME," she says, offering me a knife and an arm. My knife, my carving knife. Her arm is pale, veins pronounced.

Blue, thin.

I look into her cold grey eyes. I seek something there. Something pronounced. But all I get is a

tired

bloodshot

stare.

"No," I say, pulling on my beer. Our fridge is broken. The beer's been on the table for a week. I drink it still, even though it's

warm, flat.

I want to say something more. I want to see something there. Something profound. But all I can offer is a

tired

bloodshot

stare.

"What the fuck is wrong with you?" She screams, slamming the knife down onto the table. The knife belonged to my grandfather, then my father, and now it's

old, dull.

"Don't you even care anymore?" She seeks something with that. "You used to love me, you used to care, but now you're just a

tired

old

fool."

"Yeah," I say, noncommittal. Apathetic. Her makeup is smeared from sweat, from sex. She trembles with anger, with guilt. Her blouse is

wrinkled, torn.

I want to cut him. I want to do something bad to him. But he's not here, he's gone and ran away like a

scared

little

boy.

"Why won't you do anything?" She screams, again. She's in a rage, a fit. Her muscles tense, her jaw clenched. I almost want to laugh at her, but I stay

silent, still.

"You're pathetic," she says, quietly. "Call me names, call me a whore." She wants to feel justified with that. "If you loved me you

would

cut

me."

"No," I say. I take another pull on my beer. I'm surprised at myself. I should be the one in a rage, a fit. But I only feel

old, wasted.

I look at her again. I want to see something there. I want to remember the woman I married. But I can't. "No," I say again. "If I loved you, I

would

kill

you."

PRACTICE
by Bob Pastorella

"Remember Shelly Baxter?"

I paused for a few seconds, feigning remembering. "Yeah, I think."

Dave screamed into his radio, then came back to the phone. "You better remember her. You used to go out with her."

"Yeah yeah yeah." I closed my eyes against the smell of her hair, strawberries and cream, shook away the image of her crooked smile. "What about her?"

"Well, she did it. Hold on a sec . . ." Dave screamed into his radio again, came back. "Hey, call me later on tonight. Some lady just got hit crossing Highway 73. Dumb bitch thought she could just run across during the busiest part of the day."

"Later."

I closed my cell and stared at the computer screen in front of me. Filled with potential customers from the nationwide database, all the names and addresses blurred for a second. I blinked and everything looked normal again.

For a second, all of the names on the screen were Shelly's.

Seven months ago, she knocked on my back door just as I was leaving to go out for the night.

"Hey," she said. Her blond hair was the same old style yet different, longer maybe. The screen door made it difficult to see who was there, but her smile, reaching up higher on her right cheek, gave her away fast.

"Hey," I said, opening the screen door, "what's going on?"

"Just hanging out. Can I come in?"

I stepped aside. "How did you know I live here?"

She brushed past me, faint perfume hitting my nostrils. "I saw you coming home from work the other day. You still doing the insurance deal?"

"Yeah. You saw me. Where were you?"

"At the taco place. I can see your door from the drive-through."

"And you knew it was me?"

"Yep. Hey, can I use your phone?"

"Well, I don't have a landline."

"You got your cell?"

I nodded, reluctant. "I was about to leave."

"Don't worry, baby . . . I'll tell them not to call the number back."

I handed her my cell and stepped into the living room. One year had passed since I last saw her, maybe longer, and she knocked on my door like no big deal, and then she was in my apartment wearing her tight jeans and halter top. Sandals on her feet and a silver toe ring. Very sexy.

And calm.

Sitting on the sofa I tried to listen, but all I could make out was *come on man* and *damn it*. She snapped my phone shut and pounded her fist on my counter. When I walked back into the kitchen, she was facing away from me, propped against my refrigerator. The muscles in her triceps clenched for a second, then released.

"Everything okay?"

She turned and, for the briefest second, let her mask slip.

She smiled. "Sure. Boyfriend's a little pissed I ran out on him, but he'll get over it."

I forced my hands into my pockets to keep myself from touching her arms. "You need a ride somewhere?"

She shook her head. "Can I just crash here?"

"Well . . ."

"Just jacking with you, man. He's going to meet me back at the bar."

"The bar?"

"Yeah, Shorty's. You know, that place you hate."

"Oh yeah. Well, at least let me give you a ride."

"No. It's just right there. And besides, you look like you're about to go out."

"It's no problem. I—"

She was out the door and halfway down the steps. "Thanks for letting me use your phone. See you around."

I never saw her again.

My friend Waylon introduced me to Shelly. He had met her friend at the bowling alley the week before and set up a double date without asking me first. "Dude, I need a wingman," he said.

"That's really shitty of you, man."

"I'd do it for you."

Of course, he would have. When the night came around, he called me forty-five minutes before I was supposed to meet them. "They're here."

"At your house? Now?"

"Yes. I want your girl. She's hotter than mine."

I drove twenty miles in twelve minutes. He was right—I wanted my girl, too.

Shelly's hair was shorter then, with a slight curl. I'd seen her around, usually hanging out with people I didn't know, being loud and cutting up. "I know you," she said, holding out her hand. "Don't know your name, but I've seen you around."

I told her my name was Markus and she smiled. "You look like a Markus. Ready to party?"

Waylon drove his Tahoe, Shelly and I sat in the back. She leaned in close, whispered in my ear. "Why are you sitting so far away?"

"I don't know."

She wrapped her arm around my shoulder. "Loosen up a bit. You're like way too tense."

We played pool, ordering pitcher after pitcher of beer. She was a damn good player, better than I was, and drank like a fish.

"Don't go for that shot," she said, snaking her arm through mine, guiding the cue stick. "Tap the four ball slightly on the right and it'll sink in that corner pocket." She lined up the shot, stood behind me, and guided my arms into the cue ball. It tapped the four ball and rolled into the pocket, just like she said.

Shelly playfully punched my arm. "See?" I looked into her brown eyes, letting them get closer and closer until our lips touched, very gently. She pulled back, crooked smile beaming. "Now really kiss me."

I went in gentle again, then felt her arms wrap around my back. I touched her face and slowly ground my lips into hers, letting her tongue slide against mine.

She tasted like bubblegum.

Her hair was damp against her brow and she smelled like smoke. "Thanks for coming to pick me up. I feel like I'm going crazy." She was wearing a long-sleeved T-shirt and baggy shorts, her feet wrapped in a pair of dirty sneakers with no socks.

"What's wrong?"

"Take me to my mom's, okay? I'll tell you everything, but I have to get out of here."

I pulled out of the Walmart parking lot, watching her and driving at the same time. Shelly dug around in her purse, pulled out a prescription bottle and read the label. "Damn," she said, throwing it back into her purse.

She stared out the window the whole ride. When I pulled into her mom's, she jumped out of the car before it stopped rolling. "I'll be right back," she said, already on the front porch. She returned seconds later with a black garbage bag overflowing with shirts and jeans and a giant pillow in a pink pillowcase. She threw everything in the back, jumped in the front and grabbed my arm. "It's okay . . . right?"

"What?"

Her eyes brimmed over. "I don't have anywhere else to go."

Our second date started pretty wild and crazy. I picked her up at her mom's house and she immediately wanted to go to the mall because she didn't like what she was wearing. "It'll take me five seconds to buy this dress I saw the other day, change into it, and then we are hitting the road."

"Want me to come inside?"

"Just keep the engine running, 'kay? It's hot tonight."

Images of her shoplifting the dress, and no telling what else, kept sifting through my mind. Any second, the police would be pulling up to the front of the store, they would drag her out, and then she'd point at me and scream, "That's him, he made me do it."

When she walked out of the store, I knew she paid for the dress. It was too pretty to steal. Short and sleeveless, chocolate brown and snug, the color turned her tanned skin a shade darker, her blond hair a little brighter.

She wanted to go to Hampton's for a drink, then to Shorty's for more drinks. "Why don't we just stay at Hampton's?" I asked.

"They close too early. You don't have to work tomorrow or anything like that, huh?"

"No."

"Then I got you all night long. Unless you're tired, or a wuss."

"Definitely not a wuss. And I'm not tired."

She stopped in front of a curtained window outside of Hampton's, checking her reflection. "Damn it," she said. I watched as she reached underneath her dress and removed her panties. She smoothed the dress down her hips, turned and smiled at me. "That's much better." She tossed the panties into a nearby trashcan and linked her arm through mine. "Let's get to drinking."

"My pulse is over one hundred and my pressure is one sixty over ninety-eight. Well, that's according to the Walmart thing you sit in and it tells you your pressure for free. I don't think it's too accurate, but that's still too high." Shelly sipped her water then sighed. She was plopped on my sofa, dirty sneakers kicked off, breathing deliberately through her nose.

"Hungry?"

There wasn't much food in the icebox, but if she said the word, I'd order a pizza.

"Can't eat. Heart's beating too fast."

"What's wrong?"

"I don't know."

"You go to the doctor?"

She shook her head.

"Want to go to the hospital?"

"No."

Later that night, I came out of my bedroom and sunk into the recliner. After hitting the channel button on the remote for twenty minutes, I settled on a South Park rerun. Shelly slept soundlessly for a while, then woke up, coughing and checking her pulse. She stood up slowly and went to the bathroom. When she came back to the couch, she hooked her finger at me, inviting me over.

The first thing I noticed when I wrapped my arms around her was how hot she was.

"It's my blood pressure."

We touched and kissed a little, remembering how we liked each other's body. When my hand slid down her stomach close to her shorts, she stopped me.

"I can't," she said.

"What's wrong?"

"My heart. Something's not right. I'm scared to do anything, especially that."

My fingers felt for her pulse, and instead encountered a mass of scar tissue around her wrist. I turned her arm to look more closely. There was one scar around her wrist, white and raised. It seemed odd I never noticed it before. Along the inside of her arm was a longer scar, pink and jagged.

"What's this?"

Shelly shook her head. When she realized I wouldn't break my stare, she gave me a weak smile. "I had some problems . . . okay?"

"And this is how you tried to fix them?"

"No."

"These are recent, Shelly."

"No, the long one is. The one across my wrist is from years ago."

"I never noticed it before."

"You never bothered to look."

I stared at her arm. "What kind of problems?"

She didn't say anything for a long time. Finally, she coughed and whispered. "It's okay. My problems are not bugging me right now."

"What do you call this?" I said, running my fingers down the long scar.

"Practice."

FADING GLORY
by Brandon Tietz

"Such a pity I can't wear these anymore," Ms. Murtoil mentions from her daybed, easing a 24-carat band over the wood-like fingernail. The inner edge of the ring scrapes off some of the carnation pink finish, revealing that plank of seaweed brown underneath as it flakes away.

Around the age of sixty this happens: the nail plates of the toes and fingers will begin their swell to a nickel coin thickness, typically due to poor circulation, or: *Arteriosclerosis*. They'll progressively become more tan. Less polished. And extremely brittle.

Common knowledge if you're an elderly healthcare professional.

"Oh dear," Ms. Murtoil says in her flimsy voice, squinting at her own hand. "Looks like we'll be painting my nails again," she sighs, pushing the gold loop down her polish-dusted ring finger, where it stops short on a ballooned knuckle. Merely one in a series as each digit has at least one disfigured knot from Osteoarthritis, like huge chunks of cartilage gravel. "Interphalangeal jewelry roadblocks," they're sometimes called.

The staff at Silver Oaks has all sorts of medical monikers.

"Bryce, my dear?" Ms. Murtoil says, dumping the ring onto her bedside table next to a ruby-crusted and platinum number that no longer fits. Both of them will eventually end up in the cherry wood jewelry box with the rest of the can't-be-worns. She decides with a slight nod, "Today . . . the diamonds from Malachi, I believe," her face brightening with an expectant smile. Or senility.

Yesterday she called me Barry.

Before that, it was Barton.

The nameplates of the staff at Silver Oaks adhere to the first initial/last name formula, so Ms. Murtoil always addresses me with some variation of a "b" name.

Today it's Bryce.

This is completely normal coming from someone with Alzheimer's. Or: *Dementia*. It's not selective memory. More like a filing down of the mind. When an octogenarian resident can recall a hot August night back in 1944 but doesn't know if they had a Reuben or beef Wellington for lunch, the brain (quite literally) has begun to rot.

There's plenty Ms. Murtoil either confuses or can't remember: names, medications, what day it is. Not once though, has she misremembered a piece of jewelry.

The same woman who couldn't tell you if she's gone to the bathroom in the last hour is a human catalogue of necklaces, tiaras, and broaches, right down to the date received and country of origin. Today, she wants the diamonds from Malachi, tilting her cotton candy-laden head forward as the piece is strung around her aged neck. Ms. Murtoil habitually smoothes her hands upward from the base of her skull, clearing any stray hairs from being caught in the links even though she has the same short-and-wispy do as every other resident.

Silver Oaks has over forty female tenants; all of them have the same stark white haircut. *Melanocytes*, which are the cells responsible for producing hair pigment, eventually run out of coloring product. Like the brain, everything about you will dry up and deplete. Until you're nothing but bones.

But diamonds are forever.

Gold never tarnishes.

"So lovely to be wearing this again," Ms. Murtoil comments, smiling in wrinkles and crow's feet as I poise the silver hand mirror a couple feet in front of her, framing all those heavy stones dripping from her neck, making their individual impressions. By the time she takes these off, her chest will look hail-damaged.

"Memory foam skin," the Silver Oaks staff calls it.

As the dermal and hypodermal layers begin to degrade, your birthday suit becomes more prone to things like rashes, tears, and bruises from hip-checking tables and bumping doorjambs. Magenta veins on either side of the nose means a resident is carrying too much weight in the eyewear department. An ankle-to-knee eczema breakout suggests wool socks or a reaction to the laundry detergent. Danger is everywhere, always hiding in commonality.

In this specific case: heavy rare stones. Already, that necklace stringing the ice along Ms. Murtoil's collarbone gutters is searing a red line across the back of her neck. Segmenting and dividing liver spots.

And just like yesterday, the warning comes.

"No more than an hour, okay, Ms. Murtoil?" I say. This isn't so much a suggestion as it is a reminder, just in case she forgot (and that's quite possible). Working at Silver Oaks is about knowing people's limits. Anything past the sixty-minute mark and that chain will saw its way through the epidermis enough to leave a signature.

Reverse-side strangulation.

Ms. Murtoil admires the stones in the mirror, saying, "Please, dear, call me Glory," as she drags a couple fingers down their slopes. Those flawlessly cut edges. "How many times must we have this conversation, Bernie?" she asks, a smile broadening across her face that almost looks youthful and girlish. The eyes fixated on diamonds, frosty with memories and the denaturation of lens protein, or: *cataracts*.

Her poor vision is what allows me to slide an antique pearl broach into one of my pockets, a little Victorian number with an amethyst foliate plaque. This was part of last week's showcase along with the treble clef ruby pendant and white gold charm bracelet.

She turns her milky blue eyes to me—to "Bernie," and asks, "Did I ever tell you about how I used to be in the pictures?" but Ms. Murtoil states this less like a question, and more like a conversation-starter.

"I even did a Howard Hughes film once, in the late '30s," she says. "Although, back then I went by Gloria. People said Glory sounded too . . . um . . . well, I can't remember what they said," she laughs, a veiny, spotted hand briefly touching mine. Not flirtatious.

Forlorn.

And lonely.

The family of Ms. Murtoil rarely ever visits. Unfortunately, she's always under the belief they'll be coming that day, and thus, becomes the victim of constant disappointment. Most residents experience some variation of this.

Down the hall, Dino Gosland wakes up at six o'clock every morning to play golf with his older brother, the same one who's got machines breathing for him three states away.

Clara Cantu gets all dolled up for coffee with her longtime friend, Miss Marilyn De Colti from Catalina, even though she died over nine years ago from wasting syndrome, or: *cachexia.*

Once you reach a certain age, the brain hardwires specific routines and notions.

"The permanent delusion," the staff of Silver Oaks calls it.

This is right about the time when Ms. Murtoil announces, "My son will be bringing in the grandchildren, Bernie—so . . . we need to get me back to my old Hollywood self," delivering a motivating slap to my knee. She says, "I want to look like a star for them . . . the diamonds are a good start," and the wrinkly knotted fingers smooth the stones once more, swimming with fragmented memory.

The majority of families visit an average of twice a year: on Christmas and birthdays, and the Murtoils are no different in that regard. When you're paying an $8,000 per month residence fee, it's easy to convince yourself that taking time off work to see your mother isn't exactly convenient. Staying away requires even less effort the first time you see pressure sores or a bony hand clutching a tightening chest, also known as: *Angina*.

Mr. Murtoil sends the check for eight grand like clockwork, operating under that out-of-sight-out-of-mind mentality as his mother continuously slips further away, a sort of mutual forgetfulness.

"He will come today, Bosco," Ms. Murtoil states firmly, giving her wrists a dab of lilac fragrance before sliding one set of tendons over the other, part of the preparation routine. This would be dangerous under normal circumstances because of the alcohol content, a component that is notorious for causing dry skin and rashes in the elderly. However, part of any Silver Oaks elderly caregiver's job is prevention, and the perfume was replaced with a non-irritating substitute some years ago. A few lacerating square and princess cut diamond rings got the same switcheroo treatment.

A "safety swap," the staff calls it.

This is also used with: toiletries, oral hygiene and hair products. Relatives are the worst about this. At least once a week some family member brings in a $40 lotion or $60 coloring product that has to be confiscated. They're completely ignorant to the adverse effects of triclosan-laced soaps or retinoid-harboring anti-aging creams. We've all seen a lot of harm done in the name of "just being nice" here at Silver Oaks.

Ms. Murtoil shakily dabs the lanolin-free lipstick on her mouth, a few rosy smears going outside the lines on the upper lip, or: *The Vermillion Border,* but these are gently corrected with a tissue. Just like yesterday's smudged mascara and overindulgence of blush, the errors are carved back to their original negative space of wrinkles and loose skin.

"Malachi Abramowicz gave me these diamonds while we were courting," Ms. Murtoil says, pouting her lips. "Right before the premiere of one of my movies— and oh, *Bosco* . . . you should have seen the gown I wore that night."

Floor-length red dress. Sequined.

I've heard the story, seen the pictures.

The term "a broken record" is a direct reference to the elderly telling their tales over and over, and that doesn't just include Ms. Murtoil and her Tinseltown adventures. No resident is without a story he repeats ad nauseam.

Mr. Cardiff will talk your ear off about fighting the Nazis in WWII if you let him. His kill count usually goes up a couple each week.

Ms. Parlour used to own a French bakery. The result of these conversations is getting her secret family recipes for apricot croissants or vanilla cheesecake, but with a couple of ingredients added or omitted in the retelling. Obscured, along with the names of her grandchildren and dead husband's favorite TV show.

At Silver Oaks, the residents are provided a quality of life like none other: the most luxurious furnishings money can buy, a meal plan that borders on gourmet standards, but most importantly, an attentive staff. These are a few of the reasons why all those rich sons and daughters can go months on end without the guilt eating them alive. They've outsourced their undivided attention. Transferred their responsibility. The rest of the elderly care assistants and I—we actually listen. Not necessarily because we're interested. Depending on how much a story changes, this is how one gauges exactly how far the mind has slipped without running an MRI. This is how you can tell if a diamond necklace or Civil War pistol can go missing without reprisals.

A face powdering and majorite-adorned anklet later, Ms. Murtoil asks, "They're not coming . . . are they, Bradford?" her optimism shrinking along with her torso and appendages. Her neck. Right after your hair follicles and skin begin to dry out, your sense of hope follows shortly after. It's a medically proven fact of life.

"Moments of clarity," the staff calls it.

Ms. Murtoil hasn't had one of these in over four months. This is part of the regular status updates sent to the immediate family, along with any allergies or medications they're on. It's also the reason why her son hasn't visited Silver Oaks since Christmas, two years ago. Quite a bit lower than the average, but some people just can't handle it. Or don't want to.

"When he comes . . . you have to make sure that I'm ready, Bradford," Ms. Murtoil says, shaky, trembling hands clutching mine from a substantial loss of nerve cell function, or: *Parkinson's.*

Or maybe she's scared of being so close to the end, tears turning the blush and mascara muddy. A tissue is plucked out of a nearby Kleenex box, dabbed ever so lightly on the sagging face of Ms. Murtoil, and yet another pearl necklace disappears into my pocket. Two more sets of emerald earrings as she squeezes her eyes shut to blow her nose.

She says with a sniff, "I want to look my best . . . with my diamonds, and you can do the makeup, Bradford—and they'll . . . remember me right."

Sooner or later, every resident makes mention of how they want to be found: in their favorite dress or armed services uniform, an ensemble they feel best reflects who they were in the prime of their lives.

"The death-day suit," we call it.

Besides Christmas and birthdays, this is the only other occasion where the family is obligated to visit Silver Oaks. Beyond the legal commitment to collect their dead, the Murtoils will have plenty of jewelry to claim, but maybe not as much as they thought. It is, after all, the only thing they didn't get an exact inventory on, unlike the estate and foundations that were seized from her control, when Mr. Murtoil had her deemed mentally incapable of performing her duties, or: *legally incompetent.*

He stuck her in Silver Oaks, waiting for this geriatric bond note of a woman to mature her way into a coffin so he could collect the residuals, left her here to pee on plastic-covered couches with her jewelry and delusions of loving family. The rat bastard said to his mother, "I'll come visit you all the time."

From that point on, the record began to skip.

Those are the words I remember every time a ruby hairpin or Columbian black pearl pendant slips inside my pockets. With every diaper change and crying fit, Mr. Murtoil is giving me what any stockbroker, realtor, or financial planner would: a cut.

"When it happens . . . make me look like a star again," Ms. Murtoil requests in a desolate tone, officially reaching that point where she's stopped focusing on living and is now planning out the circumstances of her demise.

The "short-term will," we call it.

"A Hollywood star . . . just like when I did the Howard Hughes film," Ms. Murtoil says, a renewed smile emerging, waves of nostalgia flashing over milky blue eyes as she drapes the diamonds with her bumpy fingers. "Did I ever tell you about how I used to be in the pictures, Benjamin? Those were wonderful times."

LITTLE DEATHS

by Gary Paul Libero

"HERE IS YOUR COVER. It must go on prior to entering the shell. This will all be explained in due time."

The little freak speaks at me like I'm some toddler. I think there's make-up around his narrow eyes, although he may be a she. It's harder than ever to tell.

"Once inside, it is imperative that you move as little as possible."

He's not looking at me. I'm not here.

"You've purchased our finest module," the freak says. "I understand your potential final release will be here with us?"

My shrug doesn't answer his question exactly. Regardless, he keys a reply in the handheld device he's been caressing since I walked in.

"Great then! I'll just need your autograph here, Mister McEweeee?"

He extends the last name far too long, passes me the handheld device and a stylus.

"Terrific! We hope you enjoy your time with us, sir. One of our technicians will be out shortly to explain the details of your package and will assist you into the shell. I believe," he looks at his computer, "Marilyn has been assigned to you. She's a diamond!"

Charlie presented me with an envelope a week after we met with the doctors. Before they uttered a word I saw it in their faces and Charlie asked how long. They said three months.

The cancer spread.

"Pop, this shouldn't be a sad time for you. For us."

My mouth shaped the words *I love you Charlie*. Before I opened the envelope, he explained the contents.

"This place, it's where people go these days, for companionship. They're not selling call girls, nothing like that. This is high class, and high tech. The most advanced virtual intimacy a person can experience."

I pulled the gift certificate from the envelope. He watched my eyebrow rise.

"It's one of the larger accounts I've been working with. We began selling materials to them six months ago.

I don't know about this, Charlie.

"They offer a special package for," it pained Charlie to say, "the terminal."

The doctors agreed to release me for one day only. They told Charlie because of my weakened state, being away from the hospital could kill me. He told them we were willing to take the risk.

As they say, go out with a bang.

"Mr. McEwe? May I call you Ralph?" a voice sweet as apple wine asks at my back.

I turn in my waiting chair and she's there, just as the little freak promised.

A diamond.

"My name is Marilyn. I'll be assisting you today."

She flashes a smile that could put out the sun.

I slip one arm from a sleeve and she's quick to help me out of the rest. She bends down close to me, eye to beautiful eye. My old face goes beet soup. In my ear,

"There is nothing, and I mean nothing, to be embarrassed about here."

Marilyn works each button, buckle and snap holding my clothes together. Her hands in sheer gloves bring arousal to parts that haven't worked so well in many moons.

"Ralph, if I may ask," careful with her question, "what is sex like in the later years?"

My sweet, have you ever shot pool with a rope?

She laughs at the childish expression on my face. "I see. You're a quiet one. The strong silent type. I like that in a man," selling me every step into the grave.

The diamond guides me toward an oversized egg.

"As I'm sure Singh told you at the front desk, it is very important to move as little as possible during the experience. The module will guide your actions once you are sealed inside."

I nod.

Without asking she takes the shriveled wrapper in my hand.

"This is strictly for sanitation of the shells."

She guides me inside the rubber cover. It fits as I remember condoms did, and warmer.

"For most terminals, the pleasure shell experience can be intense and overwhelming." She looks down at her feet and giggles. "Do you know how Shakespeare described the orgasm?"

I shake my head.

"Little deaths," she says.

We share a smile. She guides my rickety bones into the shell and looks right through me before the egg's door slides between us. She blows me a kiss. A series of electronic sounds confirm the door is sealed.

It's quiet, then, "Good morning, Ralph," a woman says. "My name is Glo. I will be your companion during your pleasure module."

There is no face to match the voice.

"Ralph, I will need you to relax with your back against the rear of the shell. You will feel the foam material conform to your entire body, save your head and neck regions. It is imperative that you remain still during this process."

A cool air washes over my face

"Close your eyes and relax. We will begin momentarily."

That smell.

Woman.

Nurses never smell like this.

"Ready?" the voice asks.

I nod.

Blinding green light falls over me. A woman's face appears, intimately close to mine. Her body pressed against me. She's strong and ageless.

"I've been waiting for you. Do you find me attractive?"

I nod again.

I understand. Your condition restricts speech. I will speak internally, while taking care of you . . . externally.

That freak said nothing about mind control.

This is not mind control, Ralph. It's simply your pleasure module. You have nothing to fear. Just let me do the work. You don't have to think a word.

The egg vibrates and moves. I can't tell if I'm standing or lying. The foam adjusts and tightens. Her hands touch mine. She runs them over my body, my face, my cover.

I will do anything for you, Ralph. I am at your service. I want to make you happy.

Please, don't stop.

I haven't spoken in months.

I miss this connection, even if it's with an egg.

I am not an egg, Ralph. My name is Glo. I am at your service. Now, let's begin.

The doctors said this could kill me.

I hope they are right.

WE SING THE BAWDY ELECTRIC
by Rob Parker

HER LIPS SLIDE CROOKED across shatterproof teeth as she squishes my root between her biodegradable fingers and diddles my prosthetic perineum. Servos whir in cadence with our pelvic writhing, and they nearly obscure the hum and grind of webcams crusted to the blank white walls that squint and zoom in medical-grade fluorescent lights.

Her eyes, fresh from the far side of the uncanny valley are twin black lenses adrift in seminal globes, set apart with the hint of epicanthic folds. Her face framed by a mane of wild purple hair. Our bodies designed to exude adolescent virility: hairless groins, twenty feminine fingers between the two of us, her breasts frozen in pubescence: perky and palm-sized, my perfect porcelain teeth laden with braces, even. I register braces incising the polyurethane underside of my lips as our foreplay subroutines play through truncated abstractions of the mythical reality of copulation.

Our kisses are quiet and shy, and her smiles furtive, meant only for me—even as they were filtered through a massive processing unit and reproduced the world over. Simulated sweat filters to skin surface and we caress it away. Our programming a nested series of complementary subroutines such that we know exactly what the other wants. The intimacy of having no expectations, no designs, no agenda. No matter how our servos tremble, we finger force-feedback pads beneath the skin with languor, breathing slowly and shuddering.

Every time is the first time. Each new position dizzying, individual as the pattern of mass-produced fingerprints we leave all over each other. We tumble over the edge of every fetishized maw of depravity and come out the other side, wide-eyed, breathing hard. Our movements and feelings recorded, replicated, broadcast and rebroadcast in syndication. Each orgasm a flurry of pixel and data. Patterned chaos. A self-replicating archive of raw footage to be edited and recut for digital distribution.

The tender moments we keep for ourselves, light caresses that barely crease the padding of flesh over our metal and plastic infrastructure, too light to register and trigger the recording pressure plates.

Inside her, I modulate my rhythm, deep shallow, deep shallow deep-deep and her lenses widen in their globes of fluid, her mouth open slightly; the slick lump of vat-grown tongue peeking from behind her teeth as she registers my thrusts in ones and zeroes. We tingle with the thrill of having a secret, speaking a code nobody in the millions of voyeurs could catch. She digs her fingers into the interlocking plastic of my spine, twitching and kneading out a response with her fingernails. We move faster and faster with learned excitement until my programming fires a subroutine and I pull out, vocal chip procedurally emitting a configuration of grunts until I expend ropes of oily synthosperm onto her beaming, silent face.

The system operators in the next room cut power to our gyros and we drop on top of each other, feel the bottom drop out from our RAM and the cold fingers of sysops on our command prompts as they grope for sensory perceptions and scenes that would soon be edited for maximum erotic impact.

A limited awareness trickles back into us from the streaming feeds, the haptic feedback conjuring a metonymy of fleshy alien bodies: our audience. Slack jaws, gelatinous limbs attached to bulbous torsos with engorged, slavering genitals rubbed raw by technology. Eyes swiveled nervously toward the windows where atrophied forests feed upon mounds of dead and dying under the eye of a swollen sunset as they mutter obscenities in response to their simulated, our simulated sex; our love and affection camouflaged by a jungle of erections.

IN EXILE
by Chris Deal

IT WAS TEN YEARS before he saw the sun clearly. For the entirety of that time he remembered those last moments, the warmth flowing down over him as he walked off the bus, wrists and ankles chained and the whole of him connected to the person in front of and behind him. He soaked it in, willing time to slow until the world between heartbeats stretched out past the horizon, memorizing that light and that warmth on his face before it was gone and he was in the dark, the quiet.

They were children together, their parents friends and they became the same. At five they were each other's first kiss, long before they knew what came with such an act. The two ran and held hands, and they smiled, they were always smiling. The girl, her face covered with freckles, would dance and the boy would watch. He'd be quiet for a long time, just observing her. For the girl, dancing couldn't be explained. The movement of her body in time with the music felt right. The boy, he would disappear into himself for long stretches. The days he and the little girl weren't together were days when no words sprang from him; only she could bring them out. He was her audience when she imitated the people in the movies her mother took her to, the plays, and he didn't understand the appeal at first. To him, dancing was just something you did, not something you cared about. Watching her, though, the way she stuck her tongue between her lips as she perfected each move, it'd bring things out from him, words that stayed sacred between them.

The boy's mother went away when he was young and his father became given to long stretches of absence. It infected the boy, the itch for elsewhere crawling behind his eyes. He'd walk out into the woods and find a place to be alone. He smelled the ground like a beast and ate roots until his stomach retched and then he'd walk back inside. When he was older, he'd buy a ticket and show up at the bus station, the idea being he'd leave school behind, his father, the empty house, the hole in the ground, just go away and be forgotten, living on in no one's memories. He once made it four hours away. He stood in the dull corona of a street-light among the exiles, somewhere outside of nirvana. He bummed a cigarette because he thought it the thing to do and drank coffee that cost a quarter a cup and when it came time to move on, his feet were stuck. He closed his eyes and saw the girl. He bought one more ticket and got home as the sun breached the horizon.

Both knew friendship to be the most fragile of things, and as they moved apart through life, the girl and the boy would remember the other, running through fields and coming home covered in mud, and they would smile, a sacred motion given to no one else. The conversations grew scarce, the boy's words even more so. The girl kept dancing. Practiced and careful, calluses ripped across the balls of her toes. Each movement meant something, the routines told a story she shared with the world. They came to see her dance, people with money and people with love.

She left before him, kissing her mother goodbye and going where she could hone her skills. She did not give him a goodbye, nor did he seek one out. He went to work and each day was the same as those that came before, on and on like an infinity mirror. His eyes grew dull and he thought only of food and shelter. He collected maps of places he had never been and made plans to vanish, but when the day would come, he'd get up early in the morning, have a breakfast of coffee and cigarettes and go to work. When he returned home, he would sit down in his apartment and turn on his television. One night as the world slept on around him, he watched the patterns of static move over the television screen, thinking there to be something important hidden in the chaos. His body went concrete stiff when the blast of virtual snow developed into the thin lines, the crooked nose of his father. The old man's voice took a tight grip on his attention, and the son was offered a job.

The girl made friends fast in her new home, those she trained with. They danced for hours, the same moves and the same routines repeatedly until they were crisp and perfect. She was the best of them, and though some hated her for it, most smiled and asked her for help. She grew stronger in body and mind. Men watched her as she moved down the street, each step holding a world's worth of grace. One day, it was her turn. She was the person everyone came to watch, the person her friends supported, their movements giving agency to her own, and with one last pure pirouette the audience stood and roared her name. Weary but floating, she at first resisted when her friends tried to take her out to celebrate, but because of the buzzing in her very being, she relented. At a quiet bar she met a man with a pleasant smile. She woke up in the morning with the elation of the previous night gone, in its place was pain, her face bruised and the man gone. She forgot him and the haze of the night. During the long weeks of practices for her next performance she was off. Her body did not move in the way she expected it to, her muscles were given to more ache. She could feel the dreams she'd held sacred since she was a girl being ripped apart.

He only spoke when someone asked something of him. Conversations were rare and his coworkers thought him an object, less a person, and he was fine with that. Snow came in its time and he liked the clearness of it. He began to think of the large, clean fields as his own mind. He woke one quiet day, the world stretching out like a blank canvas, and he decided on a drive. He found his father in a slovenly motel room on the outer rim of town. The father handed the son a set of keys that belonged to the car he'd last seen his father drive away in and made him promise to burn it somewhere hidden. He took that junker through the roads out to the low hills beyond town, his momentum carrying him closer to the mountains that loomed like sleeping giants. As the tires hummed over the ice and the slush, there came a sharp curve. Long stretches of emptiness had dulled him, and he turned his eyes to a black bird paused in the middle of a pure, white field. When he looked back to the road, the passenger side tires were veering over the shoulder. A police cruiser was stopped just ahead, the officer hunched over his open trunk. He jerked the wheel but the force of his movement caused the tires to lock up and he kept sliding forward, the weight of his car colliding with the cruiser, pinning the officer between the two vehicles. For a thin moment he thought that this was it, that he would pull back and keep driving, not even going back home for what few objects he cared about. He would empty his bank account and travel south, racing his deed to Mexico where he would tan and learn a new tongue and maybe meet a woman he could hold at night who would remind him in her quiet movements of the first girl. He got out of the car and waited beside the officer, splayed over the hood, as more police traveled fast towards them. The paramedics put the officer into an ambulance and the police, they checked the car's plates and saw there was an alert out for it, for the driver. They asked for permission to search the vehicle and consent was given. Opening the trunk, three officers stood in silence, their eyes trapped, their faces anemic. One turned, gun drawn and finger itching ever closer to the trigger. The son was pinned to the frozen asphalt and saw as they brought a knife, a pair of brown stained jeans too small for any man, out into the open.

He kept his head down in the early days, continuing his practiced silence, and walked through each hour untouched by the informal politics of race revered by the convicted. He fell in with no group, saw no need for protection and became a target. During the slow hours the contained spent idle in the common area an initiate came at him with a straightened mattress spring filed to a harsh point. The initiate thrust and the metal speared deep into his stomach and in his blind efforts of protection he struck the offender twice in the throat. The initiate fell to his knees, blood trickling from the corners of his mouth. He kept his feet and the prisoners began to speak of him as something special. He received an additional five years onto his sentence. After one more failed attack with batteries buried in toes of a sock and another year, no man attacked him again.

CHRIS DEAL

A friend had driven her to the clinic. They sat out in the parking lot for an hour as freezing rain plinked down on the windshield. Tears flowed down the back of her throat and she could not will her legs to take her inside. Dreams and reality were always different beasts. Her company director let her stay on as a teacher and she was able to keep her apartment with the help of her roommate, a fellow dancer. She stood on the side during dance practices, watching and guiding her friends. Sometimes a fear flashed over her that they would soon surpass her. Each day she got bigger and she knew the chance she would go back on stage became slimmer. At night she would rewatch the tape of her performance over and over until every unnoticed mistake became cataclysmic and she knew the applause that came at the end was a joke on her, a series of condescending cheers. Her pillow would dampen and she held the tape in her hands, thinking of ways to destroy it like the forgotten man had done to her. Her mother came to the city and helped her pack her few things before the child was due. They drove back home listening to the wind pushing against the car. Though her mother never asked about the father, she told her everything and the mother smiled sadly and said she would not tell the girl's father. She settled in to her childhood home, getting used to the idea that she was going to be a mother. Before dawn on a Sunday she woke knowing it was time. They drove to the hospital she herself had been born in. Before those long hours she knew pain as something abstract but it became real, a tearing heat from the child working its way out of her.

She sent him letters. Each was written by hand, her calculated cursive holding dreams he didn't want in the hoops of an O. He didn't write back at first. He knew he should have, the world he found himself in. All the old timers spoke of needing an anchor on the outside, even if you won't be seeing it again. You needed something to dream about. For most it was a woman, others wanted the stars or a country they'd never been to, offspring or a cold beer. One night in his first year, he woke up to find his cellmate, the Sacred Heart inked over his chest washed in pale fluorescent light, a sliver of glass shivering in his hand, begging for a word, any word. He relented, if only for a night. He showed his cellmate a picture the girl had sent with a letter. The child was the one he remembered from the years before who had grown into the woman holding her young.

His only peers were the lifers and among the convicts their will was law. His first parole hearing was pushed back to account for the man he left dead in the commons and he thought that was good. His father came to visit and they sat together, both men older than their age, one by a looming death, the other by containment. The father apologized through a breathing tube for the sins that put the son where he now was. The son sat stone still for several long moments, looking over the crags of the old man's face. He forgave his father and it was like a long sigh, the letting go. They hugged, a deed never committed between the two. The father left with a smile. When the old man died in hospice weeks later, the warden looked over the son's record and allowed an excursion to attend the funeral. The son had been inside for a decade of his life. A guard lent the convict a simple black suit and they drove in the prison van out of the gates, the tie tight around his neck, his hands and ankles chained. When they got to the funeral home, the guard asked if he could be trusted to behave himself and he nodded in reply.

A family was gathered in the main hall, their mourning continuing still. An attendant guided the two men into a small room lined with plastic flowers, his father the centerpiece. The old man looked more alive than the last time his son saw him, and the convict stood above the coffin for several long minutes under the guard's watch. He looked down and felt blank, unsure of what it was he should have been experiencing. His mouth was dry, that he knew. His father was small in his repose. The man's uncle came in with his family, an aunt and two cousins he couldn't remember. They shook hands and exchanged forced words. He thought he would like to go back to prison but felt that would not be right, that his presence was as important here as the dead man's. He found a seat and he stared through the world around him, his mind the smooth surface of a lake at midnight. Someone sat in the chair beside him, a woman holding a young child. He looked to her, and she greeted him, her smile breaking through him, and he spoke.

. . . will always be a love letter.

ACKNOWLEDGMENTS

To The Velvet, Write Club and The Cult

to Robert Baynard, Matt Bell, Misty Bennett, Tim Beverstock, Blake Butler, Will Carpenter, Vincent Carrella, Mlaz Corbier, Jason Cross, Craig Davidson, Brian Evenson, DeLeon DeMicoli, Christopher Dwyer, Stuart Gibbel, Michael Paul Gonzalez, Amanda Gowen, Cassie Gressell, Jason Heim, Mirka Hodurova, Anthony David Jacques, Mark Jaskowski, Jeremy Robert Johnson, Nicholas Karpuk, Rick Keeney, Chuck King, Nik Korpon, David Law, Gary Paul Libero, Alex Martin, Colin McKay-Miller, Kyle Minor, Doc O'Donnell, J David Osborne, Rob Parker, Bob Pastorella, Gavin Pate, Cameron Pierce, Michael Raggi, Eddy Rathke, Bradley Sands, Roger Sarao, Sam Schrader, Michael Seidlinger, Devin Strauch, Hilary Tardiff, Brandon Tietz, Gayle Towell, Paul Tremblay, Simon West-Bulford, Mckay Williams and Nic Young

and most especially
Chris Deal, Sean Ferguson, JR Harlan, Gordon Highland, Chelsea Kyle, Jesse Lawrence, Caleb Ross, Jessica Smith, Boden Steiner, Richard Thomas, Axel Taiari, Craig Wallwork and Mr Via

and Logan Rapp

Steve Erickson

Will Christopher Baer, Craig Clevenger, Stephen Graham Jones

thank you.

PV

"The Killer" by Brian Evenson originally published in *The Din Of Celestial Birds: Stories* by Brian Evenson (Wordcraft 1997)

"Little Deaths" by Gary Paul Libero originally published in *Colored Chalk*

"Mantodea" by Matt Bell originally published in *PANK 4 (2010)* and *How They Were Found* by Matt Bell (Keyhole Press 2011)

"They Take You" by Kyle Minor originally published in *Plots With Guns*

"The Liberation of Edward Kellor" by Anthony David Jacques originally published in *Pulp Metal Magazine*

"Practice" by Bob Pastorella originally published in *Troubadour 21*

"Love" by JR Harlan originally published in *Troubadour 21*

"Crazy Love" by Cameron Pierce originally published *Lost in Cat Brain Land* by Cameron Pierce (Eraserhead Press 2010)

"Soccer Moms and Pro Wrestler Dads" by Bradley Sands is the first chapter of the forthcoming novel *TV Snorted My Brain* by Bradley Sands

"All the Acid in the World" by Gavin Pate originally published in *Perigee*

"Chance the Dick" by Paul Tremblay originally published in a limited edition of *In the Mean Time* by Paul Tremblay (ChiZine Publications 2010)

CONTRIBUTORS

MATT BELL is the author of *How They Were Found* and *Cataclysm Baby*, a novella forthcoming from MLP in 2012. His fiction has appeared in *Conjunctions, Hayden's Ferry Review, Gulf Coast, Unsaid,* and *American Short Fiction*, and has been selected for inclusion in anthologies such as *Best American Mystery Stories 2010* and *Best American Fantasy 2*. He works as an editor at Dzanc Books, where he also runs the literary magazine *The Collagist*, and as the Visiting Writer at Greenhills School in Ann Arbor. He can be found online at www.mdbell.com.

TIM BEVERSTOCK uses writing to explore his fascination with all things sweet-natured and dark. His angular, urban narratives feature characters clinging to the edge of their feelings as they dip below the surface of modern life and experience the hidden ambiguities of their existence. Between writing, he enjoys indulging in his passion for boutique beers, volunteering for a food rescue organization and reading noir fiction. He is 32 and lives in Wellington, New Zealand. For news and updates bookmark: www.beverst.com.

BLAKE BUTLER lives in Atlanta and edits HTMLGIANT. He is the author of *Ever* and *Scorch Atlas* and *There is No Year*. In November 2011, Harper Perennial will publish a nonfiction book about sleep, *Nothing*.

VINCENT LOUIS CARRELLA is an award-winning writer, game designer and father of two girls. His debut novel, *Serpent Box*, follows the mystical life of a deformed ten-year-old snake handling boy in post-depression Tennessee. Learn more at www.serpentbox.com or on Twitter @theserpentbox. Follow his Blogazine, *Giphantia*, at www.eyeattheendofmyhand.blogspot.com.

CRAIG CLEVENGER is the author of *The Contortionist's Handbook* (MacAdam/Cage, 2002) and *Dermaphoria* (MacAdam/Cage, 2005). He is currently at work on his third novel. (photo by Timothy Faust)

CRAIG DAVIDSON wrote the books *Rust and Bone*, *The Fighter*, and *Sarah Court*. His nonfiction has appeared in *Esquire* and *GQ*. (photo by Lisa Myers)

CHRIS DEAL writes from North Carolina. He can be found at Chris-Deal.com.

DELEON DEMICOLI lives in San Francisco, CA. When he's not writing, he trains in Mixed Martial Arts.

CHRISTOPHER J DWYER is the author of *When October Falls* and numerous short stories that skirt the edges of noir, horror and science fiction. His work has been featured in several fiction anthologiies and magazines both online and print, including *Twisted Tongue Magazine*, *Pendulum*, *Colored Chalk*, *Red Fez*, *Shalla Magazine*, *New Horizons*, *Gold Dust Magazine*, *Nefarious Muse*, and *Sex and Murder*. He is the former writer-in-residence of indie online magazine *Dogmatika*. He can be reached through www.christopherjdwyer.com or Twitter @chrisjdwyer.

BRIAN EVENSON is the author of ten books of fiction, most recently the limited edition novella *Baby Leg*. His work has been translated into French, Italian, Spanish, Japanese and Slovenian. He lives and works in Providence, Rhode Island, where he directs Brown University's Literary Arts Program. He is the recipient of three O. Henry Prizes as well as an NEA fellowship.

SEAN P FERGUSON is an EMT and a PST for the state of New Jersey. In his off time he reads and writes all he can. His work has been published in the literary journal *Cellar Door* and in *Colored Chalk*. He is currently working on a novel, a number of short stories, and reviews. You can follow him at www.SeanPFerguson.com.

AMANDA GOWIN lives in the foothills of Appalachia with her husband and son. Her stories have been published in *BlackHeart Magazine* and *Thunderdome*. She has always written and always will.

JR HARLAN is from Southern California. He is fond of words, women, and whiskey. He runs *Nefarious Muse*, a short fiction blog at www.nefariousmuse.com.

GORDON HIGHLAND is the author of the novels *Major Inversions* and the forthcoming *Flashover*. A member of The Velvet since 2006, he is a site moderator and one of its most frequent posters. Gordon has been directing videos professionally for over fifteen years, and lives in the Kansas City area, where he also enjoys writing, recording, and performing music. Visit him at gordonhighland.com.

ANTHONY DAVID JACQUES has bagged groceries, sold women's clothing, booked international travel, roasted coffee, repossessed cars, survived cancer and Christianity, gotten married, written a novel, and now he works as a gemologist while slaving over prose. Writing is what he does to make sense of everything else. His short fiction has been published at *Colored Chalk*, *Dogmatika*, *Troubadour 21*, *Pulp Metal Magazine* and *Outsider Writers Collective*. He is currently at work on his second novel. www.anthonydavidjacques.com

MARK JASKOWSKI lives in Gainesville, Florida, where he works rather strange service industry jobs and writes at the picnic table near his apartment. This is his first published work.

JEREMY ROBERT JOHNSON is the Bizarro author of the cult hit *Angel Dust Apocalypse*, the Stoker Nominated novel *Siren Promised* (w/Alan M. Clark), and the end-of-the-world freak-out *Extinction Journals*. His fiction has been acclaimed by *Fight Club* author Chuck Palahniuk and has appeared internationally in numerous anthologies and magazines. In 2008 he worked with The Mars Volta to tell the story behind their Grammy Winning album. In 2010 he spoke about weirdness and metaphor as a survival tool at the Fractal 10 conference in Medellin, Colombia. Jeremy runs Bizarro imprint Swallowdown Press and is working on a host of new books.

STEPHEN GRAHAM JONES started writing in 1990, in an emergency room. Ten years later, his first novel came out, and, since then, there have been six more, and two collections. He has also had some hundred and thirty stories published, anthologized, and included in annuals and textbooks. And he still finds himself in the emergency room more than he really planned. Jones teaches in the MFA program at the University of Colorado at Boulder, and has been a member of The Velvet since 2005. More at www.demontheory.net.

NIK KORPON is the author of the novel *Stay God* and the noir novellas *Old Ghosts* and *By the Nails of the Warpriest*. His stories have ruined the reputation of *Out of the Gutter*, *Do Some Damage*, *3:AM* and *Everyday Genius*, among others. He is a fiction editor for *Rotten Leaves Magazine*, a book reviewer and a co-host of Last Sunday, Last Rites, a monthly reading series in Baltimore, MD. He received a master's degree in Creative Writing from Birkbeck College in London, England, and now lives in Baltimore. Give him danger, little stranger, at www.nikkorpon.com

GARY PAUL LIBERO has been bald since 1997. He is a technology professional living in Middlesex County, Connecticut, with his wife and two toddlers. His short fiction can also be read at *Nefarious Muse*. He hopes to have a novel completed before his kids are able to read.

KYLE MINOR is the author of *In the Devil's Territory*, and co-editor of *The Other Chekhov*. His recent work appears in *The Southern Review*, *The Gettysburg Review*, and *Plots with Guns*, and in anthologies such as *Best American Mystery Stories 2008*, *Surreal South*, and *Twentysomething Essays by Twentysomething Writers*. Random House named Kyle one of the "Best New Voices of 2006," and *The Columbus Dispatch* named him one of their "20 Under 30 Artists to Watch" in 2007. Visit www.kyleminor.com.

DOC O'DONNELL is a rock 'n' roll dropout who writes dirty noir from a cramped apartment in Newcastle, Australia. To pay for the bills and booze he looks after the elderly, soaking up their tales. His work has dirtied the pages and screens of *Crime Factory*, *Pulp Metal Magazine*, *Short, Fast, and Deadly*, *Nefarious Muse*, and *Thunderdome*. Doc is the editor of www.dirtynoir.com, a crime-noir webzine. He can be contacted at: www.docodonnell.com

J DAVID OSBORNE is the author of the Lynchian gulag-escape novel *By the Time We Leave Here, We'll Be Friends*. His second novel, *Low Down Death Right Easy*, is due out this winter from Swallowdown Press. He lives in Oklahoma with his dog.

ROB PARKER currently lives in Waterloo, Ontario. He has his MA in English & Film Studies from Wilfrid Laurier University and secretly hopes that one day serious men in dark suits on the university payroll will speak in quiet, horrified whispers about the monster they created.

BOB PASTORELLA lives in Southeast Texas. He's published with *Outsider Writers Collective, Thunderdome, Nefarious Muse, Troubadour 21*, and his short story "To Watch Is Madness" is featured in *The Zombist: Undead Western Tales Anthology.* He is currently working on a vampire/noir novel. You can visit Bob at www.bobpastorella.com.

GAVIN PATE is the author of the novel *The Way to Get Here* (Bootstrap), and his short stories can be found in places like *The Collagist, Barrelhouse, The Southeast Review*, and *Dogmatika*, among others. He is an Assistant Professor of English at Virginia Wesleyan College, and lately, in the lengthening days of the impending summer, he has been steadily working on what's now only known to him as The Next Book.

CAMERON PIERCE is the author of *The Pickled Apocalypse of Pancake Island, Lost in Cat Brain Land, Ass Goblins of Auschwitz,* and *Shark Hunting in Paradise Garden.* His fiction and poetry has appeared or is forthcoming in *The Bizarro Starter Kit (Purple), The Nervous Breakdown, Verbicide, Bust Down the Door and Eat All the Chickens, The Pedestal Magazine, Nemonymous, The Dream People, Kill Author, Everyday Genius,* and other publications. Cameron also runs Lazy Fascist Press. Visit him online at meatmagick.wordpress.com and lazyfascist.com.

EDWARD J RATHKE is an adventurous dandy wandering space and time. More of his life and words may be found at edwardjrathke.wordpress.com.

CALEB J ROSS has been published widely, both online and in print. He graduated with a degree in English Literature and a minor in Creative Writing from Emporia State University. He is the author of the story chapbook *Charactered Pieces: stories*, the novels *Stranger Will* and *I Didn't Mean to Be Kevin*, and the forthcoming novella *As a Machine and Parts*. Visit his official page at: calebjross.com. Twitter: @calebjross and on Facebook: facebook.com/rosscaleb.

BRADLEY SANDS is the editor of *Bust Down the Door and Eat All the Chickens* and the author of *Sorry I Ruined Your Orgy*, *Rico Slade Will Fucking Kill You*, and *My Heart Said No, But Camera Crew Said Yes!* His contribution to this anthology is the first chapter of a forthcoming novel called *TV Snorted My Brain*.

AXEL TAIARI is a French writer, born in Paris in 1984. He studied Screenwriting and Modern Literature. After an endless string of shit jobs, he quit everything to focus on writing. His work has appeared in multiple magazines and anthologies, including *Dogmatika*, *3:AM Magazine*, *No Colony*, and *365tomorrows*. He is also the creator and co-editor of the literary journal *Rotten Leaves*. He has recently finished a noir science-fiction novel and is now trying to sell his soul to the devil. Read more at www.axeltaiari.com and www.rottenleaves.com. You can also stalk him on Twitter @axeltaiari.

CONTRIBUTORS

RICHARD THOMAS was the winner of the 2009 "Enter the World of *Filaria*" contest at ChiZine. He has published dozens of stories online and in print, including the *Shivers VI* anthology, with Stephen King and Peter Straub, *Murky Depths, PANK, Pear Noir!, Word Riot, 3:AM Magazine, Dogmatika, Vain* and *Opium*. His debut novel, *Transubstantiate*, was released in July of 2010. He also writes book reviews at *The Nervous Breakdown*. www.whatdoesnotkillme.com. (photo by John Geiger)

BRANDON TIETZ studied Illustration and Literature at the University of Kansas and deejayed under the stage name Agent Green while in college. Tietz's familiarity with nightlife and his fascination with the socialite lifestyle led him to write *Out of Touch*, a transgressive take on the coming-of-age story in which the main character feels no physical sensation. In 2009, Tietz joined the Chuck Palahniuk Writers' Workshop, where he now serves as one of the moderators. He's currently working on a new book called *Vanity*, a themed novel-in-stories.

GAYLE TOWELL is a fiction writer living in Hillsboro, Oregon, with her husband and three children. Author of *Moron and X*, she is currently working on her second novel, a quasi-sequel with the working title *Seized*.

PAUL TREMBLAY is the author of the weirdboiled novels *The Little Sleep* and *No Sleep Till Wonderland*, the short story collection *In the Mean Time*, and the novella *The Harlequin and the Train*. His short fiction has appeared in *Weird Tales* and *Year's Best American Fantasy 3*, with stories due to appear in *Cape Cod Noir* and *Supernatural Noir*. He's the co-editor of the anthologies *Fantasy, Bandersnatch, Phantom,* and *Creatures*. He still has no uvula and lives somewhere south of Boston with his wife and two kids. (photo by Michael J Maloney)

CRAIG WALLWORK lives in West Yorkshire, England, with his wife and daughter. After leaving Art College he studied to be a filmmaker before becoming a full-time editor for nine years. In his spare time he writes short stories and is working on his fourth novel. His fiction has appeared in various anthologies, journals and magazines. Follow his progress via his website: craigwallwork.blogspot.com.

NIC YOUNG lives in Cape Town, South Africa. He has packed supermarket shelves in Edinburgh, slept in the open Sahara desert, and broken an inordinate number of bones. He has been writing software since 2005, and stories since 2010. Visit him at www.nicyoung.net. (photo by Lillith Leda)

CONTRIBUTORS

FOREWORD: STEVE ERICKSON is the author of eight acclaimed novels: *Days Between Stations, Rubicon Beach, Tours of the Black Clock, Arc d'X, Amnesiascope, The Sea Came in at Midnight, Our Ecstatic Days* and *Zeroville*. Currently he's the film critic for *Los Angeles* magazine and editor of the literary journal *Black Clock*, which is published by the California Institute of the Arts where he teaches in the MFA Writing Program. His ninth novel, *These Dreams of You*, will be published in early 2012.

INTRODUCTION: LOGAN CHANCE RAPP is an administrator for The Velvet, and a writer in North Hollywood, CA. He graduated from California State University Fresno with a degree in Mass Communications / Journalism. When asked for this bio, he groaned to himself, muttered "fine" in that way where you just know he isn't "fine," but wrote the bio anyway, forgetting that the lovely editor who asked him for it is going to read this. You can find his day job writing at Sourcefed.com.

EDITOR: PELA VIA is the fiction editor for Outsider Writers Collective and a member of Write Club. Her short work has been published in *Nefarious Muse, Red Fez, Word Riot* and others. In 2010 she received a nomination for *The Best of the Net* collection. In 2011 she will be included in the Thunderdome anthology *In Search of a City: Los Angeles in 1,000 Words*. PelaVia.com

RECOMMENDED READING

KISS ME, JUDAS BY WILL CHRISTOPHER BAER During his first night out of a mental institution after suffering a nervous breakdown, Phineas Poe is picked up by a prostitute named Jude. She drugs him and removes his kidney and leaves him in a hotel bathtub full of ice with a note on the counter that reads, "If you want to live, call 9-1-1." Phineas, an ex-police officer who had recently been searching for information against the Denver Police Department's Internal Affairs Unit, later finds out that his kidney was actually replaced by a baggie of heroin. While searching for his missing kidney, Phineas actually finds love in his attacker, while he evades the angry police of Denver and tries to unlock the secrets behind his wife's recent death. 1998 Viking Press, ISBN 0670881759

HELL'S HALF ACRE BY WILL CHRISTOPHER BAER Kidnapping, snuff films, amputee geeks and a requiem of lost love . . . Cast adrift after the blood symphony of *Penny Dreadful*, Poe is looking for answers in the form of a woman. He tracks Jude to San Francisco, where he finds her involved with John Ransom Miller, a wealthy sociopath with a mysterious hold over her. Jude is nursing a revenge fantasy against a U.S. Senator with an amputation fetish who wants her dead, but she needs Miller's help, and in exchange, Miller wants Jude to help him pull off a high-profile kidnapping and make a snuff film on the side. Poe throws himself into the mix, hoping he can save Jude from herself, make sense of his past, and safely navigate a torturous internal landscape he calls hell's half acre. 2004 MacAdam/Cage, ISBN 1931561826

THERE IS NO YEAR: A NOVEL BY BLAKE BUTLER A wildly inventive, impressionistic novel of family, sickness, and the birth-wrench of art, evocative of *House of Leaves* and the films of David Lynch, from a novelist rapidly emerging as one of the voices of his generation. As the Toronto Globe and Mail says, "If the distortion and feedback of Butler's intense riffing is too loud, you may very well be too boring." 2011 Harper Perennial, ISBN 0061997420

SERPENT BOX BY VINCENT LOUIS CARRELLA In the deep mountains of Appalachia, the Flints of Leatherwood, Tennessee, spread the word of the gospels by handling deadly serpents and drinking lye in front of large gatherings of the faithful. Believing his ten-year-old son Jacob—called Toad or Spud—to be a prophet, Charles, the patriarch, takes the boy down a long and arduous path as they travel the back roads of the postwar Deep South in search of God and plumb the depths of their unorthodox brand of faith. But sudden, shocking tragedy will shatter Charles's cherished dream of building a ministry and a permanent church—and set young Jacob on a dramatically different course. 2008 Harper Perennial, ISBN 0061126268

THE CONTORTIONIST'S HANDBOOK BY CRAIG CLEVENGER John Dolan Vincent is a talented young forger with a proclivity for mathematics and drug addiction. In the face of his impending institutionalization, he continually reinvents himself to escape the legal and mental health authorities and to save himself from a life of incarceration. But running turns out to be costly. Vincent's clients in the L.A. underworld lose patience, the hospital evaluator may not be fooled by his story, and the only person in as much danger as himself is the woman who knows his real name. 2002 MacAdam/Cage, ISBN 1931561486

DERMAPHORIA BY CRAIG CLEVENGER Eric Ashworth awakens in jail, unable to remember how he got there or why. All he does remember is a woman's name: Desiree. Bailed out and holed up in a low rent motel, Eric finds the solution to his amnesia in a strange new hallucinogen. By synthesizing the sense of touch, the drug produces a disjointed series of sensations that slowly allow Eric to remember his former life as a clandestine chemist. With steadily increasing doses, Eric reassembles his past at the expense of his grip on the present, and his distinction between truth and fantasy crumbles as his paranoia grows in tandem with his tolerance. 2005 MacAdam/Cage, ISBN 1596921021

THE FIGHTER BY CRAIG DAVIDSON Everything has been handed to Paul Harris, the son of a wealthy southern Ontario businessman. But after a vicious beating shakes his world, he descends into the realm of hardcore bodybuilders and boxing gyms, seeking to become a real man, reveling in suffering. Rob Tully, a working-class teenager from upstate New York, is a born boxer. He trains with his father and uncle, who believe a gift like his can change their lives, but he struggles under the weight of their expectations. Inevitably, these two young men's paths will cross. 2008 Soho Press, ISBN 9781569474990

SARAH COURT BY CRAIG DAVIDSON Sarah Court. Meet the residents . . . The haunted father of a washed-up stuntman. A disgraced surgeon and his son, a broken-down boxer. A father set on permanent self-destruct, and his daughter, a reluctant powerlifter. A fireworks-maker and his daughter. A very peculiar boy and his equally peculiar adopted family. Five houses. Five families. One block. Ask yourself: How well do you know your neighbours? How well do you know your own family? Ultimately, how well do you know yourself? How deeply do the threads of your own life entwine with those around you? Do you ever really know how tightly those threads are knotted? Do you want to know? I know, and can show you. Please, let me show you. Welcome to Sarah Court: make yourself at home. 2010 ChiZine Publications, ISBN 1926851005

LICK ME BY DELEON DEMICOLI Through the use of dark satire, *Lick Me* is a wickedly funny tale from an original voice that shows no mercy when writing upon the immoral standards of network television that interprets news worthy headlines by ratings, while an easily influenced culture finds their "truths" in celebrity tabloids. 2009 P'NK Books, ISBN 0615266037

WHEN OCTOBER FALLS BY CHRISTOPHER J DWYER Clint Korbis has lost it all: his sanity, his grip on life, and most importantly his wife, Jenna, who disappeared without warning. Exhausted and incapable of coping with the loss, the only relief seems to be suicide, but then a series of happenings indicate that Jenna may not be dead...she may be closer than Clint thinks. 2011 Brown Paper Publishing, ISBN 0615470033

OUR ECSTATIC DAYS: A NOVEL BY STEVE ERICKSON In the waning summer days, a lake appears almost overnight in the middle of Los Angeles. Out of fear and love, a young single mother commits a desperate act: convinced that the lake means to take her small son from her, she determines to stop it and becomes the lake's Dominatrix-Oracle, "the Queen of the Zed Night." Acclaimed by many critics as Steve Erickson's greatest novel, Our Ecstatic Days takes place on the forbidden landscape of a defiant heart. 2005 Simon & Schuster, ISBN 9780743264723

ZEROVILLE BY STEVE ERICKSON A film-obsessed ex-seminarian with images of Elizabeth Taylor and Montgomery Clift tattooed on his head arrives on Hollywood Boulevard in 1969. Vikar Jerome enters the vortex of a cultural transformation: rock and roll, sex, drugs, and-most important to him-the decline of the movie studios and the rise of independent directors. Jerome becomes a film editor of astonishing vision. Through encounters with former starlets, burglars, political guerillas, punk musicians, and veteran filmmakers, he discovers the secret that lies in every movie ever made. 2007 Europa Editions, ISBN 9781933372396

LAST DAYS BY BRIAN EVENSON Intense and profoundly unsettling, Brian Evenson's Last Days is a down-the-rabbit-hole detective novel set in an underground religious cult. The story follows Kline, a brutally dismembered detective forcibly recruited to solve a murder inside the cult. As Kline becomes more deeply involved with the group, he begins to realize the stakes are higher than he previously thought. Attempting to find his way through a maze of lies, threats, and misinformation, Kline discovers that his survival depends on an act of sheer will. *Last Days* was first published in 2003 as a limited edition novella titled *The Brotherhood of Mutilation*. Its success led Evenson to expand the story into a full-length novel. In doing so, he has created a work that's disturbing, deeply satisfying, and completely original. 2009 Underland Press, ISBN 9780980226003

MAJOR INVERSIONS BY GORDON HIGHLAND Your roommate says you should date more, that all those spandex nights on stage paying tribute to hair metal and banging faceless groupies only amplify your Jekyll/Hyde syndrome. That this quicksand town of floozies, fiends, and filmmakers will survive without your commercial jingles. And your narcotics. That you should turn in your daytime security-guard badge and settle down. He's got the perfect girl, a cinnamon-scented innocent who will bring that elusive substance to your life despite the familial forces that conspire against your union. Always lurking in the periphery, the roommate remains buried in his Master's thesis, the parasitic puppeteer behind your reinvention, the search for your birth parents, and your all-too-brief film scoring career. A supporting cast of lecherous directors, deluded bandmates, federal agents, and nostalgic exes obstruct your path to closure and ironic revenge in this "revisionist character study." 2009 CreateSpace, ISBN 1448667291

ANGEL DUST APOCALYPSE BY JEREMY ROBERT JOHNSON Meth-heads, man-made monsters, and murderous Neo-Nazis. Blissed out club kids dying at the speed of sound. The un-dead and the very soon-to-be-dead. They're all here, trying to claw their way free. From the radioactive streets of a war-scarred future, where the nuclear bombs have become self-aware, to the fallow fields of Nebraska where the kids are mainlining lightning bugs, this is a world both alien and intensely human. This is a place where self-discovery involves scalpels and horse tranquilizers; where the doctors are more doped-up than the patients; where obsessive-compulsive acid-freaks have unlocked the gateway to God and can't close the door. This is not a safe place. You can turn back now, or you can head straight into the heart of . . . the ANGEL DUST APOCALYPSE. 2005 Eraserhead Press, ISBN 0976249839

ALL THE BEAUTIFUL SINNERS BY STEPHEN GRAHAM JONES Deputy Sheriff Jim Doe plunges into a renegade manhunt after the town's sheriff is gunned down. But unbeknownst to him, the suspect—an American Indian—holds chilling connections to the disappearance of Doe's sister years before. And the closer Doe gets to the fugitive's trail, the more he realizes that his own involvement in the case is hardly coincidental. A descendant of the Blackfeet Nation himself, Doe keeps getting mistaken for the killer he's chasing. And when the FBI's finest three profilers descend on the case, Doe suspects the hunt has only just begun. But beneath the novel's pyrotechnic plotting, the deeper psychic cadences of Stephen Graham Jones's prose take hold. His specific imagery and telling detail coalesce into the literary equivalent of an Edward Hopper painting. But like the other seminal works in the genre (*Fight Club, Red Dragon*), *All The Beautiful Sinners* will unnerve you, and it will then send you back to page one to experience its mysteries all over again. 2004 Rugged Land, ISBN 1590710312

DEMON THEORY BY STEPHEN GRAHAM JONES On Halloween night, following an unnerving phone call from his diabetic mother, Hale and six of his med school classmates return to the house where his sister disappeared years ago. While there is no sign of his mother, something is waiting for them there, and has been waiting a long time. Written as a literary film treatment littered with footnotes and experimental nuances, *Demon Theory* is even parts camp and terror, combining glib dialogue, fascinating pop culture references, and an intricate subtext as it pursues the events of a haunting movie trilogy too real to dismiss. There are books about movies and movies about books, and then there's *Demon Theory* – a refreshing and occasionally shocking addition to the increasingly popular "intelligent horror" genre. 2007 MacAdam/Cage, ISBN 1596922168

STAY GOD BY NIK KORPON Damon lives a content life, playing video games and dealing drugs from his second-hand store while his girlfriend, Mary, drops constant hints about marriage. If only he could tell her his name isn't really Damon. If only he could tell her who he really is. But after he witnesses a friend's murder, a scarlet woman glides into his life, offering the solution to all of his problems. His carefully constructed existence soon shatters like crystal teardrops and he must determine which ghosts won't stay buried-and which ones are trying to kill him—if he wants to learn why Mary has disappeared. 2010 Otherworld Publications, ISBN 0982649428

OLD GHOSTS: A NOVELLA BY NIK KORPON Nik Korpon brings us back to a Baltimore we haven't seen since The Wire and answers the question of what might've been if *The Grifters*' Roy Dillon had tried to settle down, go straight, and have a kid. A story of brothers and sisters or lovers, *Old Ghosts* reads like a horror story down one man's memory lane. —Seth Harwood, author of *Jack Wakes Up* and *Young Junius*. 2011 Brown Paper Publishing, ISBN 0615470025

IN THE DEVIL'S TERRITORY BY KYLE MINOR The debut collection of stories and novellas (including "A Day Meant to Do Less," a Best American Mystery Stories 2008 selection) from a young writer who is, as Benjamin Percy has said, a master of "the dark caverns of the human heart." A schoolteacher escapes East Berlin at night, swimming the Spree River three times carrying elderly relatives on her back, so she can make her way to West Palm Beach, Florida, and "ruin the lives of fifth grade boys." A young husband reckons with the likelihood that his wife's troubled pregnancy will end with her death before Christmas. A preacher bathes his ill and elderly mother, not knowing that she has mistaken him for the long-lost cousin she watched murder his brother in her father's tobacco field. In six stories that read like novels in miniature, *In the Devil's Territory* plumbs the depths of human mystery, where meet our kindnesses and our cruelties, our generosities and our pettinesses. 2008 Dzanc Books, ISBN 9780979312366

BY THE TIME WE LEAVE HERE, WE'LL BE FRIENDS BY J DAVID OSBORNE Siberia, 1953. Stalin is dead and a once-prosperous thief named Alek Karriker is feeling the pressure. Trapped in an icy prison camp where violent criminals run the show, betrayed by his friends and his body, Karriker is surrounded by death and disorder. Bizarre Inuit shamans are issuing ever-stranger commands that he must obey. Opium is running scarce and bad magic is plentiful. Razor-tooth gangsters can smell Karriker's blood and they plan to murder him more than once. The only option: ESCAPE. Enlisting the aid of an aging guard, a cold-blooded killer, and a beautiful, murderous nurse, Karriker must now secure his getaway by finding a "calf": a gullible prisoner to be cannibalized when the tundra is at its most barren. As the vice grows tighter and life in the gulag becomes increasingly surreal, Karriker must hurry to find his mark and convince him . . . BY THE TIME WE LEAVE HERE, WE'LL BE FRIENDS 2010 Swallowdown Press, ISBN 1933929057

THE WAY TO GET HERE BY GAVIN PATE "Against the ominous backdrop of a national blackout, Pate grabs us by the hand and deftly guides us through the darkness of one man's apocalypse. Stark, urban, and cinematic, *The Way To Get Here* contains enough wrecked lives to fill up a downtown shelter house and shows us that nothing is more lethal than love." —Joey Goebel 2006 Bootstrap Press, ISBN 0971193517

ABORTION ARCADE BY CAMERON PIERCE A collection of three novellas by one of the shining young stars of bizarro fiction. Cameron Pierce's work is an intoxicating blend of body horror and midnight movie madness, reminiscent of early David Lynch and the splatterpunks at their most sublime. His fiction will punch you in the brain and leave you gasping for more. 2011 Eraserhead Press, ISBN 1936383535

STRANGER WILL BY CALEB J ROSS To William Lowson, impending fatherhood means an impending stain. His work as a Human Remains Removal Specialist, professionally cleaning the stains left from dead bodies, fuels this belief. His friend and mentor Mrs. Rose, an elementary school principal, nurtures and sympathizes with his cynicism, blaming his dilemma on an imperfect world. But she has a plan around this impediment: a group of strangers-a devout collection of kindred minds who have dedicated their lives to cultivating a unique idea of perfection, and she wants William to join. But once he is in can he get out? 2011 Otherworld Publications, ISBN 1936593076

I DIDN'T MEAN TO BE KEVIN BY CALEB J ROSS Jackson Jacoby, a twenty-two year old boy without a mother of his own finds a plea in a newspaper from a woman, begging for her runaway son to return home. He calls, pretends to be the son, and embarks on a journey to visit this mother, spreading to strangers along the way tales of his participation in the human appendage trade, the history of his missing ear, and anything else that might validate his life like, he discovers, the love of a mother could. November 2011 Black Coffee Press

SORRY I RUINED YOUR ORGY BY BRADLEY SANDS Bizarro humorist Bradley Sands returns with one of the strangest, most hilarious collections of the year. In *Sorry I Ruined Your Orgy*, the pope gets sued, a headless man falls in love with a bowl of rice, and architects dismantle the earth. A war breaks out over greeting cards. A suicidal amputee tries to kill himself. William S. Burroughs becomes an amateur archaeologist and Tao Lin drinks an ape-flavored smoothie. Between a breakfast of clocks, a lunch date with Adolf Hitler, and breakdancing in outer space, anything is possible in the work of Bradley Sands. Just never wear a bear costume to an orgy. 2010 Eraserhead Press, ISBN 9781936383153

A LIGHT TO STARVE BY: A NOVELLA BY AXEL TAIARI (Kindle Edition) A dark novella, set in near-future Paris, where vampires and werewolves are hunted like rabid dogs and put down just as quickly. Their existence is common knowledge, the army and police patrol the streets looking for them, families barricade themselves at night, and even the Catholic Church has its own task force. The majority of the population has been vaccinated, making their blood highly poisonous. What little remains of the vampire society is now reduced to dealing pure blood like drugs, living in hiding, owning clean human slaves to drink from, and generally living a pathetic life. Amidst the chaos, a clan-less vampire who has been starving for too long does his best to survive, mugging and stealing goods in order to feed himself. His only real link with humanity is a woman he lost years ago. As he checks up on her one night, he finds her missing, and all hell breaks loose. 2011 Rotten Leaves Press, ASIN B004OR1U5O

TRANSUBSTANTIATE BY RICHARD THOMAS "They say Jimmy made it out. But the postcards we get, well, they don't seem . . . real." When an experiment with population control works too well, and the planet is decimated, seven broken people are united by a supernatural bond in a modern day Eden. Most on the island are fully aware of this prison disguised as an oasis. Unfortunately, Jimmy is on the mainland, desperate to get back, in a post-apocalyptic stand-off, fighting for his survival and that of his unborn child. Back on the island, Jacob stares at the ocean through his telescope and plots his escape, reluctant to aid the cause. Marcy tries to hide from her past sexual escapades that may be her saving grace. X sits in his compound, a quiet, massive presence, trapped in his body by ancient whispers and yet free in spirit to visit other places and times. Roland, the angry, bitter son of Marcy is determined to leave, and sets out on his own. Watching over it all is Assigned, the ghost in the machine. And coming for them, to exact revenge, and finish the job that the virus started, is Gordon. He just landed on the island and he has help. *Transubstantiate* is a neo-noir thriller, filled with uncertainty at every portal, and jungles infiltrated with The Darkness. Vivid settings, lyrical language, and a slow reveal of plot, motivation, past crimes and future hope collide in a showdown that keeps you guessing until the final haunting words. Transubstantiate: to change from one substance into another. 2010 Otherworld Publications, ISBN 0982607245

RECOMMENDED READING

OUT OF TOUCH BY BRANDON TIETZ Aidin is a twenty-four-year-old wealthy socialite who spends the majority of his time coercing women with money rather than charm, and has a penchant for drugs and bottle service at the sort of clubs and venues most people can't afford to get into. After a night of heavy partying, he awakes one morning completely vacant of any physical sensation, and through a near-fatal occurrence, comes to find his old life is behind him whether he likes it or not. Enter: Dr. Paradies, a progressive therapist who explains to Aidin that no surgery or prescription exists for his particular condition. She assigns him a life list—a litany of 366 seemingly random items, ultimately designed to help cope with his ailment. Thus, a new addiction ensues for Aidin as he becomes completely enamored with following orders and directions that range from reviewing restaurants to handgun training, but most notably, a young woman named Dana who appears as Item #154 on his list. Little by little, Aidin begins to understand how to use the disability to his advantage, whether it's his endless stamina in bed or how he can be beaten to a bloody pulp without flinching—he adapts. But as the list continues and the items become increasingly more cryptic, Aidin begins to suspect this might be something more than therapy. The truth behind the condition will force him to make a life-altering decision. 2010, Otherworld Publications, ISBN 9780982649480

THE LITTLE SLEEP: A NOVEL BY PAUL TREMBLAY Raymond Chandler meets Jonathan Lethem in this wickedly entertaining debut featuring Mark Genevich, Narcoleptic Detective. Mark Genevich is a South Boston P.I. with a little problem: he's narcoleptic, and he suffers from the most severe symptoms, including hypnogogic hallucinations. These waking dreams wreak havoc for a guy who depends on real-life clues to make his living. Clients haven't exactly been beating down the door when Mark meets Jennifer Times—daughter of the powerful local D.A. and a contestant on American Star—who walks into his office with an outlandish story about a man who stole her fingers. He awakes from his latest hallucination alone, but on his desk is a manila envelope containing risqué photos of Jennifer. Are the pictures real, and if so, is Mark hunting a blackmailer, or worse? Wildly imaginative and with a pitch-perfect voice, *The Little Sleep* is the first in a new series that casts a fresh eye on the rigors of detective work, and introduces a character who has a lot to prove—if only he can stay awake long enough to do it. 2009 Holt Paperbacks, ISBN 9780805088496

NO SLEEP TILL WONDERLAND: A NOVEL BY PAUL TREMBLAY Mark Genevich is stuck in a rut: his narcolepsy isn't improving, his private-detective business is barely scraping by, and his landlord mother is forcing him to attend group therapy sessions. Desperate for companionship, Mark goes on a two-day bender with a new acquaintance, Gus, who is slick and charismatic—and someone Mark knows very little about. When Gus asks Mark to protect a friend who is being stalked, Mark inexplicably finds himself in the middle of a murder investigation and soon becomes the target of the police, a sue-happy lawyer, and a violent local bouncer. Will Mark learn to trust himself in time to solve the crime—and in time to escape with his life? Written with the same "witty voice that doesn't let go"* that has won Paul Tremblay so many fans, *No Sleep Till Wonderland* features a memorable detective whose only hope for reconciling with his difficult past is to keep moving—asleep or awake—toward an uncertain future. *Library Journal, starred review for* The Little Sleep 2010 St. Martin's Griffin, ISBN 0805088504

thank you for reading
welcometotheVelvet.com

CPSIA information can be obtained at www.ICGtesting.com
Printed in the USA
BVOW07s2019270714

360538BV00003B/165/P